THE JEWISH OLYMPICS

The History of the
Maccabiah Games

By Ron Kaplan

Foreword by Ira Berkow

Skyhorse Publishing

Skyhorse Publishing books may be purchased in bulk at special discounts for sales promotion, corporate gifts, fund-raising, or educational purposes. Special editions can also be created to specifications. For details, contact the Special Sales Department, Skyhorse Publishing, 307 West 36th Street, 11th Floor, New York, NY 10018 or info@skyhorsepublishing.com.

Skyhorse® and Skyhorse Publishing® are registered trademarks of Skyhorse Publishing, Inc.®, a Delaware corporation.

Visit our website at www.skyhorsepublishing.com.

10 9 8 7 6 5 4 3 2 1

Chapter-opening Maccabiah posters courtesy of The Joseph Yekutieli Maccabi Sports Archive.

Library of Congress Cataloging-in-Publication Data is available on file.

Cover design by David Sankey
Cover photo credit AP Images

ISBN: 978-1-63220-494-3
Ebook ISBN: 978-1-63220-855-2

Printed in the United States of America

This book is dedicated to the thousands of athletes, administrators, volunteers, and supporters who have made the Maccabiah Games a truly unique experience and, for many, a stepping stone to reconnecting the religion of their ancestors.

Contents

Foreword

by Ira Berkow

For an introspective look at the Maccabiah Games, or the so-called "Jewish Olympics," one surely must start with the stereotype—the "un-muscular" Jew, as it were, the "un-athletic" Jew, the bookish nerd—even though one of the world's earliest (it is believed to have occurred some 3,000 years ago) and greatest known athletes was a Jewish lad who could employ a slingshot courageously and with gold-medal deftness, the David who smote the giant Goliath, all six cubits and a span of him, according to 1 Samuel 17.

In this regard, in the 1980 American film, *Airplane!*, arguably one of the funniest moments is when a stewardess is asking a passenger if she'd like something to read. The passenger, in turn, asks for something "light." "How about this leaflet?" replies the stewardess, "'Famous Jewish Sports Legends'?"

Of course, there are more than a leaflet's worth, to be sure, of notable Jewish athletes. The list goes beyond baseball's Sandy Koufax and Hank Greenberg; boxing's Barney Ross and Benny Leonard; football's Sid Luckman and Marshall Goldberg; swimmers Mark Spitz, Jason Lezak, and Lenny Krayzelburg; pro basketball stars Dolph Schayes and Ernie Grunfeld; tennis legend Dick Savitt; and the gymnasts Mitch Gaylord and Kerri Strug, who stunningly helped win a US gold medal while suffering a sprained ankle.

One might also include the forty-seven former Olympians—a number of whom were medal winners—who perished in concentration camps in the Holocaust. Or the Holocaust survivor Ben Helfgott, the lightweight weightlifting champion who represented Great Britain in the 1956 and 1960 Olympics, as well as in the Maccabiah Games, and Olympic race walker Shaul Ladany, a Holocaust survivor who also managed by leaping from a balcony to escape the Arab terrorists who murdered eleven of his 1972 Israeli Olympic teammates in Munich. Ladany competed in the 1973 Maccabiah Games.

In Ron Kaplan's finely researched, engaging, and compelling history of the Maccabiah Games, he indeed begins with the essential raison d'etre of Jews holding their own grand athletic competition, the first held, in 1932, as anti-Semitism was about to reach a horrible apex in Europe. It was a way to pridefully demonstrate and highlight a "muscular Judaism."

Even into the seventh Maccabiah Games, in 1965, a fencer from New York University, Carol Benjamin, then ranked third in the United States, traveled to compete in Tel Aviv. "So we get to Israel," Kaplan quotes her as saying, "and I felt wonderful. It was the first time I had been…in a country that was filled with, primarily, Jewish people…. The thing I really remember and that struck me as very amazing was, growing up you hear stereotypes of Jewish men as little old men with beards and scholars and bespectacled reading Torah and just spending a lot of time studying, not very physically strong." The perception changed for her at the opening ceremonies: "They had all these young soldiers and young people…in khaki shorts and shirts doing demonstrations. My whole impression of what a Jewish man was changed. It was striking."

Indeed, there was more to proving mere athleticism as a catalyst for the Maccabiah Games. "For thousands of years," writes Kaplan, "Jews had been forced to convert to other religions, exiled, shunned, denied businesses and educational opportunities, rounded up and pushed into ghettos, and/or brutally victimized in pogroms." The Games would also be a statement to the world that Jews were as physically capable as any other group and, as we would learn from the numerous Israeli-Arab wars, had become quite capable of fighting back.

But what separates Kaplan, the journalist and writer, from an ethnic cheerleader is the integrity of his report. For example, he explores where the Games may go wrong: sometimes a lack of high-quality athletes; the fact that the cost to get to Israel was only affordable to those with means (thus excluding some poorer athletes); the need to cut corners to allow, for example, an American citizen named Joseph Garrie, a judo athlete, studying at a college in Japan, to be the lone representative of Japan and carry the Rising Sun flag into the stadium in the opening ceremonies; the antagonism of the Ultra-Orthodox Jewish community who have sought to stop the "frivolity" of games that intrude on study; and, as Kaplan writes, "the capper: a so-called 'Jewish Olympics' by its nature excludes gentiles, which would seem anathema to a people who had been ostracized for millennia."

Kaplan also poses for consideration the age-old question, "Who is a Jew?" At the Maccabiah Games, different countries had their own requirements. The US maintained that either parent may be Jewish, while other nations, such as Australia, stated that one's mother had to be Jewish in order to be classified as a Jew. Yet, ironically, Israel's stance is that *all* Israeli citizens are eligible to compete. Arab-Israeli Muslims indeed competed against their Jewish neighbors in the Maccabiah Games.

As it were, Spitz, Krayzelburg, Lezak, Savitt, Grunfeld, and Gaylord, among other world champions, participated and won gold medals in the Maccabiah Games, and Schayes coached an American team in the Games. And both Greenberg and Koufax were supporters. In 1934, Greenberg, then the 6-foot-3, 210-pound Detroit Tigers' home-run hitter, attended a fundraising dinner for Maccabiah—his impressive presence alone was significant to the embryonic cause. Koufax, prior to the Seventh Maccabiah Games in 1965 underwrote the expenses for ten athletes.

Kaplan does not sidestep current politics—vis-à-vis Israeli Prime Minister Benjamin Netanyahu and President Barack Obama. Before the 19th Maccabiah Games, in 2013, Obama sent a congratulatory note to the Games' committee. "It's a celebration of the deep friendship among the competing nations, especially the unbreakable bond between Israel and the United States," he wrote. "In that spirit I want to wish my good friend, President Shimon Peres, a very happy 90th birthday. He's an example of the vitality and dedication to all of us and his legacy embodies the essence of these games...."

It was missed by virtually no one that the name of a certain local Prime Minister was not mentioned, and which spoke to the ideological conflict, if not great personal dislike, between Obama and Netanyahu. Underscored was Prime Minister of England David Cameron's companion congratulatory note, which *did* include a tip of the hat to Netanyahu.

And so the 20th Maccabiah Games continued: In the opening ceremonies in Teddy Kollek Stadium an estimated crowd of 30,000 watched some 9,000 athletes and delegation members from more than 70 countries—including, for the first time, Jews from Albania and Aruba to Mongolia and Suriname—march in, flags waving and attired in colorful native garb.

There were thirty-four sports included in the Games, from basketball and swimming to cricket and ice hockey. There was, alas, no slingshot competition. Maybe the organizers will consider it for the 21st Maccabiah Games in 2017. It's got a sweet Jewish history, after all.

Author's Note

Could Joseph Yekutieli, the "father" of the Maccabiah Games, have envisioned how his dream of an international gathering of Jewish athletes would grow from a few hundred in 1932 to more than 9,000 in 2013, expanding to include sportspeople of just about any age, whose only requirement—apart from being Jewish—was the desire to compete in their sport at a high level?

In the early Games, young teenagers competed alongside those old enough to be their parents. More recently, the Games were expanded to allow all athletes to compete against their contemporaries.

While everyone associated with the Games is to be commended for their involvement, this book considers almost exclusively those who participated in the "open" categories.

A word about records

The author has made every attempt to represent the results of the games as accurately as possible. With all due respect to the thousands of participants who worked so hard to compete in the Games, space does not permit the inclusion of every athlete at every event.

Just as sports records evolve over time, so does the sophistication of record-keeping. Over the course of the Games, general sports and the events within them have been added, greatly expanding the record books. On the other hand, some events were reduced or eliminated (and perhaps reintroduced) from one Maccabiah to another, depending on the ability of the countries to provide competitors.

Due to varying conditions through the eighty-plus-year history of the event, not every event has a gold, silver, and bronze winner. For example, according to the Maccabiah Basic Regulations (updated July 5, 2012), "If only three teams take part in the event, or three competitors in the individual events, only the winner of first and second place will be awarded gold and silver medals, and the winner of third place will get a diploma." Additionally, several events issued two bronze awards.

Acknowledgments

In addition to the men and women who shared their experiences through phone and e-mail interviews, I would like to thank the following for their invaluable assistance.

First place must go to Julie Ganz, my editor at Skyhorse, for suggesting I take on this project and for her cheerful—and patient—guidance.

The rest of the winning team includes:

Michele Bass, Operations Manager, Maccabi Canada

Rony Dror, Archivist, Maccabi World Union

David Brinn, Managing Editor, and Elaine Moshe, Head of Archives, *The Jerusalem Post*

Jed Margolis, Executive Director, Maccabi USA

And last, but not least, my wife, Dr. Faith Krausman, for her suggestions, support, and proofreading.

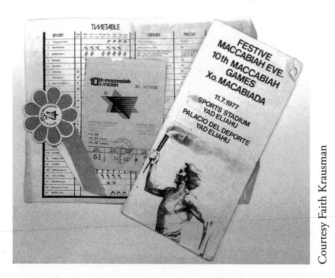

Courtesy Faith Krausman

Chapter 1

Introduction
Jews and the Organized Sports Movement

As Yogi Berra, the Hall of Fame catcher for the New York Yankees and master wordsmith, might have said with regard to the birth of the Maccabiah Games, "Thank you for making this event necessary." Because, in a way, the Maccabiah Games—the Jewish Olympics—were born out of exclusion and anti-Semitism.

For thousands of years, Jews had been forced to convert to other religions, exiled, shunned, denied business and educational opportunities, rounded up and pushed into ghettos, and/or brutally victimized in pogroms. They came to understand that their lives and livelihoods were basically suffered at the pleasure of their host nations. All it took was a disgruntled customer or a rumor about a dead Christian child whose blood had been used to make matzo, and the antagonism would begin anew.

Fast-forward to the late nineteenth century. The sons of gentile middle and upper class Europeans began to organize what the Germans termed *turnerschafts*, student groups similar to fraternities but concentrating on athletic activities: horsemanship, fencing, and shooting for the upper crust; soccer and gymnastics for the general population.

For Jews living in hundreds of impoverished *shtetls*, however, there was little time for the frivolity of sports and games. If you were male, you worked and studied Torah (and not necessarily in that order). If you were female, well, it was your responsibility to keep a kosher home and raise the children.

Observant Jews generally considered physical activities for their own sake a waste of time. Since the Hellenic occupation of the biblical land of their forefathers more than a thousand years earlier, they looked upon the preoccupation with building the perfect body as anathema.

Yet the forward thinkers among them realized they could not rely on local authorities for protection. They understood the need to take their well-being into their own hands and not merely rely on God. So they decided to seek out new opportunities away from the tiny villages and in larger cities.

Regardless of their ability to prosper in their more cosmopolitan environments, however, they were never fully integrated into society. Even in the years before the World Wars, Germany espoused the idea of a superior race. "Gymnastic exercise steeled the Aryan body in the struggle against foreign as well as internal (i.e., Jews) enemies" (*The Maccabiah Games: A History of the Jewish Olympics,* page 4). Clubs within the *Deutsche Turnerschaft* (German Gymnastic movement) set up strict quotas, so Jews found little in the way of what would one day be described as the "Olympic spirit." The best course of action was to create their own clubs.

The first all-Jewish student organization formed in 1886 at the University of Breslau. More all-Jewish societies were to come in East European university towns such as Heidelberg, Berlin, Munich, and Prague, where young men could find opportunities to fence, box, and engage in gymnastics as a means of both self-defense from their Christian counterparts and to find strength in their own numbers, relatively few as that might have been.

The first recorded general Jewish sports group, *Israelitische Turnverein* (Israel Gymnastics Club), was established in Constantinople, Turkey, in the mid-1890s and consisted of middle-class Austrian Jews living in the Ottoman capital. Over the next decade, similar clubs would open in Bulgaria, Austria, Bohemia and Moravia, Poland, and Germany.

These groups were named in honor of legendary Jewish symbols of strength and bravery. "Bar Kochba," for example, was an homage to Simon Bar Kochba, who led the Jews in a revolt against the Romans in 132 CE, while "Shimshon" is the Hebrew translation of that famous biblical strongman Samson, and "Gideon" ("mighty warrior") was a judge from the Bible. Similarly, other titles riffed on powerful imagery, such as "Hakoah" and "Haginor," Hebrew for "strength" and "hero," respectively. Maccabi, the name that would be associated with both the overall organization and the games themselves, comes from Judas Maccabi, perhaps the mightiest warrior in Jewish history, who led a revolt against the Greeks in 162 BCE and helped re-establish the Second Temple, feats that are celebrated during the festival of Hanukkah. In 1902, the Jewish sports club based in Plovdiv, Bulgaria would be the first to incorporate Maccabi in their identity.

It was roughly at this time that the Zionist movement began to formulate in earnest. Since the days of Moses, Jews had yearned to return to their historical homeland. The British Empire took control of Palestine, as it was then called, following World War I. It would take another 30 years for Israel to become an independent nation but in the meantime, there was still a number of Jews living in *Eretz Yisrael*, "the land of Israel," with the more daring seeking to immigrate there to flee their precarious situations across Western Europe and Russia. These were "tough Jews," willing to risk everything to establish a State of their own.

The First Zionist Congress met in 1897 in Basle, Switzerland, and was attended by 200 representatives from seventeen countries. While the topic of sports clubs was not a priority at that point, Dr. Max Nordau, a Hungarian-born physician, writer, and social critic, addressed the delegates about the need for "muscular Judaism" at the following convention the next year.

"Zionism rouses Judaism to a new life. Of this I am sure," said Nordau. "It achieves this spiritually through the revival of common ideals, and materially through physical education of the new generation which will return us to the lost 'Muscular Judaism.'"

Dr. Max Mandelstam, an ophthalmologist from Kiev, echoed these sentiments. "The time has come to establish, beside the study and practice of the Hebrew language, and the teaching of Jewish history and literature in its main feature, Jewish social and gymnastic societies, where Jews freely can devote themselves to the exercises of mind and body," he declared.

A gymnastics "demonstration event" was showcased at the Third Zionist Congress in 1903. According to Max Bodenheimer, another leader in the early Zionist movement and one of the founders of the Jewish National Fund, "such a gymnastic exhibition [was] worth more than a hundred speeches" in terms of expressing the need for a Jewish physical culture (*Die Welt*, August 29, 1903, p. 15).

That same year, the Juedische Turnerschaft—an organization of Jewish gymnasts in Germany—was founded. This served as the general governing body until the founding of the Maccabi World Union in 1921.

While gymnastics may have been the main form of exercise for these groups, a wider variety of sports gaining popularity, including boxing and fencing, brought in more participants.

The movement spread not only to Jewish settlements in Eastern Europe, but to British-controlled Palestine as well. In 1906, the first gymnastics club—Rishon l'Zion—was established in Jaffa in 1906 while the Bar Giora Gymnastic Club opened in Jerusalem. By the beginning of World War I, clubs had sprung up in numerous cities in Palestine, including Be'er Tuvia, Gedera, Zichron Ya'akov, Haifa, Ness Ziona, Ekron, and Rehovot. Outside Eretz Yisrael, Jewish gymnastics organizations were recognized in several regions including Germany, West-Austrian, Borbon-Galitzia, Bulgaria, and Turkey. They were based on Jewish *culture*, rather than religious ideology. "Religious" Jews still perceived these games as *mishegas*—craziness—diverting young men away from the study of Torah and the pursuit of employment and family. Worse to some was the idea of abandoning their forefathers' heritage in pursuit of assimilation into the mainstream society with just a minimum of Jewish identification.

Among the earliest organizations established in Eretz Yisrael was Hapoel in 1924 as part of Histadrut, the General Union of Labor, which had been created four years earlier to look out for the interests of Jewish labor in Palestine. Hapoel's mission was to cultivate health, physical culture, and sport among workers.

Two years later, Hapoel's founders convened to hammer out the basic framework for a "national" sport organization.

Rivalries were common. Hapoel and Maccabi battled for supremacy for the right to be the "official" athletic body. Nor should it be surprising the difficulties, especially in that era, to coordinate such an event. Needless to say, the different countries were at different levels as far as their financial ability to support the teams and athletes, especially after World War I, which left much of Europe in dire straits, and the Great Depression, which had far-reaching implications across the globe.

The stage was set for Jewish athletes to be competing on behalf of a Jewish state. As George Eisen asserted in his 1979 doctoral dissertation *The Maccabiah Games: A History of the Jewish Olympics*, "The fact that Jewish athletes could participate in the Olympic games not as representatives of an independent Jewish state, but only as delegates of various countries, was to have compelling effect upon the organization of a separate festival. By the third decade of [the 20th] century . . . the number of Maccabi clubs reached over 170. Moreover, by the 1920s, the Jewish community in Palestine had sufficient economic, social, and political strength for the organization of a sport festival of Olympic standing."

While occasional attempts had been made to organize a "Jewish games," none of them initially took hold for a variety of reasons including financial considerations, logistics, and the inability to decide on an overall governing body.

At a meeting of the 1929 World Maccabi Congress in Czechoslovakia, Joseph Yekutieli described his vision of a game for the Jewish people based on the Olympics, an answer to the exclusion that had plagued them for centuries. Yekutieli had immigrated to Palestine from Russia around 1907. Like many young sports fans, Yekutieli, then fifteen, was taken with the excitement of 1912 Olympics Games in Stockholm. He dared to dream such a spectacle could be held in the historic land of his people, serving as a point of unification for Jews.

Yekutieli held onto that dream for another decade. In 1928, he visited the Jewish National Fund, founded in 1901 with the charter to serve as a land-purchasing organization in Palestine. In a stunning example of serendipity, the Maccabi Union decided the time was ripe to hold an international competition in British-ruled Palestine. But nothing happens without red tape. Many organizations, both within and without the Jewish world, had to agree. Fortunately, Sir Arthur Wauchope, the high commissioner of Mandatory Palestine, supported the idea.

The first *Maccabiyad* was scheduled for the spring of 1932. It would not be a smooth ride.

Chapter 2

The First Games
March 28 - April 2, 1932

"Beginning March 29, Tel Aviv, the little Palestine city, will witness something the world never has seen—an all-Jewish Olympic Games, which Jews from all over the world will demonstrate their prowess in sports."

Milton Bronner, Newspaper Enterprise Association, Feb. 16, 1932

"You bring home the bacon, and I'll eat it."

New York Mayor Jimmy Walker[1]

---

1 Peter Levine, *Ellis Island to Ebbets Field: Sport and the American Jewish Experience* (New York: Oxford University Press, 1992), 264

Milton Bronner's syndicated article, which appeared in several newspapers in the late winter of 1932, heralded a new and exciting adventure as well as offering a smattering of its origin story.

Bronner explained how the impetus of the Games culminated from thirty-five years of Jewish sports clubs scattered throughout the world, with a total membership of 150,000, wanting a major event of their own. He compared it to the Olympics in terms of international scope. In fact, there was some speculation that The Maccabiah Games would serve as a test to see if the Jews of the British-controlled Mandate Palestine—as pre-State Israel was then called—could field a team to compete in the Olympics. Bronner predicted, perhaps over-optimistically, that 1,500 athletes from around the globe would make the trek to the Games, with thousands more coming to enjoy the spectacle.

Long after Bronner's story appeared, however, workers were feverishly struggling to wrap up last-minute details on the facilities to be used in the various competitions, completing it only hours before the March 28 opening ceremonies. The administrators of Mandate Palestine had generously donated the land for a 5,000-seat stadium in Ramat

Photo courtesy The Joseph Yekutieli Maccabi Archive

The Opening Ceremonies at the first Maccabiah Games.

Gan near the Yarkon River, but that decision came barely two months ahead of the inaugural event, so it didn't exactly lighten the burden for the construction process. It may be only a slight exaggeration to say the paint was barely dry in time. (Not that this was an isolated incident or unique to the times of the First Maccabiah; laborers were still putting the finishing touches on several venues for the Sochi Winter Olympics in 2014 as the athletes were beginning to arrive.)

Work on the track and field area was greatly delayed while workers awaited delivery of materials. A scaled-down athletics course was made from coal donated by the Israel Train Directorate. The gymnastics events were held on a makeshift wooden platform constructed at the Rina Gardens in Tel Aviv, formerly a reception garden and moving-pictures hall. Because there was no pool suitable for such a large-scale competition, swimming races and water polo were held at the Haifa Port, where spectators watched from rafts bobbing on the water. The 10,000-meter race was conducted through the streets of Tel Aviv along the beach on a course that was part sand. Tickets were sold at a piano shop and in pharmacies.[2]

In a 1985 interview in the *New York Jewish Week*, Lou Abelson, a member of the U.S. swim team from the City College of New York, recalled the nerve-wracking situation he and the rest of his delegation had to endure: "It was touch and go whether we would go, up to the night before we left."[3]

The *Jewish Week* article further noted "the wooden...stadium was completed by volunteers the day before the opening ceremonies," and Abelson characterized the makeshift track as "very rough. It was like a playground in Bedford-Stuyvesant after a rock group got finished with it. They hardly raked it over."

---

2 "Eye on the Maccabiah: An exhibit of Jewish muscle," *Ha'aretz*, June 23, 2013.
3 "Memorable moments: Ex-swim star recalls first games in '32," *New York Jewish Week*, June 28, 1985.

In the end, the athletes were either bivouacked in tents or set up with local families. According to Abelson, they were pretty much left to their own devices as to how to get to their activities. The American swimmers—all teammates from CCNY—were driven to the Mediterranean Sea, where their competitions were held. Others had to hoof it or utilize bicycles, depending on the location of their event. Given the uncontrollable conditions of the waters, "It wasn't good for record times," said Abelson, who returned to the Maccabiah Games in 1953 as a team physician for the American squad. He also recalled that "security was non-existent, not that you needed it." Given the historical tensions in the Middle East over the last eighty years, this may have been the only time such a sentiment was expressed.

Although Tel Aviv was a relatively large city of 50,000 at the time, it would soon be bursting at the seams. Tens of thousands of people were about to descend. They would also be visiting the small towns dotting the country that served as sites for soccer, tennis, boxing, fencing, track and field, gymnastics, and swimming. Where they would stay, what they would eat, how they would get from one place to another, and other logistical concerns, were matters of happy conjecture, for the overriding philosophy of this gathering of *mishpucha* (family) was "We'll find a way."

While the British governing authorities and Arab neighbors were skeptical, the Jews of Mandate Palestine looked forward to the spectacle. Imagine receiving their brethren from such far-off and "exotic" places as Denmark, Switzerland, and even the United States. On the flip side, what about Jews of the Diaspora, who had only heard about *Eretz Yisrael*—"the land of Israel"—from stories they learned in Hebrew school or the synagogue?

But if the road to hell is paved with good intentions, what is the road to good intentions paved with?

Undertaking the First Maccabiah posed several challenges for Palestine, as the host country, and the various countries that sought to send athletes. Perhaps the most daunting was finding the money to send ever-increasing delegations (which remains a major consideration to this day).

The Great Depression was in full tilt, holding much of the world in its tight grip. Many athletes couldn't afford the expense of going to their local tryouts, let alone travelling across the ocean. And if they *were* selected to proudly represent their nation, could they dare take time off from school or work, assuming they had jobs? At the time, a trans-Atlantic trip took four to five days each way, so it all added up to a lot of time to miss a paycheck.

According to Chaim Wein in his 1981 memoir *The Maccabiah Games in Eretz Israel*[4], the funding of the first Maccabiah "was composed of donations, sale of tickets, and royalties." The intentions were well-meaning perhaps, but nevertheless inadequate. The Anglo-Palestine Bank (later to be known as Bank Leumi) and the Jewish National Fund each contributed three percent of the budget, which was listed as 1,762 British pounds (roughly $6,075 at the time, almost $97,000 in 2014). A little less than half of that—750 pounds ($2,586/$41,300)—was earmarked for a new stadium with just 50 pounds ($172/$2,750) going towards sundry equipment, almost as much as what was spent on prizes (40 pounds/$138/$2,200). Fortunately, then as now, a great deal of the work was done by volunteers, proud to be associated with such a grand scheme, which helped reduced costs.

A 1932 column by George Joel in the *Wisconsin Jewish Chronicle* was representative of the flowery prose of the day. "With the new year already galloping towards oblivion, it won't be long before the Jewish Olympics, scheduled for March 27, will be under way," he wrote.

He discussed the challenges of raising the necessary funds and the public relations/propaganda trips undertaken by athletes and others to spread the word around Europe about the Games via an extensive motorcycle cavalcade. "To give you an idea of just how aroused the Jews all over the world are about the coming Olympiads it has been reported that a group of motor-cyclists, members of the Berlin Macca-bee, are going to drive to Tel Aviv so that they can witness the games,"

---

4 Chaim Wein, *The Maccabiah Games of Eretz Israel* (Israel: Maccabi World Union, 1981), 21

he continued. One hardy soul from Czechoslovakia was reported to be hoofing his way to Tel Aviv, beginning in August, 1931.[5]

The Maccabiyon, as the first few Games were also called, was never meant to be just a sporting event. It was a chance for Mandate Palestine to show off to their coreligionists and the world at large that Jews were strong and capable. In addition to the athletic competitions, there were equestrian shows, a marathon (unofficial) through the streets of Tel Aviv, and a Boy Scout jamboree. "Music will be furnished by an orchestra consisting of Jews from the colony of Chederah who will do their music making while riding horses."

Joel quoted Dr. Alexander Rosenfeld, vice president of the Maccabee World Union, who said, "The Jewish games will have a distinct moral and psychological value. In the first place they will show to the world a new kind of Jewish youth, a youth who has thrown off the hideous shackles of the Ghetto and has emerged physically fit and morally capable of assuming an important part on the reconstruction of the Jewish National Homeland.

The First Maccabiah Committee, circa 1932.

Photo courtesy The Joseph Yekutieli Maccabi Archive

---

5 "Sports Notes," *Wisconsin Jewish Chronicle*, Jan. 15, 1932

"The games will also demonstrate that the Jewish youth of the world, through his various Maccabee organizations, stands squarely behind the Jewish youth of Palestine in the struggle for a national existence."

Rosenfeld also pointed out the ancillary benefits that tourist dollars would mean for the local economy.

* * *

In addition to the pernicious—and spreading—anti-Semitism in Europe, there were local issues to worry about.

Although it is not in the purview of this book to discuss the historical Arab-Israeli situations and tensions, it is impossible to ignore the impact the specter of violence has had on the Games, beginning with the first ones. In 1929, a week of deadly riots broke out in April, triggered by the distrust and animosity between Arabs and Jews over economics and territorial issues, including accessibility to the Western Wall (traditionally known as the "Wailing Wall"), the last remnant of the Second Temple, which was destroyed in 70 CE. It remains one of the most sacred symbols for Jews and a must-visit spot for Maccabiah participants. More than 240 Arabs and Israelis died during the hostilities, with another 600 injured, and relationships remained strained. Some Jewish community leaders thought the timing, three years later, for a frivolous affair like these Games was imprudent and that the concept should be developed further. After much debate, and perhaps as a symbol of defiance, the Maccabi World Union leadership determined that the good outweighed the bad and pressed on for the 1932 inaugural Games. But that decision came barely four months before the projected debut.

Great Britain had agreed to support the Games on condition that Palestinian Arabs and British subjects living in Mandate Palestine would be able to participate. The Games' organizers acceded to the request, but the Arabs refused to join the event, boycotting the affair because of a perception of militarism and the distinct possibility (and subsequent reality) that more Jews would immigrate to Eretz-Israel, further deteriorating the situation between Arabs and Israelis.

Joel's column was even helpful in providing advice on "How to Get to Palestine," referring to a trip aboard the ocean liner Aquitania, departing New York to Israel on March 5, which was offering an "unusually low round-trip rate" that hundreds of American and Canadian Jews were expected to take. The regular fare for first class accommodations was listed at $540 (about $8,600 in 2014 dollars) and up, with tourist class subscriptions going for $250 ($4,000) and up. The duration of the cruise trip was listed at 43 days, "but you will be back in time to greet prosperity," as Joel quipped.

* * *

Competition between Mandate Palestine's two major sports clubs also played a role in the establishment of the Games.

The Maccabi movement had more of a middle-class leaning while their biggest rival, Hapoel, was traditionally a workers' organization. Although attempts were made to bridge the gaps and join together for the sake of unity for the Games, Hapoel decided that the Maccabi group was too "bourgeois" and withdrew its participation in the planning of the event. Naturally, each side blamed the other for the rift.

Aside from interfactional philosophical differences, there was another aspect to consider in this uniquely Jewish situation: accommodations with Mandate Palestine's religious leaders. In return for their support, Maccabiah organizers agreed that no competitions would be held on the Jewish Sabbath, which begins at sundown on Friday and lasts until sundown the following day.

* * *

In early March, the Jewish Telegraphic Agency (JTA), the wire service news organization serving the Jewish press, published an item about a larger-than-normal group from Poland—1,000 or more—heading to Eretz-Yisrael since there was a "perfect storm"—a confluence of the Games, an international trade fair, and the Passover holiday, which would take place a few weeks later in April.

The Games began in grand style. With Meir Dizengoff, the first mayor of Tel Aviv, riding a white horse, the procession travelled the mile distance from the Herzliya Gymnasium, Tel Aviv's first high school. (David Zondolovitz's statue depicting the historic if somewhat grandstand gesture was unveiled in front of Dizengoff's former official residence in 2009.)

Yehoshua Alouf, who would serve as chief organizer for the first five Maccabiahs, appeared next in the parade, followed by representatives of the Maccabi movement. Then came the delegations, bearing the banners and flags, dressed in all manner of costumes and materials, some inappropriate for the heat: Austria, Great Britain, Bulgaria, Danzig, Denmark, Greece, Yugoslavia, Lebanon, Syria, Latvia, Egypt, Lithuania, Poland, Czechoslovakia, Rumania, Switzerland, and, finally, Palestine. Trailing the individual nations were thousands of schoolchildren, released from the burden of the classrooms for this historic occasion. The march to the stadium was practically militaristic, but some locals were disappointed that not every nation treated the occasion with the proper dignity and respect it merited. Writing for *The New York Times*, Joseph M. Levy described the scene as "creating what was probably the biggest traffic jam in Palestine since Pontius Pilot inaugurated the Roman games at Caesarea . . . 2,000 years ago."[6]

At the standing-room-only stadium, Sir Arthur Wauchope, the British high commissioner, and other dignitaries including Dizengoff and Lord Melchett, a British-born Jewish industrialist, philanthropist, ardent Zionist, and president of the World Maccabi Movement, oversaw the proceedings and the playing of "God Save the King" and "Hatikvah" ("The Hope"), which would one day become the Israeli national anthem.

In addition to the March of the Athletes, the spectators, who were mashed in every conceivable space in the seats and on the field, were treated to exhibitions of dance, drills, and gymnastics and calisthenics from thousands of youngsters. "The emphasis on the public display of Jewish strength was used to demonstrate the capabilities of the Jewish

---

6 "Jewish Olympics open in Palestine," *New York Times*, March 30, 1932

people," wrote Nina Spiegel in her book *Embodying Hebrew Culture*.[7] At the conclusion of the program, 120 doves were released, ten for each of the twelve tribes of Israel as written in the Torah.

* * *

Since the Maccabiah Games were a whole new ballgame, so to speak, everything associated with it was reported with extreme interest by the press in Mandate Palestine, if not the world media. Several months ahead of the opening ceremonies, the daily newspaper *Ha'aretz* published an article about the availability of kosher food for athletes and visitors, suggesting that "All restaurants wishing to assure themselves of customers during the Maccabiah Games should contact the secretariat [of the Games] as soon as possible."[8] An announcement in a subsequent issue of the paper served notice that photographers—both amateur and professional—would have to pay for the privileges of snapping pictures. Imagine how that would go over with today's Instagram/selfie generation.

Yet even with some local media reports, how do you gauge the success of such a massive initial undertaking? By the absence of non-sporting incidents, according to one source:

> Despite the fact that during three days of the Maccabiah Games, there were some 100,000 persons in the stadium, and despite the excessive traffic to the stadium along the streets not made to handle such loads—there was not one serious mishap . . . . And during all the days of merriment in Tel-Aviv, not even one drunkard was to be found.[9]

---

7 Nina S. Spiegel, *Embodying Hebrew Culture: Aesthetics, Athletics, and Dance in the Jewish Community of Mandate Palestine* (Detroit: Wayne State University Press, 2013), 57.

8 Wein, pages 41-42

9 *Ha'aretz*, April 6, 1932

For the most part, the American media took little note of the new enterprise across the Atlantic that attracted a relatively small number of participants. Aside from Levy's aforementioned article, *The New York Times* issued no reports on the Games until the Second Maccabiah in 1935. What little news was to be found came from the athletes' home-town newspapers, especially the Jewish press.

"All political and economic worries were forgotten during the past week by Palestinians during the progress of the Olympiad sports in the Jewish city of Tel Aviv," wrote Julius H. Greenstone, Ph.D., in the April 8 edition of the *Philadelphia Jewish Exponent*. In the spirit of cooking the books, he listed the number of participants at 5,000, although this almost certainly had to have included those who took part in dancing and callisthenic exhibitions during the opening ceremonies. "The city was brilliant with flags of different countries and with the gay colors of each of the Maccabean units," Greenstone wrote. "Music and songs accompanied the contestants in the various sports and the large crowds that came from different lands to witness the performances apparently enjoyed the proceedings heartily."[10]

Reliable attendance and participation figures have continued to be a bugaboo during the history of the Games. Keeping track of which delegation was sending what number of athletes, coaches, and staff—which are rolled into the lofty figures, although this is usually not explicitly stated—was also difficult to calculate; entire delegations pulled out at the last minute, mostly due to inadequate funding, with individuals withdrawing for any number of reasons.

Attendance reports for spectators also vary widely, with reporters no doubt wishing to paint as rosy a portrait as possible, leading to a great deal of hyperbole.

Certain nations excelled in certain events in 1932. Egypt, for example, won all of the boxing matches, while track and field events were monopolized by the U.S. team, including Sybil Koff (nee Tabach-nikoff), a nineteen-year-old from Manhattan's Lower East Side, who

---

10 "In Foreign Lands: Palestine Hay During Olympiad Games," *Jewish Exponent*, April 8, 1932

won the 100-meter race, the high jump, the long jump, and the javelin. Egyptian fencer Saul Moyal, who participated in the 1928 Olympics in Amsterdam, won top honors in each of the weapons: foil, epee, and saber. Austria supplied a pair of winning female swimmers in Fritzi Loewy (100- and 300-meter freestyle) and Heidi Wertheimer (nee Beinefeld; 100-meter backstroke and 200-meter breaststroke). Wertheimer had also been a participant in the Amsterdam Olympics.

Wein noted that the "official" results of several events differ from those kept by Walter Frankel, a track and field athlete with the United States delegation. The number of athletes competing in specific events, times, distances, etc., vary from one source to another (although why an athlete would be called on to serve as a record-keeper is not addressed). For example, the official results report that Fritz Deutchser of Austria won the 400-meter race with a time of 52.9; Frankel's reckoning, however, sets the mark at 52.4. While this is not an inconsiderable difference, it can be understood when one considers the accounting was most likely done by hand, so it's quite understandable if poor penmanship, and not anything more nefarious, might explain some of the discrepancies.

Wein wrote, "Unfortunately, no complete set of entry forms and results sheets of the First Maccabiah games is available to us at present and therefore it is quite difficult to determine how many athletes did compete in these Games and who they were."[11]

He offered a list "by no means to be considered . . . complete" of scores of athletes from eighteen countries, some of whom are identified fully, others by just surname or with the title of Mr., Miss, or Doctor as the only means of identification.[12]

Another unique aspect of these early games: medals were not bestowed following each event. In fact, the current "medal count" measuring stick of success did not apply in the first Games. Instead the results of each event counted towards a point system. By that yardstick,

---

11 Wein, 36.
12 Wein, 36-40.

Poland, with 368 points, was the overall victor of the first Maccabiah Games by a wide margin, followed by Austria (281) and the United States (277). Eretz-Israel, which would always have the benefit of supplying the most athletes given the comparatively low costs involved, was fifth with 243.5 points, just behind Czechoslovakia's 245. No other team scored more than 200.

The Games served another, if tacit, purpose: With discord in Europe already beginning to gel, hundreds of athletes and tourists came to Mandate Palestine with no intention of returning to their native countries. According to one source, "following the Maccabiah, 5,000 'tourists' vanished into the cities, the settlements and the kibbutzim. The Maccabiah offered a perfect opportunity for one of the largest illegal immigrations of the Mandate Period and provided a significant addition to the Jewish population of Palestine."[13]

Such logistical and political problems would lead to a withdrawal of British support for the Second Maccabiah three years later. Nevertheless, the 1935 Games went on and several hundred additional athletes and visitors from imperiled countries under spreading Nazi influence similarly did not return to their native lands at the conclusion of the event.

---

13 "The 'tourists' of the 1st Maccabiah," *Jerusalem Post*, July 6, 1981

Chapter 3

The Second Games
April 2-10, 1935

"Between Jews and other nations the Maccabi attempt to bridge all differences and to bring together the youth of the nations in friendly and peaceful competitions. Such meetings prove to Gentile youths that anti-Semitism is the fruit of a vulgar spirit nurtured on atavistic feelings and unfounded prejudices and that Jews were created in the image of God like other human beings."

Dr. Alexander Rosenfeld[1]

---

1 "The Maccabi and Its Ideals," *Palestine Post*, April 4, 1935

For the Second Maccabiah Games, the number of participating countries increased from eighteen to thirty, with some 1,350 participants competing in eighteen events. But were these truly the *best* athletes? Or was it a matter of cost and opportunity? The Depression was still in full swing, so money remained a major issue. Some fortunate athletes were able to pay their own way while others had to rely on personal and organizational contributions, scholarships, and other means.

At a fund-raising dinner held Nov. 15, 1934, at Town Hall in New York City, Nathan Goldstein, president of the United States Maccabi Association, told the gathering it would take about $25,000 (in 1935 dollars) to send a team of thirty athletes to the affair, with $15,000 going towards the delegation's costs and the other $10,000 for overhead. He suggested one way to "salvage" some of those funds was to hold exhibition events that would serve as both a tune-up for the athletes and a money-making proposition for the cause.[2] The U.S. team would stay on for several more weeks, facing Maccabi clubs throughout Europe before returning home.

In attendance at that dinner was Hank Greenberg, the slugging first baseman for the Detroit Tigers. At an imposing 6'3" and 210 pounds, Greenberg probably would have been Nordau's perfect choice as poster boy for the embodiment of muscular Judaism. This came at a time when anti-Semitism in the United States was disquieting, given the country's philosophy of tolerance and religious freedom. Greenberg famously refused to play on Yom Kippur in the middle of the 1935 American league pennant race. His moral stance—and that of Los Angeles Dodgers star pitcher Sandy Koufax a generation later—of honoring his religious traditions became the measuring stick for Jewish athletes to come. Both men have been inducted into the Baseball Hall of Fame, as well as the National and International Jewish Sports Halls of Fame.

An item in *The New York Times* on January 18, 1935 announced tryouts in New York City and Newark, New Jersey, with a description

---

2 "Outline plans for athletes' Palestine trip," *Brooklyn Eagle*, Nov. 16, 1934

of the qualifications for participation: "[C]andidates must be of Jewish descent, citizens of the United States, and registered with the Amateur Athletic Union."[3]

On Feb. 27, 1935, New York City's 102 Engineers Armory was the site of tryouts for the U.S. track squad. Ironically, several of these tryouts were held on Saturday, the Jewish Sabbath, when the observant refrain from certain activities. This forced numerous athletes to make a contradictory and counterintuitive choice, considering the nature of the Maccabiah Games. A key item to keep in mind as well was that success at this trial was no guarantee of being selected for a total team roster of thirty athletes.

"The reason for this is a lack of funds which necessitates keeping the size of the team down to a minimum," Pincus Sober, chair of the Track and Field Committee, told the press. "Because of this, athletes who can compete in more than one event will be given special consideration by the [selection] committee."[4]

So Sober must have been thrilled when Sybil "Syd" Koff won the three events that she entered at the trial—the 60-meter dash, the 80-meter hurdle, and the long jump. Koff—born Sybil Tabachnikoff in on New York's Lower East Side in 1912—was a multi-winner in the 1932 Maccabiah, although sources differ as to exactly which events those were. The general consensus is that she won the 100-meter race, the high jump, and the broad jump. The fourth event varies according to the source as either the 50-meter race, the javelin, or the women's triathlon, which consisted of different events than the customary bike-swim-run of modern times.

All the spots on the Maccabiah team couldn't just go to the East Coast's best, though; that might well have eliminated California-based Lillian Copeland, the Olympic gold medal-winner for the discus in both 1928 and 1932, as well as other outstanding athletes from the rest

---

3 "Trials next month for Tel Aviv games," *New York Times*, Jan. 18, 1935
4 "Girl athlete leads 200 in team trials," *Brooklyn Daily Eagle*, Feb. 28, 1935

of the country. Like Koff, Copeland was also returning for her second Maccabiyad.

As a reminder of the uncertainty of the process, three members were added to the American team after additional financial "angels" came forward: Bernard Kaplan, a two-time light-heavyweight boxing champion; Harry Werbin, a distance runner; and Philip Goodman, who was added to the boxing *and* wrestling squads.

The American athletes set sail on the *S.S. President Roosevelt* on Wednesday, March 20, from New York. That was just the first leg of the arduous trip. "It took three weeks for the American team to arrive in the Holy Land by boat, train, donkey cart, and camel," according to a page devoted to Koff on the Jewish Virtual Library's website.

The *Palestine Post* of March 24 carried an update of the improvements made to the venues for the upcoming Games, including a new soccer pitch, a swimming pool at Haifa, and better standing room sight-views at the stadium where the track and field events would be held. In addition, a new 18-meter tower would house the Maccabi secretariat and press bureau.

* * *

The weather looked as if it would not cooperate, with rain throughout the morning hours, but at the last moment, the sun broke through the overcast. What clouded the occasion to a degree was the refusal by the British authorities to allow a procession through the streets of Tel Aviv similar to that of the First Maccabiah three years earlier out of concern the Arab citizenry would protest.

As it was, 40,000 joyful sports devotees filled every space in the stadium, including the 7,000 seats, the track area, the infield, and other nooks and crannies. They reveled as the delegations strode around the track bedecked in their colorful uniforms. Would the citizens of Eretz Israel once again take their fashion cues from the athletes from exotic lands as they had for Syd Koff in the first Games? "Once there, [she] competed against the world's best Jewish athletes and emerged as the

Photo courtesy The Joseph Yekutieli Maccabi Archive

The procession to the opening ceremonies through the streets of Tel Aviv.

1932 Games' greatest star . . . . Syd made such an impression that, on the streets of Tel Aviv that young Jewish women wore berets at the same jaunty angle that Koff did."[5]

Among the notables in attendance were the consuls-general of the United States, Poland, Austria, and Czechoslovakia. The joyful opening soon turned to confusion when the happy throng crowding the infield caused delays in the running of the men's and women's 400-meter relay while officials tried to clear spectators from the area.

Just as in the first Maccabiah, preparations were late in completion as the event was set to get underway, the track freshly laid just prior to being trampled by enthusiastic spectators gathered on the infield as the participants marched past them. (Track and field entrants would later complain about the "deplorable conditions" of the track.)

The local press carried Lord Melchett's address to the Opening Ceremony in full, including acknowledgement of the ills of Nazism:

"Here, in the city of Tel Aviv, which we gratefully thank for the hospitality that its has afforded us, at a time when Jewry is facing a bitter

5 Jewishvirtuallibrary.org/jsource/biography/Koff.html

oppression and bitter opposition over a large area of the Diaspora, we are able in Eretz Israel to demonstrate in a practical and visible way to show how the success of the present is based upon the struggles of the past."[6]

By the time the Second Maccabiah rolled around, the world was heading towards inevitable disaster. Adolph Hitler and his Nazi regime were well past the planning stages of making life intolerable for the Jewish citizens of Germany and other countries under their spreading domination. Fascism was an excuse to fearlessly embrace anti-Semitism.

For years, Germany had barred Jews from joining its national sports clubs. Yet they still felt it necessary to interfere with the Jewish athletic societies and those members, ordering them not to participate in the 1935 Games. In an act of defiance, 134 athletes—the largest delegation from any foreign country—went to Palestine anyway. Not only that, but they also ramped up their protest by refusing to carry the German swastika flag at the opening ceremonies.

The German delegation won the three-day boxing competition at the Maccabiah before a capacity crowd of 7,000 at the Palestine Pavilion. They were victorious despite the fact that they actually won just one match; their 37 points led all entrants, including Great Britain and Holland (two medals each); South Africa, Poland, and Egypt (one each); and the United States. Bernard Kaplan, the American light-heavyweight entry, was disqualified when he showed up late for his bout. One can only speculate if the German athletes felt extra motivation because of their circumstances.

Nevertheless, there were those athletes not from Germany who also persevered. Among the standouts at these games was Dutch boxer Ben Bril. As a fifteen-year-old, Bril had participated in the 1928 Olympics held in his hometown of Amsterdam. But at what could have been his peak four years later, he was barred from representing Holland at the Los Angeles games, purportedly a victim of anti-Semitism from a key member of the Dutch Olympic committee. Similarly, he would not be allowed to box in the Munich games. The thought of a Jew defeating

6 "Second Maccabiah Flag Hoisted," *Palestine* Post, April 3, 1935

a German in physical confrontation would have belied the notion of Aryan superiority.

Despite these obstacles, Bril was an eight-time national champion. He would be interred at the Bergen-Belsen concentration camp. He was lucky; four of his brothers and a sister died during their imprisonment. Bril died in 2003 at the age of ninety-one.

As mentioned, success at these Games was determined not by the now-familiar medal count, but by a point system. By that metric, Austria finished in first place (399), followed by Germany (375.3), and the team representing Eretz Israel/Palestine (360.5).

Although they didn't place in the top three overall, the United States led the way with thirteen first-place finishes. At the time, there was only one award per event, not the win-place-show/gold-silver-bronze configuration that has become standard in such competitions. Instead, prizes such as loving cups or crystal pieces were handed out by sponsors for specific events. The Americans brought back some hardware, including the Manischewitz Foundation Prize for track and field events. The German women's tennis team won the Greidinger Cup.

In terms of individual accomplishments, Lillian Copeland, who was injured in her preliminary heat for the 60-meter dash, still managed to add to her Israeli trophy collection, winning golds for discus, javelin, and shot put. Her American teammate Abraham Rosencranz was also a three-time winner, earning glory in the men's 800-meter and 1,500-meter races and the 400-meter hurdles. Koff took the 60-meter dash that eluded Copeland, as well as the 200-meter race.

Overall, the second Games left journalists with a lot to discuss. The *Palestine Post*, which changed its name to the *Jerusalem Post* following Israel's independence in 1948, published an amusing little "Impressions of the Maccabiah," which read like a free association exercise. Among the items: "[f]lags on radiator caps . . . bands blaring inane tunes . . . Lord Melchett, resembling yachting skipper . . . Maccabi chief with war ribbons . . . sturdy youth . . . great thrill of emotion . . . Germany has no flag, no swastika . . . a peer of the [British] realm speaking a sonorous Hebrew . . . Jewish prowess . . ."[7]

7 "Impressions of the Maccabiah," *Palestine Post*, April 4, 1935

* * *

The Second Maccabiah ended with a closing ceremony on April 10. As opposed to the first day, there were no concerns about the weather on that final day: sunny skies bathed the athletes and 50,000 spectators in a glow that belied the situations to which many European Jews would be returning.

Lord Melchett reminded the athletes of their pledge to return to their home countries despite these difficulties.

"I am well aware that in the present conditions in Europe the desire for immigration is tremendous," he said. "But it must be clear to all Maccabis that this festival cannot continue if it is to be made the occasion for infraction of laws in Palestine. I therefore appeal to each one personally to remember his promise and to show to the end the excellent order and discipline of our movement."[8]

The American team returned home on the Italian cruise ship Conte di Savoia. A group of Italian boxers were also on board, heading for an exhibition in Chicago against the city's Gold Glove team.

Bernard S. Deutsch, president of the New York City Board of alderman, who had bid the team bon voyage on their way to Palestine, welcomed the delegation back home. "You have kept your word and we're mighty proud of you," he said.

Yet, as was the case in 1932, many athletes decided not to return to their native countries that were under Germany's thrall in 1935. After all, at these Games, there were more than medals and standings at stake. With the Nazis expanding their power almost daily, it was not surprising that young people with little to encourage their return to their beleaguered homelands, decided to take a flyer and remain in Palestine, earning the 1935 Games the nickname, the "Aliyah Olympics." They decided to take a chance with new dangers rather than return to what perils undoubtedly awaited them back in their separate countries under Nazi domination. This included the entire 350-person

---

8 "After the Maccabiah," *Palestine Post*, April 11, 1935

delegation from Bulgaria (although they did send back their athletic gear and musical instruments).[9]

Sybil Koff and Lillian Copeland did not join the rest of the U.S. delegation on the return trip. According to a teammate, Koff, who was the 60 meters and 200 meters champion, remained in Eretz Yisrael for a few weeks, dickering over whether to make aliyah. Copeland, who won gold medals in discus, javelin and shot put, thought briefly of taking the plunge as well, but ultimately returned to the United States after taking a few weeks of well-deserved R&R. As evident by Koff and Copeland's decisions, a lot of the idealistic plans to stay in Eretz Yisrael were undoubtedly made in the afterglow of the feel-good atmosphere, but when reality set in—especially in pre-State years for those whose life back home was relatively secure—cooler heads evidently prevailed.

Nevertheless, it came as no surprise that some of the athletes decided to stay in Palestine. The 1935 Games were held despite the official opposition by the British Mandatory government, who were only too aware of the possibility of a mass immigration into the area, further destabilizing the relationships between Arabs and Jews. At the closing ceremonies, Lord Melchett told the assembled, "I wish to remind all Maccabis of the solemn promise which I have given upon their behalf to leave this country before the period allowed by the authorities expires."

"I am well aware that in the present conditions in Europe the desire for immigration is tremendous, but it must be clear to all Maccabis that this festival cannot continue if it is to be made the occasion for infraction of the laws of Palestine. I therefore appeal to each one personally to remember his promise and to show to the end the excellent order and discipline of our movement."[10]

If the British thought a simple call to honor would suffice, they were mistaken. Yona Olgen Hirschler was a twenty-two-year-old water polo goalie from Hungary. His efforts to joining the national team were denied because of a policy of banning Jewish athletes. Where he

---

9 www.haaretz.com/life/sports/maccabiah-2013/.premium-1.532886
10 "After the Maccabiah," *Palestine Post*, April 9, 1935

was wanted, however, was Palestine. Through some fortunate red tape-cutting, Hirchlser was able to emigrate and virtually immediately upon his arrival, was thrown into a pool in Haifa to play against a team from Libya. The Israeli team won and Hirschler was an immediate favorite and decided to remain in Palestine.

Some seventy years later, in a background piece for the 17th Maccabiah Games, Hirschler's son, Yoram, told Y-net, the Israeli news service, that he owed his life to the Maccabi organization. In a letter offering his services to volunteer for the 2005 Games, Yoram said he never would have been born had his father decided to return to Hungary. Yona's brother disappeared without a trace and it's quite probable the same fate would have befallen him. Instead Yona Hirchlser met Truda, his future bride, who had fled to Palestine from Austria in 1938. Together, they raised three children, including Yoram. Yona went on to become a founder of the Future Maccabi Union for promising young athletes.[11]

The Games That Never Were: The Maccabiah of 1938

Germany was preparing to host the 1936 Olympics in Munich. This would be their chance to show the world the awesomeness of Aryan efficiency and, they hoped, superiority.

But a great concern was raised over the Nazis' treatment of Jews and what that would mean to the purportedly democratic nature of sport. Worried about a general boycott and trying to sweep their abominable behavior and attitude under the rug, Germany nevertheless promised the Olympic Organizing Committee that all credible athletes would be welcome regardless of race or religion.

In an amazing display of short-sightedness, Avery Brundage, president of the American Olympic Committee, stated publicly that Jewish athletes were being treated fairly and that the Games should go on, as planned. After a brief and tightly managed inspection of German

---

11 "Maccabiah saved my life," Ynetnews.com, July 7, 2005

sports facilities in 1934, Brundage gave his endorsement and the Nazi Olympics were a go.

With the increasing global tensions, the U.S. Maccabi Association was queried whether they thought a boycott of the 1936 Olympic Games in Berlin the following year was a possibility. The official stance of the organization was to leave the decision to individual athletes.

Although she had established herself among the United States' elite women track and field stars, Syd Koff would take a stand by refusing to participate in the Munich Olympics.

In the meantime, given the situation, plans for the Third Macca- biah, scheduled for 1938, were abandoned.

While the Olympics section of Sports-Reference.com features a list of 47 Olympians who died in concentration camps,[12] there is no simi- lar documentation of how many Maccabiah athletes were imprisoned or died during the Holocaust, nor does such a roster appear among the records of the Maccabiah archives. The loss of many Jewish athletes during the Holocaust in part explains the small attendance when the Third Maccabiah finally took place, in 1950 in the newly-independent State of Israel at the 1950 Games.

---

12 "Olympians who died in Nazi concentration camps," sports-reference. com/olympics/friv/lists.cgi?id=3

Chapter 4

The Third Games
September 27 - October 8, 1950

"You will be able to compete with Israel sports organizations not only in athletics and games, but equally in the use of the Hebrew language and knowledge of the [Torah] in its original tongue. This Book contains the soul of Israel and the Hebrew language has been the medium of expression of Jewish thought for 4,000 years. Jewish sport is inconceivable without mastery of both."

David Ben-Gurion[1]

---

1 "Military maneuvers end third Maccabiah," JTA, Oct. 10, 1950

I t was a new set of games in a new country.

The post-war years were still fraught with security issues. The years immediately following World War II may have allowed some countries to begin returning to a sense of normalcy, but that hardly applied to the situation in the Middle East.

Israel officially became an independent nation in 1948 and was immediately attacked by the armies of four Arab countries—Egypt, Syria, Transjordan, and Iraq, setting off the 1948 Arab-Israeli War. From the moment the UN recognized this Jewish nation, many of its neighbors sought to drive Israel into the sea, a threat which has been repeated countless times over the years.

Despite these perils, Israel sought to be a true *home* land, one which offers its citizens security and the human rights to go about the business of normal life, such as the commerce of the market place, the culture of theater and music, and the diversion of sports and athletic competition.

Early on, Israel wanted to establish its place among nations in athletic endeavors. It sent twenty-five participants to the 1952 Summer Olympics in Helsinki, but only three to the Olympiad in Melbourne in 1956. It was not until the 1992 Olympics in Barcelona that Israel won its first medals, both in judo: a silver for Yael Arad in the women's competition and a bronze for Shay-Oren Smadja in men's.

But the Maccabiah Games was still "the place to be" for Jewish athletes. Some 500 athletes from twenty countries attended the 1950 affair, the first since 1935.

The number of entrants and countries participating was down substantially from a "wishful thinking" article in *The New York Times* on February 18 projecting the participation at 2,000. There's no telling how many established and potential athletes had been lost during the Holocaust, either killed outright, injured, or severely displaced. (As further evidence of the inaccuracy of figures associated with the Games, the JTA reported seventeen countries competing and 40,000 in attendance.[2])

---

2 "Third World Maccabiah Opens in Israel," JTA, Sept. 29, 1950

Another consideration: the World War had been supplanted by the Cold War. A single entry—from Czechoslovakia—represented all the Jews from those countries now finding themselves behind the Iron Curtain.

These Games featured a new Ramat Gan Stadium, a facility that would accommodate 80,000 spectators (though not necessarily in seats), the number reported by the Associated Press in February. An article in the *Palestine Post* two months later put the figure at a much more modest 50,000, with seats for only 15,000.[3] "The stands are arranged in wide terraces rising to a height of 14 meters so that every spectator will have an uninterrupted view of the whole area," reported the *Jerusalem Post*.[4] The cost of the facility was budgeted at 200,000 IL (Israeli pounds), more than $710,000 in current U.S. dollars. In addition to the stadium, new parking lots, large enough to accommodate 2,000 cars, were also prepared. Once again, the swimming events were held in Haifa while other events were staged in Jerusalem, Petah Tikvah, Sarafand, and other towns. A "Maccabi Village," which served as housing for the athletes, was created out of a military camp in Tel Aviv, situated a short distance from the three towns where sporting events would take place.

The old Maccabi Stadium was also getting a facelift, with seats for 5,000 and room for another 16,000 standees. The construction crew might even have included some Jews from Ireland: "Irish working in Palestine are getting ready their orange-white-green rosettes and clearing their vocal chords for the cheers expected of them when an Irish team enters the sports arena in Tel Aviv this year for the Maccabiah Games," was the cheerful start of a brief story published in *The Irish Times*.[5] The crew consisted of five athletes: two boxers, two wrestlers, and a swimmer. None of them won their respective events.

---

3 "Interest in Maccabiah growing," *Palestine Post*, April 4, 1950

4 "New Stadium Being Readied for Maccabiah Opening," *Jerusalem Post*, Sept. 24, 1950

5 "Irishmen will cheer in Jewish capital," *The Irish Times*, April 8, 1950

In listing the nations that had arrived in advance, *The New York Times* referred to Ireland as "Eire" in an item dated September 30. There was also a delegation from Saar, an area bordering France and Germany which had been designated as a "protectorate" after World War II. However, the French delegation was unable to participate; poor planning resulted in their having to return home before the ceremonies.

International reporting was once again spotty. *The New York Times* ran relatively small items, omitting most of the gymnastics events. The "Paper of Record" did include an advertisement for a fourteen-day trip to the Holy Land, encompassing the sporting event, for $858, round-trip. Ten thousand visitors were expected to visit during the festivities, which coincided with the Jewish holiday of Sukkot, the Feast of the Tabernacles. Tourists brought in an estimated 1.5 million pounds in spending, according to some sources.

The newly-renamed *Jerusalem Post* proudly described the countries that were sending athletes, including a breakdown of what sports were represented. The roster included Switzerland, Argentina, India, and Morocco. Another *Post* piece switched things around, listing which of the sixteen participating countries which would take part in the various events. Swimming topped the list with all sixteen nations taking part, followed by track and field, basketball, and boxing.

Despite the excitement surrounding the return of the Games, the Opening Ceremonies posed some problems. Traffic jams snarled the surrounding road, delaying not only the crowd from taking their seats with ease, but also some of the dignitaries. Yosef Sprinzak, the acting President of Israel, arrived twenty minutes after the scheduled start time. After remarks by Ramat Mayor Abraham Krinitzi, the athletes began to march into the stadium, led by the American delegation with Henry Wittenberg bearing the American flag. "The Americans, wearing grey trousers with dark blue blazers and felt hats, strolled onto the oval as though across a college campus," said a report from the *Jerusalem Post*, which dutifully noted the attire of the rest of the nations: "The Austrians dressed in buff and strutting in a sort of goosestep" is not the kind of imagery one would like to envision. "The Swiss in blue blazers, arched smartly, and the Swedes were the brightest in dress in the parade." That's more like it.

Israel, as the host, brought up the rear with its Games-high delegation of more than 240. "Israel, which had as many entries as the eleven other countries combined, placed in every event and monopolized the field events, where there were few entries from abroad," pointed out an item in the Oct. 5 *New York Times*, perhaps reflecting the mood of other countries that saw their chances for glory fade away by the sheer number of Israeli opponents.

The media also took note that the Americans were the only group that "did not dip their flags" as a sign of respect when passing the officials' reviewing stand. According to U.S. law, the "Stars and Stripes" "may be lowered only in certain circumstances," and this, evidently, did not qualify.[6]

Following remarks by Prof. Selig Brodetsky, the president of the Maccabi movement, Pres. Sprinzik officially opened the Games, to the traditional release of birds. The official flag was raised but then lowered as bugles played a dirge in memory of those who had died since the Games were last held in 1935. The Maccabiah torch was carried by Erich Feurer, a champion track star at the 800- and 1,500-meter level and the anchorman of a relay team that had transported the light almost 24 miles from Modi'in, the burial ground of the original Maccabis.

The United States sent a contingent of sixty, including forty-three athletes. Only three of those were entered in aquatic events. But what they lacked in volume, they made up for in concentration, medaling in all of their events. Aaron Kurtzman won the 200-meter breaststroke, improving on the Maccabi record set in 1937 by 8.3 seconds, finishing with a time of 2:45.5. Morley Shapiro, a sixteen-year-old diver from the University of Southern California, won men's diving, while Robert Fisher, fourteen, finished third in the 100-meter backstroke and crawl and 400-meter freestyle.

---

6 "30,000 Watch Maccabiah Open With Flags of 16 Nations Flying," *Jerusalem Post*, Sept. 28, 1950

Henry Wittenberg, a New York City police sergeant, was the first athlete chosen to represent the United States at the Games that year. Mayor William O'Dwyer offered congratulations at a ceremony at City Hall. Wittenberg, who won the heavyweight wrestling championship at the 1948 Olympics, proved himself worthy of the honor, copping the freestyle title when his opponent, Canada's Fred Oberlander, was forced to withdraw because of illness. It was a much easier time for Wittenberg than his eleven-minute defeat of his Israeli opponent, Moshe Feldman, a few days earlier.

Prior to leaving for Israel, the U.S. basketball team played an eight-game tour of South America in an effort to raise funds for their Maccabiah excursion, winning each contest. More importantly, they won the Maccabiah gold medal, defeating Canada, 56-34, in the final event of the 1950 Games. Both teams had been previously undefeated on their way to the championship contest.

One of the members of the U.S. squad was Ed Gard, a former member of the Long Island University hoops team. Early in 1951, Gard would be one of a small band of players and professional gamblers arrested on bribery charges in one of the most notorious point-shaving scandals in sports history. He served nine months of a three year-sentence for his role as an intermediary between ballplayers and gamblers and was praised by the New York District Attorney's office for his assistance in breaking up the plot.

The Games were still early enough in their development that almost every event involving speed or distance might see a new record broken. "Shattered" was a word frequently seen in stories about each day's new adventures.

Among other highlights of the Third Maccabiah:

An Israeli female gymnast, identified in the official records only as "Shifrut," won four disciplines, including floor exercises, horizontal bar, parallel bars, and vaults.

Oswaldo Shellemberg (Argentina) won three freestyle races: the 400- 800-, and 1,500-meter, setting a new Maccabiah record in the 800s at 10:56.

Susie Nador of Great Britain also won three swimming crowns: 100-meter backstroke and the 100- and 400-meter freestyle.

Ben Helfgott, a Holocaust survivor competing for Great Britain, won a gold medal in the lightweight weightlifting category.

León Genuth (Argentina) bested the U.S.'s David Lasky for the middleweight title, while Lasky's teammate Jerry Steinberg "lost the light-heavyweight crown to a deaf mute from South Africa, a Maxie Ordman," according to the item in the October 6 edition of *The New York Times*, offering evidence of journalism's somewhat politically incorrect nature during that period.

Denmark won five of the eight Greco-Roman wrestling titles, with Israel winning most of the gymnastics, and the U.S., South Africa, and Israel splitting most of the track and field events evenly.

Twenty-year-old Martin Korik, USA, won the pole vault with 12'4". He also won the decathlon, dominating with first-place finishes in the 1,500-meter race and 110-meter hurdles, a second-place finish in the javelin, and a third-place finish in discus.

Ira Kaplan, USA, won the 100-meter run. He finished second in the 200 behind Dave Sandler of South Africa. Sandler's brother Sol, won the quarter mile.

Henry Laskau, the veteran U.S. walking champion, won the 3,000-meter event.

In the high-profile basketball finals—which would evolve into perhaps the marquee event of the Games—the United States beat Canada, 56-34, for the gold medal.

In an article that would be unthinkable today for security considerations, the Israeli press warned those attending the closing ceremonies of impending traffic problems and instructed them on which routes to take to Ramat Gan Stadium. Thankfully, forecasts of rain and high winds for the sendoff proved erroneous and the crowds were treated to clear skies. No doubt it made life easier for the sixty military parachutists who were dropped into the stadium as a final display of Jewish strength.

It was no surprise that Israel took the overall top spot at these Games, amassing well over 600 points, more than twice that of runner-up Great

Britain. South Africa concluded the Maccabiah in third place with the United States coming in fourth. Prime Minister David Ben-Gurion presented the Israeli team with the Benjamin Browdy Trophy; England received the Prof. Selig Brodetsky Cup for their efforts.

Additional trophies were presented, donated by nations and individual patrons of the spectacular. Israel won the Rokeach Cup for soccer and the Eva Peron Cup for tennis. South Africa took home the Hebraica Argentina Cup for water polo. Britain received the Pierre Gildesgame Trophy for weightlifting and the United States carried away the Lord Nathan Cup for basketball; Denmark, the Greek Maccabi Cup for wrestling; and Sweden the Maccabiah Switzerland Cup for team handball.

The games officially came to a close with the lowering of the Maccabiah flag and the extinguishing of the cauldron.

Chapter 5

The Fourth Games
September 20-29, 1953

"I hope that the results of the Fourth Maccabiah will bring satisfaction and pleasure to organizers, participants and spectators alike, and that the occasion will also advance the cause of international friendship."

Lester B. Pearson, Canadian Minister of External Affairs[1]

---

1 "50,000 See Opening of 4th Maccabiah," *Jerusalem Post*, Sept. 21, 1953

"Come back to us for the next Maccabiah and bring along representatives of Rumania, Hungary, and Russia . . . . Carry back with you the message of the creation and courage and independence of Israel"

David Ben-Gurion, Prime Minister of Israel[2,3]

The Fourth Maccabiah Games marked the beginning of its current quadrennial format. While additional nations joined in the fun, those from the Soviet Bloc were still noticeably absent. The Cold War was in full swing and Russian leaders did not want outsiders having access to what was going on behind the Iron Curtain or outside influences interfering with Soviet Jews.

Ada Cohen wrote a succinct background piece in the Philadelphia *Jewish Exponent* explaining Israel's slow crawl to relevance on the international sports stage. Most of their competitions were held relatively local—Greece, Turkey, and Yugoslavia, for example—with mediocre results. The best hopes for athletic prowess lay on the basketball court. Israel's hoopsters took second place at the Moscow European Championships in 1953, to the utter joy and surprise of Jewish fans around the world.

"Clearly no more powerful antidote could have been provided against the anti-Israel teams' successes which were disseminated all over the USSR by Soviet radio and television (but not newspaper) commentaries. In view of the importance which Israel attaches to the fanning of the Jewish spark in the hearts of Soviet Jewry, people here were impressed to hear from sports officials who accompanied our team that they had frequently seen tears in the eyes of spectators among whom they sat watching our side play."[4] Cohen wondered if Israel's success in basketball might not be due to the tough nature of a people who had to endure generations of hardships in Germany, Asia, Russia, and even at home.

---

2 "Ceremony Closes Maccabiah Games," *New York Times*, Sept. 30, 1953
3 "60,000 See Maccabiah Close," *Jerusalem Post*, Sept. 30, 1953
4 "Israel Sports Scene," *Jewish Exponent* (Philadelphia), Sept. 11, 1953

Another example of constant unsportsmanlike conduct came, not unexpectedly, from Israel's Arab neighbors, who in some cases chose forfeits, fines, and sanctions over the ignominy of possibly losing to the Jewish State on the field or court.

On the other hand—and at a time that was removed from the Holocaust by less than a decade—Israel made no secret of its disdain in facing Germany in a sporting situation. In a 1952 international chess tournament, Israel's efforts to "eschew Germans" resulted in a match against the much tougher Russians. "Its consolation was that it acquitted itself well in the games against the USSR better than any other country, lost not a single game in the second preliminary round, and found that all of the U.S. and most of the Soviet players were Jews."[5]

Nevertheless, there would be no Soviet Jews taking part in the pageantry of the opening ceremonies, held on Sept. 20.

Raising funds to send athletes from most countries to Israel was always going to be an issue. An estimated 300 people showed up for a $10-a-plate dinner sponsored by a Jewish sportsman's group in Ottawa to send hoopster Mark Molot and discus/shot put practitioner Bob Abelson in Ottawa, Ontario, more than enough to pay the $1,100 cost for sending each young man. Many Jewish newspapers throughout the U.S. similarly reported on local efforts to raise funds, via dinners of every size to exhibition games and events by the athletes.

An article in the August 6 issue of *Newsday* about efforts to send Adelphi University track athlete Mort Diamond to the games pointed out the fiscal realities of what was involved in sending a team to Israel.

"Of the 25 men chosen from all parts of the United States, expenses for only 15 will be paid by the United Jewish Appeal. Remaining athletes must depend on their own resources, or on contributions from friends and organizations interested in the Maccabiah 'Olympics.'"[6]

A group of senior college hoopsters met in April in Queens, New York, the proceeds of the game going to the U.S. Committee for Sports

---

5 Ibid.
6 "Fund Drive to Send Diamond to Israel," *Newsday*, Aug. 6, 1953

in Israel—the fund-raising arm of Maccabi USA—to help athletes attend the Games.

Col. Harry D. Henshel, head of the USCSI, estimated the organization had received $150,000 in contributions, which would be spent on "food for the 1,000 competing athletes from all the nations for 14 days, not to mention every item of equipment which possibly could be needed," such as "750 cots . . . and 20 tons of frozen meat."[7]

Sports columnist Bill Wolf of the *Philadelphia Jewish Exponent* described the plight of the U.S, team in the upcoming Games, as well as the ancillary benefits of this event that differentiated it from other global enterprises, such as the Olympics.

"The thing that impressed [the U.S. team] most was the opportunity to meet athletes from many countries and get acquainted with their ways in sports. Many strong friendships developed and are due to be renewed again in September . . . .

"One of the big questions—at least from this side of the ocean—will be whether the athletes from the United States will be able to make a better showing than last time. The Israeli squad led the entire field of countries represented. Both England and South Africa finished ahead of the American aggregation."[8]

In a special proclamation, the Tel Aviv municipality called on residents to decorate their homes with flags, ribbons, and other displays to welcome the athletes and an expected 3,000 visitors. Foreign Minister Moshe Sharett and the mayors of Tel Aviv and Ramat Gan arranged a round of functions for the athletes and representatives from abroad.

An estimated 850 participants, including athletes, coaches, and other support staff, from twenty-three countries attended the 1953 Games. Israel provided 279 contestants, with the largest foreign delegation—110 athletes—coming from the United States, more than double the 41 that participated in the previous Maccabiah. The group

---

7 "Fourth Maccabiah Games Facsimile of Olympics," *Christian Science Monitor*, Aug. 6, 1953

8 "Sports," *Jewish Exponent* (Philadelphia), April 17, 1953

featured some returning "alumni" who were competing in their third set of Games and a number of winners in the 1950 competition.

Nearly sixty athletes departed from NY (now John F. Kennedy) International Airport on September 14, following a sendoff at City Hall from Mayor Vincent Impellitteri. In the days before non-stop flights to Israel, the first leg of the journey terminated in England, but the second plane developed engine trouble two hours out and was forced to return to London Airport.

The British team also contained a number of champions from the earlier Games. Israel, as the nation with the most athletes, had a hand in every event while Mexico was represented by a solitary weightlifter.

A dozen Olympians who, because they were not Jewish, would be confined to demonstrations of their particular specialties (as opposed to participating in events) were also traveling with the U.S. delegation. This was considered a major coup for Israel, who had never had the opportunity to see such high-profile performers, with all due respect to those who competed at the Maccabiah.

As the nations marched into the stadium according to the Hebrew alphabet, the media, as they had in previous Games, kept particular track of the attire and deportment of each nation. Haskell Cohen, a noted public relations man specializing in sports, marveled at the spectacle. "The uniforms of the teams were very colorful and often reflected the customs of their various homelands," he wrote in a syndicated column for the JTA. "For example, the Indians wore blue turbans; the Swiss bedecked themselves all in white and the Irish were dressed in traditional bright green. The South Africans wore orange and green, the British blue and white, and the Americans blue and gray."[9]

The sportsmen and women were joined by 6,000 members of various military, political, religious, and social organizations, including the rival Maccabi and Hapoel movements, with 1,500 apiece. The crowd was treated to a twenty-one-gun salute and a choral recital of Handel's "Judas Maccabeus" as well as the traditional release of birds and presentations of bouquets of red carnations to each national delegation.

---

9 "The Fourth Maccabiah," *Jewish Advocate* (Boston), Sept. 17, 1953.

President Itzhak Ben Zvi opened the games and welcomed the athletes and spectators; Sharon Nethanel, chair of the Maccabi World Union's executive committee, also gave remarks.

They were almost a few teams short: nine of the countries reached Israel only hours before the ceremony and barely had time to change for the event.[10] Other athletes would arrive the following day, mostly likely in an effort to save money.

All told, thirteen national delegations competed in the swimming events, with smaller number in water polo, football, basketball, hockey, boxing, wrestling, weight lifting, fencing, bicycling, bowling, tennis, and table tennis.

As a further reminder of the differences between the Olympics and the Maccabiah, Haskell Cohen wrote about the phenomenon of having everyone stay in the Maccabiah Village in his September 17 JTA story:

"In this cosmopolitan setting . . . athletes found customs and languages no bar against better understanding of each other and the furtherance of good sportsmanship. English and Yiddish were adopted as the universal languages in efforts to simplify the language barriers."

Maccabiah Profile: Allan Jay,
Great Britain, Fencing

Allan Louis Neville Jay was born in London, England, on June 30, 1931. He became involved in his sport only by chance when he was fourteen years old. During a summer term at Cheltenham College, which he attended from 1944 to 1948, he was given a few options for extracurricular activities. One was cricket, which Jay claimed never to have liked. Gardening was another choice, but similarly held no interest. He finally signed up for shooting. The problem was, it was a very popular program. "Too many boys went

---

10 "Maccabiah Games Open in Israel's Olympic Stadium," *Christian Science Monitor*, Sept. 21, 1953

for shooting, so the rubbish got the push and I was among them." Then came a life-changing opportunity. "I heard that fencing had been added to the list and if it had been tiddlywinks, I was in it."

Growing up in war-time England had a great impact on Jay as a youth. "At one stage in the war, I went to a Jewish school which had been evacuated to Wales. At the other stage, Cheltenham College had a Jewish House where my father had been a pupil, which is why I went there." Jay's father died in action in 1943.

"We received a certain religious education [at Cheltenham] as Rev Blaslafski came once a week for an hour or so. My parents were not religious and neither am I although I am proud to be Jewish," Jay wrote.

A multi-weapon artist, Jay represented England at five Olympics, from 1952-68, serving as the country's flag-bearer for the closing ceremonies at the 1964 Games. Upon his retirement as an active participant, Jay served as team manager for another three Olympics. He won two gold medals (team and individual epee) at the 1960 Olympics in Rome after finishing fourth in the foil at the 1956 games in Mexico City. He was the World Champion in foil in 1959 and won silver for epee that year. Since then, Jay has served in numerous administrative positions for national and international fencing organizations.

"You will immediately spot that I did not perform well in 1958," Jay wrote in an e-mail interview. "Indeed I did not perform at all, spending all my time studying to pass my solicitor's finals, which miraculously I did at the first shot. It was the happiest day of my life, including winning the World foil championship in 1959 (another miracle)."

Jay remembered how he first heard about the Maccabiah Games.

"I had been living in Australia for around 20 months, and had represented Australia in what was then known as the British Empire Games. I returned in June 1949 and immediately telephoned Tony Cotton . . . who had been the fencing captain at Cheltenham College in my time. He asked me what I was doing that Saturday and when I said 'nothing' he told me that the Maccabiah trials were being held that weekend and suggested that I come along, which I did."

Jay beat Ralph Cooperman—the reigning Junior British foil champion—"and I was on the team."

Jay—who was elected to the International Jewish Sports Hall of Fame in 1985—competed in the 1950 and 1953 Maccabiah Games, winning a total of six gold medals for individual and team accomplishments. He might have come back for more, but "[u]nfortunately . . . they always seemed to take place at the same time as the World Championships, which clearly had priority."

The trip to Israel in 1950 took two stages: A train from England to Marseille, followed by a ship to Haifa. "The SS Artza, an immigrant ship. Three or four days. It [was] impossible to train as the ship would have been rolling around," Jay recalled in his notes. "We returned on the SS Negba. If not luxurious, it was like heaven compared to the Artza." That would be the first of many trips to Israel for Jay.

At the 1950 games, many of the visiting teams were housed at a former British army camp. "But the fencing took place in Haifa and we were billeted with families," Jay said. "I was billeted with a judge . . . whose son became national fencing coach and subsequently president of the Israel Fencing Federation."

It turned out well in at least one regard. "In the camp, the food was terrible, with the exception of the black bread and orange juice. The British Ambassador kindly invited us to a reception and we went mad for the food and drink offered."

The Jewish State was barely two years old when the Third Maccabiah was held, but the situation then was almost as precarious as it remains today, with the threat of attack from its Arab neighbors always in the background. And even though you might be participating as a Jew, among Jews, you are representing your country, with whatever relations it might have with Israel. How do you balance such a situation?

"At the time of [my] first Maccabiah, I was politically unaware," Jay admitted. "But I do remember that with one exception—Great Britain—all participating countries had their flags round the stadium for the Opening Ceremony. Great Britain was [still] unpopular because of the Cyprus camps for illegal immigrants [where illegal Jewish aliens had been interred in the years of Mandate Palestine].

We refused to march unless our flag joined the others and, just in time, [one] appeared, having been brought by a fire engine."

As for the actual competition, Jay remembers the events with a champion's mixture of gratitude and self-assurance. "I won the epee individual title both in 1950 and 1953. I was a very young fencer of virtually no experience. In later years, I got to the top, with other [competitions], but I had my disasters, too." Nevertheless, Jay credits the Maccabiah Games for a spark of interest in continuing to compete. "Certainly I enjoyed my two Maccabiahs and to tell the truth, initially I really got hooked on fencing because of the travelling possibilities."

These days, the octogenarian Jay continues to be involved in the fencing world. "I am more than happy to say that I have been able to be of considerable help to the Israel Fencing Federation over the years and, at my request, the International Fencing Federation appointed me to be the official IFE Observer at the Ma'alot world cup competition."

* * *

Bernie Mayer of the Pioneer Club of New York and Bob Rittenburg of Harvard University set new Maccabiah marks in the shot-put and triple-jump, respectively. They also established new "Maccabee World" marks "which are marks established anywhere in the world by members of the Maccabee Sports organizations. All foreign contestants technically appear as representatives of the Maccabee clubs of their countries."[11]

The United States tennis team won every match save for women's singles finals, in which Anita Kanter fell to future Wimbledon champion Angela Buxton of England. Buxton made sport and social history in 1956 when she teamed up with Althea Gibson for the first mixed race women's doubles team to win Wimbledon and the French Open.

---

11 "Israel Shows Way, With U.S. Second," *New York Times*, Sept. 22, 1953

Henry Wittenberg, winner of his wrestling weight class at the 1948 Olympics and 1950 Maccabiah, won gold by pinning his Israeli rival in less than two minutes. It was one of three top finishes by American men on the mats. Israel won six of ten boxing matches staged in a circus tent in Ramat Gan. The only American win came when Arnold Slomowitz upset the favored Israeli Yiftah Zeid in the light-heavyweight bout on a technical knockout.

The U.S. won its fifth straight basketball game, dusting off Canada 74-29, to move into the finals. One of the wins was an 86-23 pasting of Great Britain at a time when scoring 50 points was a big deal. Another was an even harsher basting of Turkey, 125-17. Israel, in the meantime, was doing just as well: They downed England, 79-28, to face off against the American five.

The gold-medal game received more attention in *The New York Times* than any other event at the '53 Maccabiah. It proved to be the toughest and most exciting challenge for both squads with the U.S. eking out the 25-23 victory.

The Americans took the gold on a buzzer-beater by Paul Groffsky of the University of Michigan. Unlike the fast pace of their previous games, the U.S. group was stymied by Israel's tactic of freezing the ball, practically forcing the Americans to foul out of frustration of the keep-away tactics. After Israel scored the game-tying basketball, U.S. coach Tubby Raskin set up the final strategy. With three seconds left, Irwin Blumenreich, who played his b-ball at the Rego Park Jewish Center in Queens, NY, drove to the basket but missed his shot. Fortunately, Groffsky was right there to tap it home just before the final whistle.

Although you could attribute Israel's traditional success at the early Maccabiah to the sheer number of athletes who participated compared with those from other countries who had to come up with extravagant resources, the host nation had a lot to celebrate at the conclusion of the 1953 Games as well. Israel took top honors in most of the events, including track, swimming, soccer, boxing, wrestling, handball, and shooting.

A soccer game between the Israelis and an "all-star" team comprised of eleven of the best players from other nations marked the final event of the 1953 Games. The soccer ball was delivered "par avion," as a small plane dropped it onto the middle of the pitch to begin the game.[12]

During the halftime break, Parry O'Brien impressed the crowd with his prowess, tossing the discus 177'1", which he said was his best ever. His shot put attempt was not as dramatic, at 55', lower than his previous exhibition demonstration at the 1952 Olympics in Helsinki.[13]

O'Brien and fellow non-Jewish Olympians—sprinter Harrison Dillard and swimmer Beulah Gundling—received awards in appreciation for exhibitions of their specialty.

At the conclusion of the events, Israel was the winner by measure of the point system with 254, followed by the United States (182), and Great Britain (104), with no other nation breaking 100. In terms of medals, however, Israel won 32 gold medals against the U.S. total of 18, the same as South Africa. Great Britain won 16; Argentina was next with five.

Various organizations, governments, and private benefactors distributed numerous awards at the closing ceremonies. The United States won the President Juan Peron Cup for accumulating the most points in track and field events, which Laskau accepted on behalf of the Americans.

Fred Oberlander, a wrestler from Canada, was named best athlete of the Games. Less official was the prize that awaited American Bob Rittenberg, who would receive an award from San Francisco sportswriters for outstanding showing by an American in track and field. Rittenberg had record-setting performances in the triple jump and low hurdles, was second in the broad jump and high hurdles, third in the high jump, and also ran a leg in the relay that won the mile.

---

12 "Maccabiah Games Close as O'Brien Gives Exhibition," *Hartford Courant*, Sept. 30, 1953

13 "Ceremony Closes Maccabiah Games," *New York Times*, Sept. 30, 1953

The JTA reported that as a reward for setting a new high with his javelin throw of 59 meters, Sidney Kiwitt, a twenty-two-year-old from New York, received an Israel bond "and a kiss from Miss Tel Aviv, winner of a local beauty contest . . . . The kiss was a surprise to the youthful athlete."[14]

Other trophies included the Palestine Foundation Fund Cup, denoting highest marks in swimming, which also went to the U.S., as did the Lord Nathan Cup for tennis; the Keren Hayesod Trophy for highest points scored among women; and the Berl Locker Cup for "best team score in men's events. The U.S. basketball team received a trophy presented by the Dubek cigarette factory and Israel won a trophy for boxing.

The Israeli ladies won both swimming and track and field, but there is no mention in the mainstream press about awards given to women's teams, aside from the aforementioned Hayesod Trophy. In an April column, the *Jewish Exponent*'s sports columnist bemoaned the lack of Jewish women in American sports, some twenty years ahead of Title IX which states that "No person in the United States shall, on the basis of gender, be excluded from participation in, be denied the benefits of, or be subjected to discrimination under any education program or activity receiving federal financial assistance."

"[I]n general there is a marked lack of Jewish women in sports," wrote Bill Wolf. "To find the reason, the question of Jewish women cannot be examined alone. Their situation is part of a general situation that exists for all American women with respect to athletics. And that is: Men have a much greater opportunity to take part in sports . . ."[15]

The Games ended with David Ben-Gurion offering a sentiment that would be echoed for years to come: that Jewish athletes from countries behind the Iron Curtain would one day be able to travel to the land of their ancestors to compete in these Games. A send-off show consisted

---

14 "60,000 Attend Closing of Maccabiah games in Israel," JTA, Sept. 30, 1953

15 "Sports," *Jewish Exponent*, April 24, 1953

of folk dances, an air show, and a gymnastics exhibition by several hundred young Maccabeans.

The *Jerusalem Post* printed a critique of the 1953 Games, noting, among other things, the seeming unfairness of the current method of declaring an overall winner.

"It is essential to omit all points calculations in assessing the Maccabiah results," wrote Akiva Kalman. "This provided no little irritation to our visitors from overseas for Israel's advantage in this respect was so obvious."[16] He offered detailed lists of how many first-, second-, and third-place finishes each country earned, both *in toto* and per sport. He also criticized the inaccurate information disseminated prior to the Games in an effort to stir up interest: "The preliminary bulletins issued by the organizers of the event, during the preceding months, named outstanding sports personalities who were coming to the Maccabiah. Many did not [come]."[17]

16 "Maccabiah in Retrospect," *Jerusalem Post*. Oct. 5, 1953
17 Ibid

Chapter 6

The Fifth Games
September 15-24, 1957

"I had prepared a long speech and it was not bad but I won't make it. All I say to you is: Be strong, be unified, be proud and conscious of your Jewishness and send your youth to build and defend Israel for the greatness and glory of our people."

Israeli Prime Minister David Ben-Gurion[1]

At a time when communications technology was much less sophisticated, veteran sportswriter and author Harold U. Ribalow tried to help the cause in attracting worthy candidates for the American

1 "World Title Falls in Last day of Games," *Jerusalem Post*, Sept. 25, 1957

team. In a syndicated article which appeared in the Jewish press around the United States, Ribalow wrote:

> "Each month this columnist receives a number of letters from readers who, themselves, feel that they are good enough for the Maccabiah squad, or know others who are, they think. Once in a while, a rabbi will drop me a line asking where some of the better athletes of their own congregations can apply for entry forms. Well, I hope that this column makes clear that a letter to the U.S. Committee for Sports in Israel will be delighted to hear from all Jewish sports stars all over the land."[2]

Ribalow, who was recognized for his services with a "Pillar of Achievement" award from the International Jewish Sports Hall of Fame in 2009, was prescient as he pointed out an issue that was true for each Maccabiah, but even more so in recent years.

"It should be recalled that not all Jewish athletes are necessarily Jewishly educated or know very much about Zionism or Israel." He compared those who received the opportunity to compete at the Games to contest prize winners and the benefits beyond medals and athletic glory.

"It makes different people out of them" he wrote. "They continue to read about Israel and worry about its people and write letters to friends made there. They become, in a way, walking friends of the State, and always think well of it." Precisely what Israel had in mind.

In his year-end wrap-up, Ribalow—who published several editions of *The Jew in American Sports* from 1948 through the 1960s—noted:

> "[W]e cannot help but be impressed by the vast number of Jewish athletes from all over the world. In reading the English-Jewish papers in Great Britain, Israel, South Africa and other lands, we constantly come across the names of Jewish stars. Quite obviously,

---

2 "Answering the Israel Maccabiah Call" *Wisconsin Jewish Chronicle*, Aug. 9, 1957

in the Hydrogen Bomb Age, the Jew tries to compete—and often succeeds—with athletes of all other nations and faith. He does well enough, too," the writer wound up.[3] As was prevalent in Ribalow's discussion of the Games, he failed to recognize the accomplishments of female athletes in his discussions.

* * *

Exactly how much it cost to send an American athlete to the Games varied dramatically depending on the source. According to Jack Abramson, a member of the Maccabiah Games Committee, "Each [U.S.] athlete is an investment of about $15,000."[4] An item in the *Tucson Daily Citizen* "estimated it will cost $1,500 per athlete."[5] The *Los Angeles Times* put the figure at $1,800 (which may have included the difference necessary to transport the athlete to the East before moving on to Israel) in a small item extolling the assistance of individuals who served as volunteer organizers and coaches under a dire headline entreating tax-deductible contributions.[6]

Without volunteers and donations, in fact, it seems as if the Games wouldn't have been possible. American Mens Wear Manufacturers donated the uniforms to the American team. Another "fashion" item came from of *Women's Wear Daily*, which announced that Ruth Abramson, vice president and designer at Diamond Tea Gown company in Montreal, Quebec, would be attending the Games, serving as the coach for several women's teams including swimming, gymnastics, tennis, track and field, and fencing.[7]

Thanks to these contributions and more from companies and individuals alike, the Games became a reality. An editorial in the *Jewish*

---

3 "The Year in Jewish sports," *Wisconsin Jewish Chronicle*, Sept. 27, 1957

4 "Swimmer laments old age at 14," *New York Times*, Sept. 7, 1957

5 "Paul Ash is invited to Israel," *Tucson Daily Citizen*, July 31, 1957

6 "Lack of Funds May Keep U.S. Athletes at Home," *Los Angeles Times*, Aug. 18, 1957

7 "Trade talk," *Women's Wear Daily*, May 23, 1957

Advocate of Boston indicated the importance of the Games for positive international relations. According to Edward B. Lawson, ambassador of the United States to Israel, "the American Maccabiah teams [serve] as a 'band of assistant ambassadors' who will be helpful 'in creating better relations between the people of Israel and the United States.'"[8]

* * *

There were either 1,200 (JTA), 1,000 (*The Times of India*), 600 (*Wisconsin Jewish News*), or perhaps some other amount coming from twenty-six countries to take part in the Fifth Maccabiah. The JTA reported their ranks were split evenly between the host nation (thereby putting the Israeli roster at 600) and . . . everyone else, including 100 each from the United States and Great Britain (the *Times of India* published the number of Israelis as 350). The presence of a large number of world-class Jewish athletes elevated the quality of competition, as did "The co-operation of top international referees, . . . an outstanding feature" of the Games.[9]

Once again the Soviet Union refused to allow its Jewish athletes to participate in the Maccabiah event. Even importunings from the Russian-born Joseph Yekutieli, the "father" of the Maccabiah Games, could not sway the decision-makers. Nor did any other Eastern bloc nation send any athletes. However, one boxing referee from Poland was allowed to go to Israel. In addition to Russia—which had not sent a delegation since the Maccabiah in 1932—Turkey also boycotted the 1957 affair, joining many of Israel's Arab neighbors.

The male athletes were housed in more than two dozen tents set up at the Maccabiah Village near Ramat Gan while the women were taken in by local families. All the delegations would be treated to a four-day sightseeing tour within Israel, sponsored by the Maccabiah management.

---

8 "Athletes as Diplomats," *Jewish Advocate* (Boston), Aug. 1, 1957

9 "Greatest Jewish Sports Festival Begins Today," *Times of India*, Sept. 15, 1957

In this post-9/11 world, it seems inconceivable that a newspaper would publish a schedule detailing place and time for such a high-profile affair, as did the *Jerusalem Post*. Swimming, water polo, and diving were all held at the Gaiel Gil Pool in Ramat Gan. The popular basketball games were hosted at Ramat Gan Stadium. The town also was the site for boxing, wrestling, volleyball, and lawn bowls. Tel Aviv was the hub for track and field, weightlifting, fencing, tennis, cycling, and table tennis, while cricket was played on a pitch in Haifa; Jerusalem featured the gymnastics competitions; and shooting and team handball at other scattered points. Soccer, being a popular sport in Israel, had several "adequate" fields throughout the country.

The Times of India took note that "Some non-Jewish Olympic stars will also show their prowess, though they are not scheduled to appear in the competition."[10] Among them was Robert Eugene "Bob" Richards, also known as "The Vaulting Vicar" and "The Pole Vaulting Parson" who medaled at the 1948 (bronze), 1952 (gold), and 1956 (gold) Olympics. He also competed in the decathlon in 1956 but did not finish. Richards accompanied the U.S. team to the 1957 Games and held exhibitions and clinics on vaulting and other track and field events.

Another interesting feature came from the renowned journalist Gay Talese, who offered one of the more charming profile pieces in which young swimmer Jane Katz of New York City bemoaned that she was past her prime—at fourteen.[11] Katz insisted she was a superior athlete at the age of twelve.

Despite her reputation as a night owl—she professed to rarely getting to sleep before 2 a.m.—Katz won a bronze for the 400 meters freestyle and helped the U.S. contingent win silver in both the 4 x 100 medley and 4 x 100 freestyles relays. These medals came despite the fact that the team was able to put up only three female swimmers in its fifty-person delegation.

---

10 Ibid
11 "Swimmer Laments Old Age at 14," *New York Times*, Sept. 7, 1957

Katz had started out fast in the individual 400, leading most of the way before tiring. Still, her time of 5:39.8 was her best at the distance by 13 seconds.

Perhaps Katz was onto something when she suggested she was past her prime: despite considerable opinion of the sports media that pegged her as a swimmer with great talent, she never did compete in the Olympics.

Another of the more compelling stories at the 1957 Games was that of Isaac Berger, a twenty-two-year-old weight lifter born in Jerusalem before immigrating to the United States as a thirteen-year-old. He won a gold medal at the 1952 Olympics in Melbourne and would win silvers in 1960 in Rome and 1964 in Tokyo.

For now, though, Berger broke the world record in his featherweight class with a lift-and-press of 117.1 kilograms, bettering the previous mark by more than five kilos. And he did it in the most dramatic fashion: on the last day of the 1957 Maccabiah Games before a packed house, while all manner of other activities were also flashing around him.

"The large crowd, including Premier David Ben-Gurion, was virtually silent as Berger lifted the bar to his chest," reported Moshe Brilliant in *The New York Times*. "His groans were heard in the stands as he strained to raise the weight over his head. There was a deafening roar when the judges raised white flags to indicate he had succeeded."[12]

Race-walker Henry Laskau, who had won the previous two 3,000-meter events at the Maccabiah, was the flag-bearer for the American team, which consisted of a 100- (or so) person delegation.

With the cast of characters set before the Games began, the fans awaited the pomp and circumstance of the opening ceremonies. Little did they know that they were in for a bit of a scare. In perhaps the only misstep of the opening ceremonies, a fuel canister was accidentally ignited by the Maccabiah torch and exploded, sending a smoke cloud

---

12 "Berger Sets Weight-Lift Record In Finale of Maccabiah Games," *New York Times*, Sept. 25, 1957

above the stadium. The flame was swiftly extinguished by alert firemen on hand.

And thus, the Games began, and once again there were several highlights across a variety of sports. For the third straight time, the American men won the basketball final, beating Israel, 79-62. As had been the case in 1953, the American teams entered the finale without a loss, a considerable accomplishment given that they had never practiced as a unit before arriving in Israel. They clicked and overpowered their opponents with ease, including a 72-33 victory over the Dutch team. Israel, although also unscathed leading up to their last game, had a more conservative experience, with closer scores.

Despite its paucity of numbers, the twelve-person Canadian team still managed to take third place after the first day of track and field events, behind Israel and the U.S., thanks to Morris Limonchik's discus throw of 39.07 meters and Freyda Berman, another precocious athlete who, at fifteen, won the 200-yard dash in Maccabiah record-setting time.

For every Jane Katz or Freyda Berman, there was some "old-timer" making one last appearance. One such Maccabiah legend was Henry Laskau, a forty-one-year-old from New York, who won his third straight 3,000-meter racewalk at the Israeli event.

Laskau had been born in Germany and escaped from a concentration camp in 1938, the sole survivor of his entire family. He made his way to America via France and Cuba and served in the U.S. army after becoming a citizen in 1943. Although he had been a runner in his younger days, his interests turned to racewalking and he became a master at his sport, winning forty-two AAU championships from 1947 to 1957. He represented the United States in the 10,000-meter walk in 1948 and 1952, and the 20,000-meter walk in 1956. The Maccabiah gold was his final trophy.

Abie Grossfeld of the United States dominated the gymnastic arena, winning seven out of seven golds, including all-around, floor, high bar, horse, vaults, parallel bars, and rings. As a team, the Israeli women swept every event, although this can most likely be attributed to the lack of competitors from other nations. The hosts also took all but two of the shooting medals, a nod to the still-young nation and their train-ing for national security, perhaps?

Ben Helfgott, a concentration camp survivor, won the weightlift-ing gold medal in the lightweight class for Great Britain for the third Games in a row. His countryman, British Olympian and world cham-pion Allan Jay, won three gold medals.

Agnes Keleti, a Hungarian gymnast who had won four golds at Mel-bourne Olympics, similarly thrilled the crowd on the last day of com-petition with her work on the parallel bars. She had opted not to return home after the Olympics, having left for Australia just as the Hungar-ian Revolution had begun. Instead, she remained "down under" before traveling to West Germany and then on to Israel. Following the '57 Maccabiah, Keleti made aliyah, taking a job in a school for physical training teachers.

British tennis star Angela Buxton, whose doubles triumphs at the French Open and Wimbledon the previous year with Althea Gibson, an African American, also competed in 1957. The unlikely partner-ship of Buxton and Gibson became the subject of Bruce Schoenfeld's critically-acclaimed *The Match: Althea Gibson and Angela Buxton: How Two Outsiders—One Black, The Other Jewish—Forged a Friendship and Made Sports History.*

Buxton, who battled anti-Semitism in her tennis career in Brit-ain's class-conscious society, had also won the women's singles event in 1953. For some inexplicable reason her name does not appear in the "official results" in the archives of the Maccabi World Union for either the '53 or '57 Games.

Perhaps the most impressive accomplishment, however, was that of Herman Leisin, a Dutch Greco-Roman wrestler who had participated in five Maccabiahs, winning gold as a bantamweight in 1932, 1935, and 1950. In the Third Maccabiah, he also won gold as a featherweight in freestyle wrestling. In the '53 Games, Leisin won bronze as a light-weight Greco-Roman competitor. He finished his career with a silver in 1957 at the age of fifty.

At the conclusion of the Games, Joseph Finklestone published a cri-tique in the *Boston Jewish Advocate.* Although he took great pains to be diplomatic, there was, nevertheless, undertone suggestion that the current setup of the Games had a great many problems, not the least of which was a perception by the hosts that whatever they did was proper and without fault, preferring to shift the problem to expectations of the visitors. Finklestone disagreed, and echoed previous reports that using the point system for determining the overall winner was inherently unfair, since this greatly benefitted Israel, which was able to provide an extraordinary amount of athletes. "In boxing, for example, there were . . . only two competitors from abroad, and thus most of the gold medals went to the Israelis [Canada and India won the other two]. In the [soccer] competition there were only three teams . . . and this made the contests almost completely unreal."

During my interviews with Maccabiah athletes from the earlier Games, one complaint that was often repeated had to do with the food. Finklestein's assessment confirmed that. "There were differences of opinion among the competitors as to whether the amount of food they received was adequate, but nearly all agreed that the food lacked variety and that greater efforts should have been made to provide the various contingents with their own national diets," he wrote. "I am not prepared to put all the blame on the Israeli officials but the fact remains that the majority of the foreign competitors suffered from various forms of stomach ailments . . . ." Even the *Jerusalem Post* agreed with Finklestein's evaluation when it came to the culinary shortcomings. They also pointed a finger at unscrupulous business practices. "[A charge] of £2 per day was considered exorbitant for the amenities the [Maccabiah] village offered . . . . Much of the athletes' pocket money went on excessive taxi fares over which there was no control."[13]

The writer suggested that while Israel was to be praised on the aggregate, there were still a lot of issues that needed to be resolved, such as an efficient method of transporting the athletes to their various programs in a timely manner, given the distances from their housing, which were sometimes in other parts of the country. "Planning of the Sixth

---

13 Ibid

Maccabiah should be started now, and not a year before the games in 1961," Finklestone urged.[14]

One prime example of Maccabiah dysfunction: The fittingly named Ike Matza arrived too late to participate in the 800-meters heat. This would continue to be a problem as athletes had to contend with an infrastructure that was inadequate in getting them to their events in a manner that would not put even more stress on them in addition to the tension of the competition itself.

South African sprinter Harold Bromberg received the Swislogsky Medal as outstanding athlete of the Games for breaking the Games' 100- and 200-meter records. Bob Rittenberg, a hurdler, and Laskau accepted the Pierre Gildesgame Cup for the highest point score, while Israel, no surprise, won the President Ben Zvi Trophy for overall point score.

Despite their overwhelming participation, in some cases Israel was not up to the quality of many of their competitors from the Diaspora, especially in track and field. They may be a proud people, but they were not delusional when it came to assessing their performance. Yes, they may have been the overall "winners," but they understood when it came to *world-class* athletes that they were no threat to the rest of the world. The *Jerusalem Post* reflected, "If the Fifth Maccabiah served as an inspiration to youth here to participate more in sports, it will have served a very useful purpose. The scarcity of young Israel stars in the Maccabiah was a great disappointment."[15]

---

14 "Maccabiah in Retrospect," *Jewish Advocate* (Boston), Oct. 17, 1957
15 "Maccabiah Athletics Tops But Lack of Local Stars Felt," *Jerusalem Post*, Oct. 1, 1957

Chapter 7

The Sixth Games
August 29 - September 5, 1961

"I envy you the opportunity to go to Israel to participate in these games. I know it will be a great thing to see the progress Israel is making."

New York City Mayor Robert F. Wagner[1]

---

1 "135 Maccabiah Games Athletes Get Plaque, Praise from Mayor," *New York Times*, Aug. 24, 1961

With those words, New York City's chief executive sent a delegation comprised of American and Canadians (and one South African) off to Israel with a bon voyage speech at City Hall. The delegation flew via El Al, the official airline of Israel, on three separate flights.

"This cooperation brings enduring friendships and sending a team abroad gives the Israelis an opportunity to see the products of our youth of which we are so proud," Wagner said. "My very best wishes go out to you and I know you will uphold the highest traditions of sport."

The group included Rafer Johnson, winner of the decathlon at the 1960 Rome Olympics, who would serve in an advisory capacity to the athletes. Johnson gave his assessment of the American situation prior to departure.

"We should broaden our base beyond track and field and swimming, the sports in which we concentrate," he said. "I feel that we should send overseas teams that specialize in sports that are popular in the nations visited."[2]

Johnson returned in his capacity as an advisor for track and field events as well as ambassador to the Maccabiah for the United States as he had done in 1957. He explained to the media, "The importance of international competition for goodwill cannot be overstated."[3]

The Jewish press was especially effusive with their praise for Johnson's participation in the Games. *The Wisconsin Jewish Chronicle* published an editorial that said, in part,

> There's something extremely lofty and idealistic about the fact that an American Negro will help coach an Israeli Jewish team. We've been trying to find the exact word to express it: Democratic. Brotherhood. Cooperation. Integration. Anti-discrimination. Tolerant. Any of these, and others, you could toss in would all be right and proper. But there's still another word which escapes

---

2 Ibid
3 "Johnson sees Yang as Next Champ," *Daily Independent Journal* (San Rafael, Calif.), Aug. 24, 1961

us—but still haunts us—which would truly exemplify the spirit
behind this . . . .

We have it: the word is Friendship. Wouldn't it be wonderful
if all the people in all the nations were athletes to develop that
'wonderful feeling of friendship?'[4]

Nevertheless, there were still those that did not attend. Arab states
and the Soviet Union were "absent by choice" from the Games, which
were attended by thirty-two other nations, one editorial pointed out.
The Soviets, the article suggested, "while maintaining correct diplomatic relations with Israel and sending Jewish athletes to the Olympic
games, shows little interest in the kind of cultural exchange the contests
in Israel represent."[5]

With time winding down until departure, the press again tried
to spread the word about fundraising events designed to send worthy athletes to Israel. The *Van Nuys Valley News* of August 6 carried
a brief article complete with a heroic photo of college basketball star
Billy Wold. Readers were informed the young man would need $300
to make the trip. A local businessman had pledged $1,800 but had
apparently reneged, according to *The Oregon Statesman*.[6] Meanwhile,
the Pacific Coast Maccabiah Committee set a goal of $40,000 to send
forty local athletes.

According to Associated Press items, the United States would provide the largest foreign contingent with almost 130 athletes, more than
double the number they sent in 1957. Israel, of course, led all countries
with 300 of the reported 1,100 participants, but even that didn't please
the Israeli organizers. Several of the Jewish State's leading soccer and

---

4 "Rafer Johnson has a Word for It," *Wisconsin Jewish Chronicle*, August 25,
1961

5 "Maccabiah games Near Tel Aviv," *Daily Telegram* (Eau Claire, Wisconsin), Aug. 28, 1961

6 "Financial Help Asked for Beaver Hoopster," *Oregon Statesman*, Aug. 8,
1961

basketball players and gymnasts would be competing abroad in other competitions. Dr. Robert Atlasz, Sports Director for these Games, called the poor turnout, "a disgrace."[7]

Max J. Lovell, national chair of the U.S. Maccabi Committee, said that the cost of sending each athlete to Israel stood at $1,500, all raised by "public subscription."

The youngest athlete for the United States was Debbie Lee, a thirteen-year-old swimmer from California. The oldest was Isadore Keil, sixty-eight, a marksman from Delaware, who broke his streak of twenty-eight consecutive years competing at the Grand American Trapshoot in Vandalia, Ohio, for a chance to participate in the Maccabiah.

Once again, hopes were high: Twenty-six countries were expected to send 1,000 athletes, coaches, and support personnel in eighteen sports. As usual, the numbers fluctuated almost daily among the various news outlets, as did the figure for those attending the opening ceremonies, which the JTA reported at 40,000 (and the *Jerusalem Post* at 30,000.)[8]

In a preview of the Games, *Jerusalem Post* reporter Paul Kohn reminded readers of the problems of past events, including a "misleading" point system to determine the overall "winner" as well as complaints about food and transportation for athletes to their events. He also offered a scouting report in which he adjudged the U.S. as having the strongest overall team, as if to alert Israelis, like modern-day investment commercials, that past performances were no guarantee of future success. Still, there was plenty of fun to be had, putting aside the minor inconveniences that, like gnats, regularly pop up at the Games. "In Tel Aviv, anyway, you cannot miss the young men and women in their fantastic variety of dress and headgears, flirting with sabras [Israeli-born

---

7 "Maccabiah Leaders Protest Absence of Israeli Athletes," Jerusalem Post, Aug. 22, 1961

8 "40,000 Attend Opening of Maccabiah Games; U.S. Athletes Participate." JTA, Aug. 30, 1961

Jews] and each other through a babel of languages and taking a lively interest in all they see," Kohn wrote.[9]

The Maccabiah Village, a long-delayed dream, was finally open for business and would hopefully address some of Kohn's concerns. The facility—built at a cost of 2.1 million Israeli pounds—would house about 400. The new facility would include a community center, dining room, patio, L-shaped swimming pool, and nearby shopping.

The space was designed for up to three to share a room comfortably, but in a kind of "mixed blessing" scenario, many more athletes were coming than were originally anticipated, which sent organizers scrambling for places to put them. So in addition to squeezing more people into each room, the overflow of male athletes would be set up at the Wingate Institute and Tadmor Hotel, while the women would be situated at the Validor Hotel and with local families, giving them an extra taste of Israeli life.

Abba Eban, Minister of Education and former Israeli Ambassador to the United States and United Nations, addressed the crowd in Hebrew, English, French, and Spanish. Max J. Lovell, national chair of the United States Maccabiah Games Committee, received a message from President Kennedy, praising the committee for this remarkable endeavor.

> Please extend my greetings to the team of American athletes who will take part in the Sixth Maccabiah Games in Tel Aviv.
>
> Friendly rivalry at international sports events provides a healthy atmosphere for encouraging young people of differing nationalities to recognize the many common bonds and interests which united them regardless of language or country of origin. In practicing the highest ideals of sporting competition, they in return help to strengthen the basic concepts of a free society.

---

9 "Next Week's Maccabiah Games Will B Biggest Ever Held," *Jerusalem Post*, Aug. 25, 1961

The United States Maccabiah team has my best wishes for a trip which will contribute to international good will and advance the spirit of sportsmanship.[10]

Adrianne Ayares of Baltimore, Maryland, got the U.S. team on the board by winning its first event when she beat Tova Epstein of Israel in tennis in straight sets, 6-3, 6-1 the day before the opening ceremonies. Milton Friend, of Maiden, Massachusetts, won the first gold medal, though, when he came out on top in the small-bore rifle competitions.

Not everyone had a rosy experience at the Games, of course. There were so many standout candidates for U.S. men's basketball, the organizing committee decided to take two teams to Israel, one to play in the Games themselves, the other to play exhibition matches around Israel. Sports author and former basketball player Charley Rosen did make it to Israel, but in retrospect, perhaps wishes he hadn't. The 6'8" Rosen was playing outside of his comfort level with a different defensive zone than he'd been used to at Hunter College. He wrote in his memoir, *Crazy Basketball: A Life in and Out of Bounds*, "As a result I was so lost on the court that I was eventually designated as an alternate and never played in the tournament—which the USA won.

"Worst of all," he concluded, "I came down with a virulent case of amoebic dysentery and lost twenty-one pounds in the fifteen days we spent in Israel."[11] This would seem to corroborate a repeated complaint about the quality of the food at the Games.

* * *

10 Letter from President John F. Kennedy to Max J. Lovell, National Chair, U.S. Maccabiah Games Committee, Aug. 23, 1961
11 Charley Rosen. *Crazy Basketball: A Life in and Out of Bounds*. (Lincoln, NE. University of Nebraska Press, 2011), 26

Maccabiah Profile: Marilyn Ramenofsky, USA, Swimming

Marilyn Ramenofsky is another member of that exclusive club of Olympic and Maccabiah medal-winners.

Ramenofsky is currently a researcher at the University of California at Davis studying the physiology and behavior of bird migration. I had the opportunity to speak with her just before she embarked on a three-month expedition to northern Alaska.

Ramenofsky set three world records in her event. In the 1961 Maccabiah, she won a bronze in the 400-meter freestyle and gold in the 400-meter freestyle relay to help the U.S. to a dominating performance as they won all but two swimming events. Three years later at the Olympics in Tokyo, she won a silver in the 400-meter freestyle. Ramenofsky returned to Israel in 1965 to win gold in the 200- and 400-meter races.

She was inducted into the International Jewish Sports Hall of Fame in 1988.

Ramenofsky grew up in Phoenix in the 1950s and '60s, a town she termed "a pretty backwater place."

"Swimming was just a secondary sport; golf and tennis were much further ahead and swimming was pretty much reliant on parks and recreations." She took up the activity as a way to spend more time with her older bother and sister.

"As time went on, I got more and more interested in swimming. My brother, Max, went to Dartmouth. [Being] on the east coast, there was more information about the Maccabiah Games." Her brother's college coach suggested he apply for the U.S. team. He, in turn, told his coach about his younger sister's interest and talent in swimming and was told to have her get in touch with the national organizers, too.

Marilyn Ramenofsky—an inductee of both the National and International Jewish Sports Halls of Fame—modestly claimed Max was the superior athlete, yet he did not make the team, while his little sister was picked for the third slot because, as she said, "there were really so few Jewish women swimmers at that point."

"In those days, you submitted your times. You didn't have to compete like you do for the Olympic Games; it was pretty remedial but it was a great opportunity for me."

Despite all her success and memories, Ramenofsky said one of her biggest thrills was receiving the package of the official gear from the U.S. team.

"It was wonderful! When you make the team you get all the gear, and that was really exciting. [It] came in a great big box and I remember we opened the box in the living room. An early Chanukah. There was the uniform for the Opening Ceremonies, and the track suit, and the swimsuits, and God knows what else."

Prior to leaving for Israel, the swimming team met for two weeks of training at Kutsher's Country Club, a popular spot for Jewish vacationers. "For a kid coming from Arizona with more or less a cultural Jewish tradition, ending up in the Catskills was an event," said Ramenofsky, who up to that point had little in the way of formal coaching. "You don't step onto the international stage without training, she said. "I was a fish out of water, but I just lapped it up. Everything was so new to me. It was enough for me to get a taste of it and realize it was something I really wanted to do."

Ramenofsky remained on a high straight through the plane ride and touching down in Israel for her first trip abroad in 1961.

She shared a notion expressed by many Jews from the U.S. venturing to Israel for the first time, finding the accommodations and infrastructure "a bit backward."

"There was no village. When I went back in '65, they had built the Maccabiah Village. In '61 the women's team was housed in this kibbutz in Ramat Gan, so we weren't even housed with the other athletes. The food was strange to me. It was kosher; I didn't grow up in a kosher family. It was simple food. A big difference from today's sports nutrition. The people were quite aggressive, but generous [and] very warm. . . . Things were very primitive, very simple. I remember being in a bed that was not what I was used to.

"You get all dressed up and usually the Opening Ceremonies are long and it's really hot, and you have to line up ahead of time, but it's so exciting. They line you up by size, the women up front and the men behind, and you march into the stadium.

"The 'biggies' were there and they sit up in the box and you walk by and you turn your head and look and it was so emotional. We're Jews, right? And there's this bond that's ancient and you don't get that at the Olympics. Yeah, I mean, it's exciting and yeah, you're an American, but we're a polyglot."

Ramenofsky thought she was "pretty informed [about Israel]. I just came out of my freshman year in high school. I was fascinated by it, growing up in a culturally Jewish home."

"[Israel] was not the cultural center it is now. Tel Aviv was, but we were outside of Tel Aviv. We were taken to Jerusalem but there was a barbed wire fence between the east and west and we were told not to go near it because they couldn't promise our safety."

The team was not briefed on what to expect before they arrived in Israel. "It was a pretty dead time in terms of those topics." She said the same thing about the Tokyo Olympics. "You just went. You were an American, right? You didn't need to worry about such things."

She recalled Rafer Johnson and John Thomas as "ambassadors" to the 1961 team. "Can you imagine what it must have been like for them? They had travelled, of course, but to be in Israel in 1961, two African Americans? They were not only great athletes, but they were ambassadors. It was so touching."

After the giddiness of the opening ceremonies, it was time to get down to business. "I don't know that I had expectations. I was pretty much there to swim my best and that was a pretty time-consuming thing because it was apparent early on that I really wasn't as trained as the others. I had never been in an international competition before. I was at the bottom of the rung."

"I knew it was going to be stiff, especially from the Americans, and it was. These kids were on big teams that were training year-round. We weren't even training year-round in those days. Very limited.

Her success at the Maccabiah led to a further desire to compete.

"But again, this is pre-Title IX, so after high school, there were no college options. There was no NCAA. To do it, you really had to stay with your AU [Athletic Union] team and so I stayed home, taking courses at Arizona State University and qualified for the European Tour and also for the Maccabiah team and because they were the same summer I went to Europe and then Israel for a number of events."

By the Seventh Maccabiah, Ramenofsky was an old hand at nineteen, with a world record in the 400-meter freestyle under her belt.

"In '65 I was more at the top of my game. The U.S. team paid my way to come and compete in a certain number of events in Israel. I was there for a very short time. The pool was different; I imagine [the previous one] was condemned by then."

Unfortunately, the scheduling conflicts with the World Championships that year caused her to miss the opening and closing ceremonies. She wanted to try again after the Tokyo Olympics, believing she had somehow "failed" in her second-place performance

"It's coming to the fore right now how the whole U.S. Olympic attitude is geared towards Gold medals, so if you don't get one. . . .," she said, comparing it with the Maccabiah experience.

"What I loved the most [about the Maccabiah] was seeing and meeting Jewish athletes, Jewish people from around the world. Seeing that Jews did not all have dark hair and dark eyes. There were blonds, people from Australia, from all over the world. And that was inspirational, "and certainly different from the Olympics. There was a coming together of international people for a common goal. And then, of course, with the whole backdrop of being Jewish. There was a lot of feeling. I think in terms of cultural identity and emotion, the Maccabiah games have it all over the Olympics.

"You have a bond," at the Maccabiah Games, she said. "I met people who were born on a boat that was docked at Cypress; [it was] the whole story of *Exodus*."

Ramenofsky occasionally speaks to various groups—including synagogues, women's clubs, and youth groups—about her experiences at the Maccabiah Games. "I think there might be an athlete that could qualify for the Maccabiah Games but doesn't know about it. I don't know how advertised it gets on the West Coast . . ., but it's important for them to know about this."

She still has boxes of souvenirs. "The medals are nice, something to hold. I keep them in a drawer. I know some people display them. My kids are interested in that. But I don't think I'm a very showy person. I don't know what I'll do with them when I pass on. I guess it'll go to them."

* * *

Ramenofsky's observations about the difference between male and female athletes were reinforced by a profile piece about sprinter Judy Shapiro in the March 10 edition of the *Van Nuys Valley News* that made note of her wishes to compete in that year's Maccabiah as well as the fact that she was not on the romantic market (the headline for the accompanying picture made the point that she was "Talented and Pretty").

The piece read, "While some female athletic stars may scare away prospective boyfriends, Judy has a neat solution for this type of situation.

"'My coach, Dennis Ikenberry, kind of doubles as my boyfriend,' she admits with a smile, and agrees that it is a most convenient arrangement."[12]

Other stories proved to be less condescending. The first of the "second-generation" Maccabiah participants was Michael Wittenberg, son of Henry Wittenberg, who had taken first place in the 1950 Games as a freestyle heavyweight wrestler, a feat he repeated three years later at the advanced age of thirty-five. The senior Wittenberg also won a gold medal at the 1948 Olympics and a silver at the 1952 event.

Michael Wittenberg, a nineteen-year-old freshman at Cornell University, upheld the family honor, winning gold in the Greco-Roman as a light heavyweight. He was one of four named to the team by the

---

12 "2:17.3 Half Run by Judy Shapiro." Van Nuys *Valley News*, March 17, 1961

chair of the wrestling committee—his dad. Wittenberg's Cornell team-mate Phil Oberlander, was named to the Canadian squad. He would go on to win a gold in his weight class. Like Wittenberg, Oberlander's father, Fred, was also a Maccabiah champion wrestler and coach of his nation's team.

Albert Axelrod, a fencer from Scarsdale, NY, had the honor of carrying the American flag during the opening ceremonies. Over the course of his athletic career, Axelrod was a five-time Olympian, earning a bronze medal in the 1960 Games in Rome.

Hopes were generally high for the American lot, which featured such high-profile names as Axelrod; former Wimbledon champion Dick Savitt; Gary Gubner, a triple-threat in the shot put, discus, and heavyweight weightlifting categories; decathlete Mike Herman; and the men's basketball team, all of whom were expected to win their events by pre-Maccabiah prognosticator AP reporter Norman Miller.

Gubner did not disappoint. He set a new record in the discus with a throw of 164'4.5" and another record when he heaved the shot 60'1.25".

More records fell as Canadian Stan Levinson, a twenty-three-year-old salesman from Toronto and another former Olympian (1956), won the 100-meter race with a final push at the finish in 10.6 seconds, sprinting back from fifth place to break the ribbon.

Steve Damashek, like Gubner an NYU student, won the 400-meter in a Maccabiah record time of 48.8 seconds. In fact, four of the five gold medal winners had connections to NYU.

The *Sandusky* (Ohio) *Register* heralded one of its own: "The Huron County of Plymouth is mighty proud of native son Bill Bachrach. . ." who won the 10,000-meter race, the first time he had ever attempted that distance.[13]

---

13 "Plymouth Native Snares First in Maccabiah," *Sandusky Register* (Ohio), Aug. 31, 1961

But those were the only three medals that Team USA won in ten track and field events that day. Israel won twice, along with honors for Canada, France, Holland, Australia, and Italy.

The next day, the "Yanks," as the media took to calling the American squad, set several more records in addition to Gubner's shot mark. Among them were decathlete Mike Herman's broad jump of 24'6", and Lt. Lew Stieglitz, USN, who won the 1,500-meter race in 3:55.

Herman and Elliot Denman were also NYU students and winners of their respective events. Elliot won the 3,000-meter walk in 15:03, while Herman won the decathlon the next day with a total of 6,258 points, more than 1,000 better than his results in the previous Maccabiah. In fact, Herman was so far ahead of his closest rival, Israel's Hanan Frenkel, that he eased off in the final event, the 1,500-meter run, to keep something in the tank for the Sunday relays.

He added to his legendary versatility by winning the pole vault and broad jump, finishing second in the triple jump, a bronze in the high jump, and another silver as a member of the relay team.

Paul Zemechan won the 110-meter hurdles in 15:05, another Maccabiah record.

When the smoke cleared, the American men had won 14 out of 21 events. The U.S. women's track team, by contrast, did not win any gold.

In the years before junior and youth divisions were added to the program, two American fourteen-year-olds competed against their elders and won the male and female platform diving events: Dickie Morse from Nashville, Tennessee, and Kathy Flicker of Millburn, New Jersey.

Records continued to fall as four U.S. swimmers won their events: Barbara Chesnaeu, a student at the University of Pennsylvania from Miami, won the 200-meter breaststroke in 3:00.7, a full seven-second improvement over the previous mark. Lindsay Miller of Encino, California, was even more impressive in the 400-meter event, earning her spot in the finals with 5:13.2 in her heat, lopping more than 24 seconds off the record. Her victory in the finals seemed anti-climactic at 5:15.1. Ellen Welland of New Hyde Park, New York, and Marilyn Ramenofsky of Phoenix, Arizona, finished second and third respectively for a U.S. sweep.

On the men's side, David Abramson, a seventeen-year-old from Brooklyn, NY took the 400-meter freestyle wire-to-wire in 4:33, knocking off :13.8, while John Zakis of Paterson, New Jersey, copped the 100-meter backstroke.

The only events in which the United States did not excel was boxing, and with good reason: they had no entrants in the sport. Israel won six of the nine gold medals, with Great Britain, India, and Holland winning one apiece.

In fencing, the United States won gold in the foils, with Italy finishing second. The roles were reversed with the epee. Canada won bronze for each weapon.

The American group also excelled in gymnastics, where Ron Barak of Los Angeles won four golds—two on the rings, and two on the high bar—despite competing on an injured toe. He grabbed more gold glory when the competition resumed after the Sabbath for the pommel horse and parallel bars. He would finish the Games with a total of eight golds, one silver, and one bronze.

In one of the more tension-filled events, trap-shooter Isador Horowitz of Shreveport, Louisiana, tied with two Israeli competitors, Maxiim Kahan and Dan Kahan, who each hit 93 out of 100 targets. Horowitz won the individual gold in a shoot-out, but Israel came away with the team title.

The U.S. basketball team had a pretty easy time of it, winning their preliminary contests by substantial margins, including a 104-41 walloping over Argentina led by Duke University's Art Heyman's 23 points. The Israelis also made their way to the finals without a loss, beating Uruguay by a much narrower margin, 64-52, to put them up against the U.S.

The Americans beat Israel 83-68 to retain their title from 1957.

The United States wound up with 58 gold medals, twice that of the host nation. Sixteen of those came on the final day of competition, led by the swimmers, who won five, for a total of eighteen in twenty races. They also had outstanding performances in track and field, tennis, basketball, wrestling, weightlifting, fencing, gymnastics, and shooting events.

The U.S. team also won twenty-nine silver and twenty-four bronze, compared with Israel's forty-seven and thirty-eight, respectively. The high totals can be attributed to the vastly greater number of Israeli athletes.

South Africa's eleven golds were good for third place, followed by Great Britain (ten), Holland (seven), Australia (six), and Canada (five).

On September 5, Israeli Prime Minister David Ben-Gurion sent off the athletes with a "thank you" speech before another estimated crowd of 40,000 at Ramat Gan Stadium. Ben-Gurion said he hoped the 1965 Games would include the participation of athletes from North Africa, Eastern Europe, and the Soviet Union. "He said the allegiance of the participants in the outgoing Maccabiah to their respective countries had not been impaired by their attendance here and nothing would happen if Jews from communist bloc and Moslem countries would come for a few days to show their prowess."[14]

He also made his now-standard plea that young people consider moving to Israel, although he mixed his admiration with a touch of cajoling: "You must learn Hebrew. You cannot be a real Jew if you cannot read the Bible in Hebrew," he warned. "I hope that the next Maccabiah will include contests in Hebrew, the Bible, and Jewish history."[15]

"Iron Mike" Herman was named outstanding male athlete of the Games. Madelaine Bergman, "Australia's fleetfooted schoolmarm,"[16] received the honor for female athletes for winning two golds (200 meters, 800 meters) and two bronzes (100 meters, 800 meters hurdles). The U.S. received a silver trophy for having won the most gold medals. Lord Nathan of England, honorary president of the World Maccabi Union, formally closed the Sixth Maccabiah Games.

---

14 "Herman Honored at Ceremonies Closing Sixth Maccabiah games," *New York Times*, Sept. 6, 1961

15 "Sixth Maccabiah Ends, U.S. Takes Most medals," *Jerusalem Post*, Sept. 6, 1961

16 "Mike Herman Gets Top Honors for U.S. at Maccabiah Games," *Florence Morning Press* (Florence, SC), Sept. 6, 1961

Rafer Johnson, who would remain in Israel for several months after the Games to train Israeli athletes, and John Thomas gave an exhibition of their track and field prowess, to the delight of the fans.

The athletes returned to their respective countries having spent today's equivalent of $5 million, according to Pierre Gildesgame, chair of the World Maccabi Union, who said the Games' budget had been balanced by the spectators at the opening and closing ceremonies. He also said, however, that the Israeli government was not as supportive as he had hoped; the monies they have given towards the production and running of the Maccabiah had not increased from the 40,000 Israeli pounds ($72,000 in 1961 dollars) given towards the 1957 Games.

Chapter 8

The Seventh Games
August 23-31, 1965

"This is it. I came out of retirement to compete here again because my heart is in Israel."

> Henry Laskau, forty-eight, after winning a gold medal for race-walking for the fourth consecutive Maccabiah Games.[1]

Planning for these Seventh Maccabiah Games began in August, 1963 with the appointment of Pierre Gildesgame as chair of the

---

1 "At 48, Maccabiah Great Calls it Quits," *Alton Evening Telegraph* (Illinois), Aug. 30, 1965

Maccabi World Union. Almost immediately the quadrennial speculation began as to how many nations and athletes would compete.

The Seventh Maccabiah saw many firsts, not the least of which was
fifteen-year-old Mark Spitz making his international competitive debut
in spectacular style. Most of the other changes were infrastructural.
Ramat Gan Stadium expanded from 35,000 to 50,000 seats and featured a new track and soccer pitch. There was also a new Olympic-size
swimming pool as well as a multi-purpose arena for basketball, fencing,
boxing, wrestling, weightlifting, gymnastics, and judo, a new addition
to the Games. Unfortunately, all presented problems almost as soon as
they were completed: Ramat Gan Stadium and the smaller arena *still*
did not have enough seats to accommodate fans for the more popular
sports. The pool lacked a 10-meter high dive board, which would force
that event to be held elsewhere.

In addition to judo, golf made its official debut, held on the lush
greens at Caesarea. Other new facilities included a shooting range and
a lawn bowling green.

"Not since these Games began has there been as much interest as
Tel Aviv makes a dramatic race against the clock to complete all the
facilities required," wrote Ernest Mehl, sports editor, in the *Kansas City
Times* in February,[2] continuing the cycle of shortsightedness and indifferent management of leaving too much to be done last-minute. (At the
opening ceremonies, Ramat Gan Mayor Avraham Krinitzi marveled
that the stadium was ready on time.)

Mehl pointed out another potential concern: the dates of the Maccabiah conflicted with those of another major sporting event, the University Games, scheduled for August 20-29 in Budapest, Hungary.
What effect would that have on the participation of the athletes who
fell into those demographics?

Nevertheless, with about a month left before the opening ceremonies, Dr. Robert Atlasz, former sports director and now chair of the
organizing committee for the Games, reported that more than 1,000
athletes would be joining in the event, including 300 from Israel. Such

---

2 "Sporting Comment," *Kansas City Times* (Mo.), Feb. 23, 1965

a large showing, although gratifying, created a logistical headache, as it was much more than could be housed at the Maccabiah Village, which was opened for the 1961 Games (and was too small to serve the athletes who came for *that* one). Despite Gildesgame's plans to expand the capacity of the Maccabiah Village from 600 to 1,000[3], the overflow would have to be relocated to a "housing estate for young couples a stone's throw away."[4]

Meals would have to be served in two shifts, but the organizers promised better nutrition, the food being one of the usual complaints, especially from athletes from the Diaspora who were not used to the customary Israeli breakfasts. The *Jerusalem Post* reported that 35 tons of food had been ordered, including 50,000 eggs and 20 tons for vegetables and fresh fruit.[5]

Another new twist for 1965: athletes would be housed according to sport rather than nationality. On the face of it, it was an interesting notion, giving them the opportunity to bond with people with whom they shared an additional common interest. Practically, however, it didn't always work because of language difficulties.

In a gesture of gratitude towards the host nation, Haskell Cohen, the head of the U.S. contingent, praised the Maccabiah Village, acknowledging the "difficult obstacles which had to be overcome."[6]

Once again the Soviet Union declined the opportunity to send any athletes to the Games, Jewish *or* gentile (for exhibition events). Poland became the first Communist bloc nation to be represented at the Maccabiah, but only in a nominal sense since almost all of Poland's Jews had disappeared following the Holocaust.

Absent from the Games—in addition to Iron Curtain countries—would be the South African soccer team. FIFA had banned them from

---

3 "135 Athletes from U.S. will participate in Seventh Maccabiah in Israel," JTA, Dec. 18, 1963
4 "The Biggest Maccabiah Ever," *Jerusalem Post*, July 28, 1965
5 "3,000 calories a day for Maccabia athletes," *Jerusalem Post*, Aug. 19, 1965
6 "Seventh Maccabiah Games open in Israel today; 36 countries represented," JTA, Aug. 23, 1965

participating in official competitions because of that nation's apartheid policies. Other athletes from South Africa might be allowed to compete depending on their individual sports' governing bodies.

The international committee for the Seventh Games set a budget of one million Israeli pounds (roughly $2.465 million U.S. in 2014). As an example of the fundraising efforts, George Konheim of Beverly Hills, chair of the West Coast Chapter of the U.S. Maccabiah Committee, held a meeting at his home.

"It takes $1,800 to provide an athlete with a uniform, transport him from the West Coast to New York, house him for two days during the staging at the group, fly him to Israel and put him up in the Maccabiah Village," he said. "We have a lot of qualified athletes on the coast, and we want to give everyone an opportunity to participate.

"It is important now to raise funds so that none of these fine young men and women are left behind when we leave for Israel . . . ."[7]

In what was undoubtedly one of the more bizarre publicity stunts, the Van Nuys *Valley News* reported that "Sandy Koufax has been named a member of the United States team that will compete in the World Maccabiah games in Israel next month—but conflicting commitments with the Dodgers probably will keep the ace pitcher from being with the Americans."[8]

As if the Dodgers would allow Koufax, their ace pitcher, future Hall of Famer, and arguably the most famous and important Jewish athlete of his generation, to take time off in the middle of the season.

Koufax was given the honor at a luncheon sponsored by the West Coast Chapter of the United States Maccabiah Games Committee as a "thank you" for supporting the program by underwriting the expenses of ten local athletes.

The 1963 estimate of 1,000 athletes ballooned by 50 percent by the time the opening ceremonies were held. The United States, as usual,

---

7 "Fund Drive Kickoff Meet Here Sunday," *Times* (San Mateo, Calif.), June 12, 1965

8 "Name Koufax to Maccabiah Games Roster," *Valley News* (Van Nuys, Calif.), July 25, 1965

presented the largest delegation apart from Israel, with almost 200 athletes, requiring the use of three jets from El Al, the official airline of Israel, to transport them from New York. And as had been and would continue to be the case, last-minute details were necessary virtually hours before the athletes arrived.

As had become commonplace, statistics offered by even the same outlet could differ wildly from day to day. An August 23 item in the JTA announced the number of athletes and countries at 1,500 and thirty-six, respectively. The next day, the count had changed to 1,400/twenty-nine. An editorial in the August 19 edition of the *Daily Globe* of Ironwood, Michigan put the attendance figure at a whopping 3,600.

Following in the footsteps of his late predecessor, President Lyndon Johnson sent a message to the U.S. team as they were leaving for Israel on August 17:

> I am pleased to extend my personal greetings and congratulations to the members of the United States Maccabiah Team.
>
> In an age of tension and friction at the international level, the opportunity for young people of all nationalities to meet in an atmosphere of friendly competition and shared hopes takes on increasing importance.
>
> I know all Americans share my confidence that you will perform in a manner which will do credit to your country and further the cause of international goodwill.[9]

Israel's president, Zalman Shazar, opened the 1965 Games for a crowd of 55,000, with the Israel Defense Orchestra providing the ceremonial music.

As the athletes marched into the stadium, the Israeli press once again seemed obsessed with the fashions of the foreign delegations, and critical of their own: "The largest contingent of all, the Israelis, were good

---

9 Message from President Lyndon Baines Johnson, July 29, 1965

in the march but gained low points for elegance as some wore sandals and others wore shoes. . . ."[10]

A wire service report painted a marvelous picture as it described the delegations' attire. "The stadium, enlarged for the games, was ablaze with color as Israelis in sky blue uniforms, Irish in bright green and Danes in glaring red mixed with the navy blue of the Britons and the gray and black of the Brazilians to form a veritable rainbow."[11]

Deborah Turner, a former gold-winning British subject who had made aliyah, conveyed the Maccabiah Torch into the stadium, the last of 500 runners to bear the flame from Modi'in. Tanhum Cohen-Mintz, one of Israel's best basketball stars, invoked the athletes oath. After brief speeches by Mayor Krinitzi and Gildesgame, 500 doves were released to ecstatic cheers.

Mark Spitz wasted no time in setting a new Maccabiah record in his first event, held the same day as the opening ceremonies, when he took the 400-meter freestyle, knocking 6.3 seconds off the old mark to finish at 4:26.2.

Yvonna Tovis, a seventeen-year-old who had established residency in Israel just six months earlier after immigrating from Czechoslovakia, grabbed the only swimming gold medal the Americans failed to win. Otherwise, the U.S. squad won eleven of thirteen medals.

Spitz aside, the darling of the Games might have been Kathy Cole, a fourteen-year-old from North Miami Beach, Florida. "Little Kathy, who looks like she might be swallowed by the first big wave . . . has bagged three . . . silver medals in the first two days . . . ." reported AP sportswriter Murray Rose.[12]

Cole's third medal came in the 400-meter freestyle behind Marilyn Ramenofsky's record-setting 4:54.4. Ramenofsky, who had won Maccabiah decoration in 1961, was on hand only long enough to compete

10 "Seventh Maccabia Opens," *Jerusalem Post*, Aug. 24, 1965

11 "Maccabiah Games Are Opened by Shazar," *Anderson Herald* (Indiana), Aug. 24, 1965

12 "Girl, 14, Wins Three Medals," *Ironwood Daily Globe* (Michigan), Aug. 27, 1965

in a few races; she had interrupted her competition at the European Championships for the opportunity to return to Israel.

The next day, Cole won two golds, one for the 100-meter freestyle and the other as a member of the 400-meter medley relay. She also earned a bronze in the 100-meter backstroke for a record-setting seven medals, which outshined even Mighty Mark.

Some forty years later, Spitz looked back on his experience as a Maccabiah athlete in a video produced by Maccabi USA, one of a series of "in their own words" projects from men and women who had been named "Legends of the Maccabiah," an honor Spitz received in 2011:

> I credit my success as an Olympian from the fact that my experience was gained internationally at the age of fifteen then again at the age of nineteen.
>
> My first impression when I was fifteen years old was that I was competing for the United States. It was the first time I traveled outside the United States and it was an opportunity for me to explore my abilities as an athlete, to experience swimming under conditions that I had not experienced before, against international competitors, which I had not experienced as well. From that point of view, it was a great learning experience.
>
> I came back in a different capacity in 1985 as a guest to run the torch in and light the cauldron and again as a guest twenty years later. I was not there as a coach or anything, I was there in spirit and it was a great honor for me to play that role.
>
> What I represent is a vision of someone that is marching behind me and all those that came into the stadium, that some day they may go and reach higher levels as an athlete not only at the Maccabiah Games, but onto other sports and levels they want to achieve, maybe even go to the Olympic Games. That's what's important: that we give something back so that we're there as an image, not only globally for what we've accomplished, but spiritually and emotionally for those that are looking at us."[13]

13 Mark Spitz testimonial, maccabiusa.com/about/legends/2011-legends-of-the-maccabiah/mark-spitz/

Gary Gubner, a gold medal-winner at the 1961 Games in the shot, discus, and heavyweight weightlifting, had been named to the team, but had to drop out because of business commitments. Other returning "alumni" included gymnasts Abe Grossfield (1953, 1957; Olympics in 1956 and 1960) and Ron Barak (1961/1964 Olympics).

George Davidson of Lafeyette College was the first coach named by the United States for the 1965 Games. He was expected to lead the men's basketball team to another gold medal, a trophy they had never lost at the Games.

Davidson was no stranger to Israel, having spent time there at the behest of the U.S. State Department and U.S. Committee Sports for Israel to build up the country's hoops program in 1964. The team he put together for the 1965 Games included four "ballers" who were drafted by NBA teams, including Tal Brody of the University of Illinois (Baltimore Bullets, later the Washington Wizards), forward Ron Watts of Wake Forest University (Boston Celtics), guard Steve Nisenson of Hofstra University (NY Knicks), and seven-foot center Dave Newmark, a freshman at Columbia University (Chicago Bulls). Of the four, only Watts and Newmark actually played in the NBA. Watts appeared in one game in the 1965-66 season and twenty-seven the following year. He was selected in the expansion draft by the Seattle Supersonics but never played for them. In addition to the Bulls, Newmark played for the Atlanta Hawks and the Carolina Cougars of the ABA. He also played a season in Israel for Hapoel Tel Aviv in 1973-74.

The U.S. breezed into the finals unscathed. In one game, they outscored their Venezuelan opponents, 142-42, with their other lead-up contests fairly easy as well. Brody gave some indication of what the Bullets would miss, contributing to a balanced offense that went on to take the gold medal over Israel, 74-66.

* * *

Maccabiah Profile: Carol Benjamin, United States, Fencing (1965); Half-marathon (2013)

Carol Benjamin, née Abby, picked up fencing at the age of fifteen in high school in Long Island, New York, where the family belonged to a reform synagogue. She described her upbringing as "traditional, but not necessarily observant."

Benjamin became proficient in her sport fairly quickly and started entering competitions on a wider scope. She went to New York University, in part, "because it had a great fencing team."

"A lot of the fencers I encountered were Jewish and it was through them I learned about the Games." At the time she went to Israel in 1965, she was ranked third in the country, so trying out wasn't necessary. This represented her first trip to Israel and she recalled, "My entire family was beside themselves with excitement, especially my grandparents.

"It made such an impression on me," she said. "I was only nineteen. When I got there, being in the airport—the whole thing was incredibly exciting. We get on the plane, and it's midnight, the whole team . . . They did nothing but feed us the entire way across. It was amazing. At midnight, they gave us corned beef sandwiches. Then at 5:30 in the morning, they fed us bagels and lox. And then at 9:30 in the morning, they fed us a chicken dinner, which I couldn't eat." All to help acclimate the athletes to the time change in Israel. Benjamin said she couldn't eat again so soon. "I gave my dinner to a muscle-bound guy across [the aisle] from me," she quipped.

"So we get to Israel and I felt wonderful. It was the first time I had been . . . in a country that was filled with, primarily, Jewish people. It was very inspiring. The thing that I really, really remember and that struck me as very amazing was, growing up you hear stereotypes— it wasn't that far away from World War II—stereotypes of Jewish men as little old men with beards and scholars and bespectacled reading Torah and just spending a lot of time studying, not very physically strong."

That perception changed at the opening ceremonies.

"They had all these young soldiers and young people . . . in khaki shorts and shirts doing demonstrations. So my whole impression of what a Jewish man was changed. It was so striking."

Photos courtesy Carol Benjamin

Carol Benjamin had a 48-year gap between her two medal-winning appearances in the Maccabiah, the first in 1965 as a fencer (center), the second as a half-marathoner in 2013.

Benjamin returned to Israel for the 2013 Games as a half-marathoner in the "masters" category for athletes who had "aged out" of open competition. "This time" she said, "it was very similar in the sense that everything was growing but the sophistication level was much higher. Last time, there were soldiers with Uzis all over the place. This time I felt completely safe, but you just took it for granted that the organization to protect everyone was much higher. The sense of being safe was very apparent now and less apparent then. Nobody seemed worried at all. This time some people expressed concern—they're always involved in skirmishes—but I wasn't worried at all."

Benjamin said she knew everyone on the fencing team back in 1965, when there was a relatively small number of athletes compared with 2013. "I was a kid but I had a bunch of chaperones, basically. This time, the United States had a tremendous number of athletes.

"The Games were held in a much more concentrated area last time; this time they were all over. Last time, we all stayed at the Maccabiah

Village; this time some were in one place, some were in another."
(The Masters athletes are allowed to arrange their own accommodations and many do not stay with the rest of their country's team).

Benjamin observed that the level of fencing competition wasn't as
high as what she had experienced in other international meets, primarily because of the lack of countries putting up fencers. Some of
the world's best lived in Russia, Germany, and other nations in the
USSR regime, but "there were no Communist countries [in attend-
ance]," said Benjamin.

Just as she had in 1965, Benjamin had to send in several times from
sanctioned races to qualify for the 2013 Maccabiahs. "My times were
pretty good; I was coming [in] one, two, three for half-marathons in
my age groups—I always have to add that," she said. With that confidence, she thought she had a shot at making the Maccabiah team.

Benjamin had the acceptance letter—which had arrived on her sixty-
seventh birthday—on hand during our conversation: "Dear Mrs.
Benjamin: We are delighted to hear from the overall track and field
half-marathon chair that you have been recommended as a member of 19th Maccabiah Games USA Masters half-marathon team.
On behalf of the organizing committee, it gives us great pleasure
to inform you that your recommendation has been accepted. Your
appointment is now official. Let us be the first to offer you congratulations . . ." The letter was signed by Jeff Bukantz, first vice president
of Maccabi USS and chair of the U.S. delegation.

Benjamin said getting accepted the second time was more meaningful. "I'm not sure entirely why. It just meant so much. This is a con-
tinuity of all the training that I did, the connection to Israel, it was
wonderful."

So forty-eight years after her international fencing debut at the 1965
Games, Benjamin returned for her first international half-marathon.

One of the things she noticed upon her return to Israel was the
abundance of trees. And the food: "The first time terrible food, was
not exciting. Good tomatoes, but overall this time was incredibly
delicious."

There were other changes as well.

"The first time around, I couldn't get into East Jerusalem, so I couldn't see the [Western] Wall," she recalled of the first trip that took place two years before the Six-Day War united the city. "This time I was at the Wall, sticking messages in," she said, referring to the Jewish tradition of leaving prayers and good wishes for loved ones, inserted in the hundreds of cracks in the Wall. Much of the touring in 1965 was based on the athletes' discretion and availability.

Benjamin and her fellow distance runners had been warned to train for the hot Israeli conditions, which she did. Fortunately, the event was held in the slightly-cooler evening. Still, it was 80 degrees and humid, and the course was more hilly than she had expected.

As for the Masters program that gave her the opportunity to go back to Israel? "It's great," she said. "It gets many more people involved. People who may have been athletes and continue being athletic and would love to go to Israel under these conditions.

Master athletes are expected to make major financial contributions that go towards sponsoring a younger athlete who would not otherwise be able to participate in the Games. "When I was a kid, there was no way in the world I would have been able [to go]"; she and her brothers were all in college at the time and her parents would not have been able to send her to Israel. "A man in my community donated a whole bunch of money to the Maccabiah Games and earmarked some of it for me it once I had made the team."

"Now we were thinking, we'll just pay the whole thing [for a younger athlete], but my kids talked me into fundraising. I am the worst fund-raiser in the world." Benjamin's daughter helped out in that regard.

The Games are important. "It helps, just like it says, to promote good feelings and interactions among young people and older people" who may be interested in donating money and time, as well as mentoring younger athletes. "It helps to promote athleticism and positive interaction and healthy interaction among young people who are Jewish in this country and with kids from other countries. And it works."

Although Benjamin said she would love to participate in the 2017 Games, that pesky fundraising business might be the deal-breaker.

* * *

Overall, the U.S. finished with the most medals that year: sixty-eight gold, forty-five silver, and thirty-three bronze, for a total of 146. Israel was next with 107 (thirty-two/forty-five/thirty), followed by Great Britain's forty-six (eighteen/ten/eighteen). South Africa won thirteen gold medals; no other country won more than four top prizes.[14]

For the United States, the story was just as much about what they left behind in the form of athletic equipment. As Haskell Cohen said, "We wanted to win as many . . . as we could, but it was important for us to promote good will and physical fitness. I feel confident we have succeeded in all respects."[15]

The standard Maccabiah post-mortem reiterated the disappointments regarding the poor organization of some of the events. "At times the crowds did not know what was going on as events were cancelled or switched to other days." Although the Games were covered by an increasing number of news agencies, the organizers didn't appear to understand the importance of making the process easier. "At one stage, overseas journalists were forced to sit on the stadium steps in order to obtain results of track and field events. A member of the organizing committee of the Maccabiahs commented that no one had asked them to come here anyway."[16]

The addition of Tal Brody to their national sports program for decades to come more than compensated for what Israel was lacking in the medal count that year. It would take awhile, since Brody would lead the U.S. basketball team to another gold medal in the Eighth Games. But the Holy Land had made such an impression on him that ultimately he made aliyah and became one of the most important sports figures in Israeli history.

---

14 "Maccabia and muddle," *Jerusalem Post*, Sept. 3, 1965

15 "U.S. Aces Dominate Games," *Bronwood Bulletin* (Texas), Sept. 1, 1965

16 "Maccabia and muddle," *Jerusalem Post*, Sept. 3, 1965

Chapter 9

The Eighth Games
July 28 - August 7, 1969

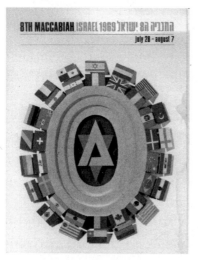

"For every [Israeli] soldier who is killed in the war, we hope 10 boys and girls will remain to replace them because we are going to urge and educate the young people to come and settle in Israel."

Pierre Gildesgame, Chair, World Maccabi Union[1]

As in the 1965 Games, the 1969 Maccabiah opened to fanfare and heightened security in a period of frequent Arab bomb attacks

---

1 "Maccabiah Open in Tel Aviv Among Festivities," *Wisconsin Jewish Chronicle*, Aug. 1, 1969

in Tel Aviv and other cities in Israel, two years after the Six-Day War dramatically expanded the Jewish State's territory.

"Despite continual warfare along its troubled ceasefire lines with Arab countries, the Jewish state welcomed the players with all the pomp it could muster," reported the Associated Press.[2] On May 16, many of the Maccabiah athletes made a plea for peace to UN Secretary-General U Thant at a ceremony held in honor of Jerusalem Day, which commemorates the city's reunification following the 1967 War.[3]

The Eighth Games started off in a more solemn mode than previous kickoffs, with a memorial service for Israeli military who had died in the service of their country since 1948. In addition, there was a tribute to Jews who were unable to attend because of political restrictions of their various homelands. They were represented at the ceremony by athletes originally from those countries—including Egypt, Morocco, Poland, Czechoslovakia, Hungary, and Russia—who were fortunate enough to have fled to the Jewish State.

Iran and India, whose governments refused to issue exit visas to its Jewish athletes, were similarly absent from the festivities. India's Prime Minister, Indira Gandhi, prevented the three-member team from attending the Games, fearful of how such a rapprochement with Israel would sit with Arab nations.

Joseph Yekutieli, whose imagination was the impetus for what had become an ever-expanding event, lit the ceremonial torch in Modi'in. From there, the flame was conveyed by runners to Ramat Gan Stadium in Tel Aviv, roughly 24 miles, or slightly less than a marathon away. Deborah Turner, a British gold medal-winner in the 100-meter race at the 1961 Games who had made aliyah, handed it off to Amon Avidan, captain of Tel Aviv Maccabi basketball, who lit the cauldron before a packed house, as President Zalman Shazar officially opened the Games,

---

2 "War Backgrounds Maccabiah Games," *Independent* (Long Beach, CA) July 29, 1969

3 "1,400 Athletes from 31 Countries will Send Peace Plea to Thant at Maccabiah Opening," JTA, May 13, 1969

with youngsters performing exhibitions of mass calisthenics. Flocks of birds were released as a symbol for peace.

Twenty-seven nations sent some 1,450 athletes to compete in the Eighth Games. Pierre Gildesgame made the traditional plea for the athletes to consider making Israel their permanent residence once the Games were over. "For every soldier who is killed in the war, we hope 10 boys and girls will remain to replace him," he told the crowd of 40,000.[4] (*The Jerusalem Post* reported an estimated 65 participants had made the decision to make Israel their new home following these Games, "but the number is not final and might even be doubled."[5] Gildesgame had reported that about 15 percent of the participants from the Seventh Games had made aliyah.)

Israel's Prime Minister Golda Meir echoed Gildesgame's sentiments. "This country belongs to all of you. We need you here for its upbuilding and re-creation," she said.

She also praised the thousands of young men and women who were serving in the Israeli military. "You should know that they are there also for you—giving their lives for the whole Jewish people," Meir said both in Hebrew and English.[6]

The Spitz kids, Mark and Nancy, made for a most economic addition to the U.S. swim team, accounting for 10 percent of the team while accruing a combined eight medals on the first day alone. After carrying the American flag during the opening ceremonies, Mark won the 100-meter freestyle, seven-tenths of a second off the world record at 52.09. He was also a member of the gold-winning 4x200-meter relay team, setting a new Maccabiah record of 8:30.9. The next day, Spitz added to his hardware with golds in the 100-meter butterfly and 200-meter freestyle.

Nancy Spitz—at fifteen, the same age as her brother in his Maccabiah debut four years earlier—took silver in the women's 100-meter

---

4 "Eighth Maccabiah games Open in Israel Among Festivities, memorial Observance," JTA, July 29, 1969

5 "Lessons of the Maccabiah," *Jerusalem Post*, Aug. 10, 1969

6 "Maccabiah ends with Premier's call to youth," *Jerusalem Post*, Aug. 8, 1969

freestyle, finishing second to South Africa's Missy Caplan, and followed that up with a gold in the 200-meter freestyle. Nancy took another gold in the 800-meter freestyle, narrowly beating fellow Americans Marla Rappaport and Rebecca Seitlin.

Following his splash on the swimming scene at the '65 Games, Spitz's appointment to the '69 squad barely received notice in the sports sections. Hell, Buddy Taylor—the U.S. team *trainer*—got a huge write-up in the *Pittsburgh Courier* of June 1. *The Van Nuys News* published a piece about swimmer Ellen Epstein, a North Hollywood high school junior who had been named to the team. The un-bylined article, which took great pains to mention Epstein's academic and extracurricular accomplishments as well her athletic skills, also served as a request for donations to help subsidize the trip.

Overall, the U.S. dominated in the water once again. Among their gold-winning performances:

Nancy Spitz, 200-, 400-, and 800-meter freestyle

Marian Spira, women's 100- and 200-meter butterfly, 400-meter individual medley

Richard Miller, 100-meter backstroke

Larry Gibbs, 200-meter backstroke

Murray Greiner, 100-meter breaststroke

Paul Katz, 200-meter butterfly

Mark Spitz, 100-meter freestyle, 200-meter freestyle, 100-meter butterfly

The men's 4x100-freestyle and medley relays and 4x200-meter freestyle 400-meter relay

The women's 4x100-freestyle relay

There were some noteworthy story lines from non-U.S. swimmers as well. In a stroke of bad timing, 1968 Olympic team member Yoel Kende was recalled to duty by the Israeli army and was unable to compete in the finals of the 100-meter breaststroke. As hungry as Israel was to have a good showing on this international athletic stage, this was an important statement on national priorities.

In the years before the specialty of sports medicine and positive reinforcement techniques became en vogue, Great Britain was an early adapter of hypnosis as a tool to improve an athlete's mental focus. David Ryde, the London-based doctor serving as the nation's physician, suggested the technique for swimmer Katherine Ingram and diver Angela Tyler, both sixteen, who had sustained hand and foot injuries, respectively. Although neither won a medal, his therapy allowed them to continue competing where more traditional methods of merely wrapping the injuries might have impeded their performance.[7]

In gymnastics, the U.S. won six of seven events, led by Mark Cohn of Philadelphia, who captured the all-around competition and pommel horse while teammate Barry Seiner, also from Philly, earned top honors for the horizontal bars and floor exercise. Fred Turoff, another Pennsylvania "neighbor," won gold for horse vaults and rings.

Over on the track, Canadian Abbie Hoffman set a new Maccabiah record in the 800-meter run with a mark of 2:08.9, while Israel's Shaul Ladany walked to the 3,000-meter gold in 13:35.4, also a new Games record. Ray Roseman of Great Britain improved on his personal best in the 1,500-meter run by 4.3 seconds to win the Gold. He had already won the 5,000-meter event.

Stan Wald, a record company director from South Africa, won gold in the 100-meter race, but lost by a tenth of a second to the U.S.'s Michael Fratkin in the 200s.

One of the oddities of the Maccabiah has been the fluctuation of how many athletes participate in any given event. In some cases, there just weren't enough to hold a competition and in very rare occurrences for team sports, an athlete from one country might find himself filling a sport for another. In 1969, only three men started the decathlon; the winner was Jerry Novilowsky of Austria.

David Berger was a member of the United States team in 1969 when he won gold for middleweight weightlifting. Like fellow American Tal Brody, he would make aliyah and compete for Israel in the 1972 Olympics. Sadly, he was one of the eleven members of the Israeli team who would be murdered at the 1972 Munich Olympics.

---

7 "Hypnosis Helps Girl Swimmers," *Tucson Daily Citizen*, Aug. 5, 1969

The level of tennis talent continued to improve, with the United States enjoying a golden sweep. Allen Fox, a former Davis Cup member for the United States, won men's singles and teamed up with Ronald Goldman for the doubles crown. Julie Heldman—the No. 2 female player in the U.S. and winner of the Italian Open—won out in the women's events, winning singles, doubles with Marilyn Aschner, and mixed doubles with Ed Rubinof. Heldman was inducted into the National and International Jewish Sports Halls of Fame in 1989 and 2001, respectively.

Over on the hardwood, the U.S. team got off to a promising start by manhandling their opponents from Brazil, 89-30, led by Brody's 29 points. They also beat Uruguay, 94-90, with Brody posting 28 this time. Then they absolutely crushed Mexico, 104-29, and handled Argentina 92-33 to move into the finals.

The U.S. team was selected relatively early, in April, in hopes that the twelve-member squad would have a chance to gel, with occasional practices before leaving for Israel. A small wire service item mentioned that they had asked for longer beds for the '69 games.[8]

Following his 1965 experience, Brody eschewed playing in the NBA, trading in USA's red, white, and blue for the blue and white of Israel. He was only on Team USA because he still had to fulfill his military obligations. The Army gave him the permission and time off to participate in the 1969 Games. (Compare this with Kendo's situation with the Israeli army.)

Israel, in the meantime, was making its way to a gold medal showdown with the U.S. by knocking off Argentina (82-42), Canada (79-52), and Australia (107-67).

Israel upset the mighty U.S. squad, 74-70, on the last day of competition to win the gold. The Americans, led once more by Brody, with 21 points, had closed a halftime deficit of 39-26 to make things interesting.

---

8 "American Cagers Voice Opinions," *Lubbock Avalanche-Journal* (Texas), May 25, 1969

Maccabiah Profile: Tal Brody,
United States/Israel, Basketball

Tal Brody deserves a chapter of his own.

He was among the top basketball players in the U.S. in 1965, selected by the Baltimore Bullets (now the Washington Wizards) as the 12th overall pick in the same draft that included such NBA stars as Bill Bradley, Gail Goodrich, Rick Barry, Billy Cunningham, Dave Stallworth, and the Van Arsdale brothers, Dick and Tom. Bradley, Cunningham, and Barry would eventually be inducted into the basketball Hall of Fame.

After Maccabi USA invited Brody to play with the team for the Seventh Maccabiah, he asked the Bullets' owner (and fellow Jew) Abe Pollin for permission, persuasively arguing what a wonderful opportunity it would be.

As so many who have participated in the Maccabiah Games over the years would say, it was a life-changing time for Brody. He would not go on to NBA glory. Instead he would make aliyah and help Israel become an international powerhouse on the hardwood for the next fifteen years. They won the European Championship for the first time in 1977.

Their opponent in that game was CSKA Moscow, the Soviet Army team, a major force in international competition. A match like this could have served as the inspiration for *Rocky IV*, in which an underdog, despised by the opposition and used as a propaganda tool to hail Soviet superiority, won in a stunning upset.

The Soviet Union had had no diplomatic relations with the Jewish State for years and was, in fact, supporting Israel's Arab enemies. They routinely refused to send a team to the Maccabiahs, nor would they grant visas for Israelis to come to Russia. So a neutral site for the game was found in Belgium.

Like in *Rocky*, Israel shocked Russia and the basketball world by beating the mighty Russians by a dozen points, 91-79.

Interviewed immediately after the victory, Brody is credited for one of the most inspirational remarks in the Jewish state's history. "We are on the map," he said in Hebrew to a television reporter. "And we are staying on the map. Not only in sports, but in everything."

After he retired as an active player, Brody remained in Israel where he became one of the sport's greatest ambassadors, and his post-playing career has included numerous positions as a national spokesperson. He has received numerous accolades in recognition of his great achievements on and off the court, including induction into the International and U.S. National Jewish Sports Halls of Fame in 1996 and 2011, respectively.

Brody grew up in Trenton, New Jersey, in the 1940s and '50s, where he had a traditional Jewish upbringing: Shabbat dinners, synagogue on the holidays, religious school on Sundays, and a bar mitzvah.

He picked up basketball at an early age. By nine years old, he was playing in several youth leagues at the local Jewish community center, Police Athletic League, and Boys Club. He recognized that this was what he wanted to do with his life, an ambition that was reinforced by his coaches.

He heard about the Games as he was wrapping up rookie camp with the Bullets following an outstanding college career at the University of Illinois.

"I was practicing with some of the players during the summer, waiting for preseason camp to begin. I got an invitation to play in the Maccabiah Games in the summer of 1965. We had the tryout at Kutsher's Country Club and our team was chosen: twelve good basketball players, and we did win the Gold Medal."

He convinced Pollin and Buddy Jeanette, the Bullets' owner and general manager, respectively, that this was would be a fantastic opportunity for him to improve his game against international competition. In fact, Brody was trying to work out a trade to the Philadelphia 76ers, where he would probably have more playing time than he had been getting as a bench player in Baltimore.

Brody tremendously enjoyed touring around the country, "feeling that history of Israel, the culture, the history, the religion—all the things that related to me." When he was approached by the Maccabi Tel Aviv basketball team, a team that had never gotten past the first round of the European Basketball Championships, he picked up the gauntlet. They believed he was the missing piece that could push them to the next level.

"Considering that the NBA was not the NBA of today—today you're the 12th, 13th player [in the draft], you probably sign for $2 million—at that time the average salary was $30,000 and the minimum was $12,000—when they came to me with this challenge . . . it appealed to me."

Brody said he was "completely indebted to Maccabi USA because they brought me to Israel. If it wasn't for the Maccabiah Games, I never would have had a chance to go to Israel . . . . I would have missed the most beautiful moments of my life. It's not only stepping foot on the ground in Israel, it was seeing that the possibility of taking on that challenge and feeling a part of this country—the religion, the culture, the history, I felt a part of it."

Brody's father had moved from Europe to Mandate Palestine, residing there for three years before coming to the United States. "It wasn't like I was completely ignorant of Israel," Brody said, "but just like everybody in the United States before the Six-Day War, you knew very little about Israel."

Things certainly were different in Israel than what he had been used to back in the USA. Gone were the sellout crowds at Illinois. "All of a sudden, you're playing outdoors on asphalt and you're playing games where you get rained out—which was a real shock when I wrote back to my friends—or in windstorm or in cold weather in Jerusalem. Even when I think about it today, I don't know how I did that. It was a completely different atmosphere. The competition wasn't like the Big 10, that's for sure.

"That first year in Israel was such a wonderful experience. I went to Israel to play basketball, but I stayed because I saw what basketball was doing for the country. After my first year, I decided to come back for a second. Everything that was happening to me during those two years, I thought I was going to make aliyah [in the summer of 1968]."

That would have to wait, though, until Brody fulfilled his military obligation. During that period, during which he played basketball in various armed forces tournaments, he was given a furlough that allowed him to compete for the U.S. in the 1969 games, where they lost in the finals for the first time. He returned to Israel for good in 1970.

Brody said he never considered that he was giving up a life in the NBA. "Not really. You can't compare the NBA with thirty teams and minimum salaries of $470,000 and the average salary between $5 and $7 million today with what it was in 1965."

"Knowing everything which I have [accomplished] in Israel, all those moments in this country, going through, what, five wars and two-and-a-half Intifadas, and my daily life, family life, I would give up that [NBA money] and take the road to Israel . . . . You can't put into dollars and cents what I've been through."

Although Brody said he "felt great" representing the United States at the Maccabiah Games and other tournaments, he had no "funny feelings" playing for Israel in the Ninth Games in 1973.

Photo courtesy The Joseph Yekutieli Maccabi Archive

Heroes of the Maccabiah: Tal Brody, left, and Mark Spitz at the opening ceremonies in 1965.

Brody has seen some amazing transformations during his long association with the Games. "When I came [in 1965], Mark Spitz and I led the delegation. At that time there were 1,200 athletes from twenty-five countries. During the [2013] Games, to see over 9,000 Jewish athletes from close to seventy countries is an amazing feeling. Just as I have that feeling of taking that ride and seeing what has happened since I made that decision to come to Israel and take a team that . . . made it to the finals to the 'cup of cups,' the first landmark that Israel can be a basketball [power].

"[I]n 1977, when picking up that trophy, it was like picking up all of Israel when we won for the first time the European Basketball Championship."

Brody has parlayed his reputation into helping various organizations. He is chair of the Children at Risk program; honorary president of B'nai Herzliya, where more than 1,000 boys and girls from 5-18 play basketball, which grew to an organization that features all sports for 8,000 youngsters in the area; and board member on the Committee for Maccabiah Games. He's also a part of the Maccabi World Union.

"To see that from the raw beginning to today, that we have basketball from Elat to Gilil Eliyon. Basketball has spread all over this country. From a stage where you get rained out of games to a stage where we get into Madison Square Garden, where we have 18,000 people cheering for our team against the New York Knicks; it's beautiful to be part of that ride."

* * *

Despite the success of some events like the basketball matchup, returning Maccabiah competitors couldn't expect the Games to go by without some form of controversy. In 1969, there were two: the sensitive issue of "who is a Jew" and the rights of amateur athletes.

Two members of the Belgian water polo team were "outed" regarding their Jewish identity. According to a strict interpretation of *Halacha*, Jewish religious law, a person is considered Jewish only if he or she is born to a Jewish mother or undergoes a conversion process under the guidance of an Orthodox rabbi. Each country sets its own "standards" when it comes to qualifications on their teams. Israeli national law holds that either parent may be Jewish.

The situation came about when the Canadian water polo team, following their loss to the Belgians, registered a complaint about Paul and Mark Rigaumont, a pair of brothers whose Jewish father had competed in the event at the Maccabiah Games in 1953, 1957, and 1961. Their mother, however, was not Jewish.

Gildesgame ruled that the athletes were not Jewish. The Maccabiah organizing committee upheld the decision at which point the entire Belgian team withdrew rather than continue without the brothers. Team manager Abie Polak said, "We withdrew our team because we came with 11 athletes whom we support 100 percent. We feel they should play in the Games and we cannot allow them to be put aside."[9]

Another Belgian—a table tennis participant—withdrew voluntarily after opponents accused him of not having a Jewish mother.

Over on the basketball court, officials from the Brazilian delegation accused their opponents from Uruguay of fielding players who were not "officially" Jewish.

The Uruguayan team had made it to the semi-finals before they were barred from future games. The situation wound up in a Tel Aviv district court, which overturned the ban on the basis that the Organizing Committee had failed to defend its decision. A lawyer for the Uruguayans argued that there was nothing in the Maccabiah rules that "specifically" limited the Games to Jewish athletes, and that an Arab actually competed for the Israeli team (and won a gold medal). A spokesperson for Maccabiah explained that according to their bylaws, the Israeli national team was forbidden from discriminating against non-Jews.[10]

In a stunning case of red tape, the court returned the decision to the World Maccabiah Union rather than the International Maccabiah Games Committee (the body that rules on by-laws and rules in competition) so the original ban held, ultimately pitting the United States against Israel in the finals.[11] Shimon Caspi, who served as honorary treasurer of the Games, would resign in protest of the ousters a week after the event.[12] In a sad turn of events, he died two days later at the age of fifty-seven.

A post-Maccabiah evaluation offered several suggestions for future events. For one thing, the Jewish identity controversies served as a wake-up call for the Games' officials to be more diligent in vetting the athletes.

Perhaps a bigger issue, at least from a United States perspective, was one that had far-reaching implications on college sports.

---

9 "Feud Mars Maccabiah Games," *Tucson Daily Citizen*, Aug. 2, 1969

10 "Judge Overrules Racial Ban," *New York Times*, Aug. 5, 1969

11 "Controversy over Jewish Identity of Athletes Roils Maccabiah Games," JTA, Aug. 4, 1969

12 "Maccabiah Treasurer Quits over Disqualification of Non-Jewish Athletes," JTA, Aug. 11, 1960

The men's basketball program came up against bureaucratic red tape with the National Collegiate Athletic Association. Under NCAA rules, student athletes were not allowed to participate in "any organized outside basketball competition except during the permissible playing season." The penalty was the loss of the players' eligibility.

The rules were put in place in response to the point-shaving scandals of the 1950s and '60s since potential dubious contacts were often made during the summer seasons when players took part in various exhibitions. The lone exception: the Olympics.

The Maccabiah Games, although scheduled during the summer, obviously fell within these parameters. Needless to say, this put the Americans in a bind. "I'm not happy with a situation over which we have no control," said Robert Rosenberg, president of the United States Maccabiah Committee.

Basically, the team was left with three options, none of them favorable: disobey the rules and have the players bear the brunt of any penalties; withdraw from the basketball competition; or draw up a new team comprised of players outside the NCAA's jurisdiction.[13]

Yale University decided to challenge the edict on behalf of Jack Langer, a twenty-year-old, 6'8" center from Fort Lee, New Jersey who had been named a member of the Maccabiah squad.

Langer was the only one of the eleven players to defy the ban. Actually, according to DeLaney Kiphuth, the school's athletic director, "It's not Langer who is defying the ban; it's Yale."

The school's administrators fully supported Langer, vouching for him before the NCAA that the Maccabiah Games should be a special case, given its educational and cultural mission.

"These games rank very much higher than the Pan-American Games and just below or equal to the Olympic Games. There is a religious issue, too," said Kiphuth.

"When the [U.S. Maccabiah basketball] team comes back from Israel, we'll see what the effect the defiance of the ban has had," he said.

---

13 "2 Sports Groups enmeshed Again," *New York Times*, June 11, 1969

"It might even be that we will be placed on probation and lose our NCAA television appearances.

"We're not looking for a fight, nor are we backing away," he said.[14]

So Langer played for the silver-winning Team USA. And sure enough, the NCAA stuck by its guns. He was banned by the Eastern College Athletic Conference (ECAC), which followed NCAA guidelines. Despite this, Yale used Langer in its season-opening game against Fordham University on December 3. After the game, ECAC officials said they would review Langer's case; Yale would face losses for any game in which Langer played if the ban was upheld.

Other teams were in a similar bind. That same summer, the NCAA ruled that the St. John's University basketball team could not travel to Spain and Italy for a exhibiton tour, drawing the ire of their legendary coach Lou Carnesecca.

"It was an injustice to the kids not only at St. John's but to players all over the nation. . .," said Carnesecca. "It's making us look foolish in the eyes of the Europeans. How can anyone expect us to solve the Vietnam War when the NCAA and the AAU [Amateur Athletic Union] can't patch up their differences in a power struggle?"[15]

Sports Illustrated took up the issue in its "Scorecard" section of September 15, pointing out the differences between the letter and spirit of the NCAA rule. What harm could it be for Langer and other players to compete in an event that is clearly of no conflict, but rather a "turf war" between the NCAA and AAU? A month later, Sol Leiber, national basketball chair of the U.S. Committee Sports for Israel, responded with a letter to the magazine in which he tried to straighten out some misapprehensions.

"I would like to clear up a misunderstanding that has grown out of one of your statements. . . . While it is true that the AAU does sanction the Maccabiah Games and our selection committee, we have never called upon the AAU for any assistance in making our team selections.

---

14 "Yale Defies N.C.A.A. Ban on Games in Israel," *New York Times*, July 28, 1969
15 "Carnesecca Hits N.C.A.A. Ruling," *New York Times*, Dec. 2, 1969

A number of coaches misread your article and erroneously assumed that that was the reason the NCAA did not sanction our team."

Ultimately, Leiber wrote, "We feel the NCAA should give us the same consideration they give to the Olympics and Pan American Games."

* * *

At the wrap, the host nation led with 151.5 total medals, against 138.5 for the United States. The U.S., however, came out on top with 63.5 gold medals to Israel's 48.

They were followed by Great Britain with 10½ gold/8 silver/13 bronze and South Africa with 8/18/25. No other country won as many as twenty combined medals.

The '69 Games concluded with a closing ceremony at Ramat Gan Stadium, full of dancing and singing. Prime Minister Golda Meir gave the visitors a sendoff after which they paraded (euphemistically) through the streets and enjoyed a display of track and field events and gymnastics set to music.[16]

Following the formal finale, the athletes took part in a "Jerusalem Day" tour of the Old City, where they walked through the Arab market and visited the Western Wall, the Knesset, Hebrew University, and Israel's monument to John F. Kennedy, before concluding the tour on Mount Scopus.[17] It was the first time since Israel declared statehood that Jews had access to that part of the country.

Looking ahead, another logistical consideration would be scaling back the number of competitions. "It has been decided that the 21 sports included in the Maccabiah were too great a burden on the organizational resources," wrote Gideon Hod in *The Jerusalem Post*. "The 9th Maccabiah will have fewer sports, and, it is hoped, will be better organized."[18]

---

16 "Maccabiah Games End," *New York Times*, Aug. 8, 1969

17 "Maccabiah Competitors Tour Jerusalem," *Kansas City Times* (Missouri), Aug. 7, 1969

18 "Lessons of the Maccabiah," *Jerusalem Post*, Aug. 10, 1969

Chapter 10

The Ninth Games
July 9-19, 1973

"The success of the ninth Maccabiah Games will be our answer to the Munich tragedy."

Chaim Wein, Organizing Chairman[1]

The 1973 Maccabiah Games were held in the shadow of the Munich massacre, in which eleven members of the Israeli delegation were murdered by Palestinian terrorists at the 1972 Olympics.

---

1 "U.S. Hoop Star to Light Opening Torch," *Lowell Sun* (MA), July 9, 1973

More than 1,750 athletes from twenty-eight nations came to participate in twenty-two sports and events at forty-five venues scattered through the country. As usual, Israel supplied the largest contingent—335 athletes, including twenty-seven who had emigrated from the Soviet Union, which once again declined to participate as a nation. The United States led the visitors with 263 and was expected by many to sweep the swimming competitions.

The assembled athletes and spectators experienced both joy and sadness as the opening ceremony paid tribute to their lost brethren, including Moshe Weinberg, wrestling coach, and Yossef Romano, weightlifter, who were killed at the Olympic Village trying to protect their teammates; weightlifters Ze'ev Friedman and American expat David Berger; wrestlers Eliezer Halfin and Mark Slavin; Yakov Springer, a weightlifting judge; Yossef Gutfreund, wrestling referee; Kehat Shorr, a shooting coach; Dutch-born Andre Spitzer, a fencing coach; and Amitzur Shapira, track coach. Berger and Romano had finished first and second as middleweights at the 1969 Maccabiah. (In a bittersweet display of empathy, Holland's Marion Dringer, who came in second in the women's foil, gave her silver medal to Spitzer's widow.)

Ex-American basketball star Tal Brody, now captain of the Israeli national team, carried the Maccabiah torch on its final leg of the journey from Modi'in. He was accompanied by Esther Shahamorov and Shaul Ladany, two of the surviving members of that 1972 Olympic squad.

Upon hearing the screams of his comrades, Ladany—who already had a brush with death as a young boy in a Nazi concentration camp—had leapt from a balcony and alerted authorities to what was transpiring. Shortly after the Olympics, Ladany set a world record in the 100-kilometer walk and would go on to win the 20- and 50-km walks at the 1973 Maccabiah.

The ceremony began with a memorial prayer by Israel's chief rabbi, Shlomo Goren, followed by the lighting of eleven torches representing their eleven fallen countrymen. A military chaplain offered another prayer: "Remember, O Lord, the souls of the eleven sons of Zion, cherished champions of Israeli sport—who were slain at the hand of evil murderers in the city of Munich."[2]

Chaim Wein, the Game's organizing chair, later remarked, "The success of [these Games] will be our answer to the Munich tragedy."[3] Golda Meir and Abba Eban also paid homage to the slain athletes, after which Israel's president, Ephraim Katzir, officially opened the Games.

A *Jerusalem Post* article reporting on the ceremonies noted the colorful attire by the 1,600 athletes who marched into Ramat Gan Stadium. The piece also marked the shifting times: "The change in fashions since the last Maccabiah was accented by the flared trousers and long hair of many of the men."[4]

Despite the heartache, Israel was in a celebratory mood as the games approached. The Jewish State marked its 25th anniversary in 1973, an infant compared with other countries, yet millennia old in religious and cultural significance. All sorts of celebrations were planned, with entertainment provided by such international luminaries as Barbara Streisand, Pablo Casals, Leonard Bernstein, and Rudolf Nureyev. It would prove to be a tourist's heaven and promised to yield economic benefits from Israel's top "industry." One of the fundraising events in California was a dinner-dance held on the SS Queen Mary in June.

These Games took place during a relative lull in hostilities, one that would be shattered just weeks later by the Yom Kippur War. Nevertheless, seeing to the safety of thousands of athletes and spectators continued to be a major concern and the Israeli authorities beefed up security with hundreds of extra personnel.

In 1973, the leading controversy was the withdrawal of invitations to several athletes from South Africa. Despite the claims that the Maccabiah was an event for Jews rather than nations, the organizing committee still had to abide by the rules of the various governing organizations which oversee individual sports in this case the International Amateur

---

2 "Americans Reap Harvest of Medals First Day of Maccabiah Action," *Danville Register* (Virginia), July 10, 1973

3 "Security is tight for Jewish games," *Tuscaloosa News*, July 8, 1973

4 "Colourful March past opens Maccabiah," *Jerusalem Post*, July 10, 1973

Athletic Federation as well as those that governed boxing, weightlifting, wrestling, and track and field that barred athletes from that apartheid state.

Athletes from Spain and Rhodesia—countries that had no formal diplomatic relations with Israel—marched in the opening ceremony sans national flags; the rationale was that they were not competing as citizens of their countries, but as representatives of local Jewish sporting associations.[5]

Members of the South African team who were sanctioned by their respective sports' governing bodies condemned their national leadership as well as the Maccabi World Council for "knuckling under" to the IAFF. Harry Kampert, a life member of the SA Maccabi Council, resigned on principle, stating, "I and many other Jews are furious at this iniquitous and immoral move. The South Africa Maccabi should put all our athletes on the plane and challenge Israel to stop them from competing."[6]

The Games were budgeted at an estimated four million Israeli pounds, about $960,000 in U.S. dollars at the time. A similar amount went into upgrading Ramat Gan Stadium with new lights, seats, grass, and "improved services."[7]

In 1973, the Games had their own quirks when it came to some of the participants. Linda Sharp, a "Miss Province of Victoria" beauty queen, competed in seven track events. One of the more unusual scenarios involved Joseph Garrie, a twenty-year-old judo practitioner from California, who was the sole representative of Japan, where he was attending college. He won silver in the up-to-70 kg division.

Cricket was part of the sports menu for the first time, played on pitches in Ashdod and the old Maccabiah Stadium in North Tel Aviv. The U.S. sent a team built almost exclusively of men from California

5 "International Maccabiah 'Olympics' Open in Israel," *The Cumberland News* (Maryland), July 10, 1973

6 "South African Athletes Barred from Maccabiah; Community Protests," JTA, June 15, 1973

7 "Maccabiah athletes arriving next week," *Jerusalem Post*, June 28, 1973

who, in the words of Joe Siegman, a veteran Maccabiah athlete and organizer, were "baseball has-beens." Nevertheless, they boarded the plane full of confidence, however misplaced it might have been.

"We feel that we are the darkhorses [sic]," said team captain Jack Tabbush of Encino. "But then we have some very good players. . . . Many of [them] have been playing cricket for a good many years and are conversant with the game, and we could very well pull off a few surprises over in Tel Aviv."[8]

The American squad did not win a match.

Maccabiah Profile: Joe Siegman
United States, Cricket/Lawn Bowls

So what the heck was the United States doing fielding a cricket team?

That head-scratcher was put to Joe Siegman, now seventy-nine, in discussing his introduction to the Maccabiah Games in 1973.

Siegman was living in Los Angeles, working as a publicity agent for stars such as Carroll O'Connor (Archie in *All in the Family*) and Ed Asner (Lou Grant in *The Mary Tyler Moore Show*). He was one of the founders of the popular Hollywood Stars Night, comprised of actors, musicians, and other entertainers who played baseball exhibition games for charity.

The Chicago native had a long love affair with the national pastime. He lettered in high school, played American Legion ball, and one year at the University of Chicago before injury curtailed him from further advancement. He then turned to softball. In Chicago, that meant a 16-inch ball and no fielders' gloves. When he moved to L.A. and was invited to play he was surprised to learn the ball had "shrunk" to 12 inches and gloves were required.

---

8 "Tabbush Leads Cricketeers," *Valley News* (Van Nuys, California), July 3, 1973

With that in his background, Siegman felt qualified to try out for the American cricket club that would compete in the 1973 Games, undaunted (and uninsulted) by the invitation put out to "over-the-hill baseball players."

Speaking from his home the California, Siegman recalled, "It was a kick in the head to play cricket. How hard can it be? It's English baseball! Well, it turned out to be very little like baseball." Siegman met up with what movie blurbs might describe as "a rag-tag group"—all Jewish, but all originally from different parts of the world, including India, Ireland, and England. It took about a year for the team to learn the game sufficiently if not proficiently.

Although his maternal side hailed from Israel and he had many relatives living there, including his brother who had moved there some ten years earlier, Siegman had never been there. "It was Camelot, of a sort. It was fantasy," he said of his first trip.

"We were treated like we were going to the Olympic Games. Now, we come to Israel and we're pretty much all saturated in supporting Israel. I'm anxious to see my brother and my aunts and uncles I've only heard about. I didn't know where Netanya was or Tel Aviv. Or Sefad [his mother's home town]. It was exciting. My wife and my kids went with me."

Aside from the obvious talent divide, another thing that separated the Americans from the rest of the cricket competition was their age. Most of them were well into their professional careers (Siegman was thirty-eight at the time), while their opponents were either still in college or recently graduates.

The U.S. cricket team didn't win a match, but Siegman said it gave him a new appreciation for the sport as well as for the Maccabiah Games and Israel. One of the things he learned that was true for many athletes was discovering that there were "Jewish guys just like us, in other parts of the world, except we all spoke funny to each other."

There were plans to return for the 1977 Games, but tragedy struck when John Martyr, the British organizer of the club, died suddenly after a team meeting. With no one willing to take over the reins, the cricketers disbanded.

Siegman was not quite through with the Games, however. Someone suggested they look into another popular sport in the Los Angeles area: lawn bowls, a game in the bocce family. "Bocce is checkers, lawn bowls is chess," he said.

Photo courtesy Joe Siegman

Joe Siegman, second from right, has been involved in the Maccabi movement for more than 40 years. He is shown here with a Maccabiah Games mixed competition, which brought the best of two countries together, including, from left, Israeli national team member Tzvika Hadar, American singles champion Mert Isaacman, and the 2002 U.S. Pairs championship team of Siegman and Neville Sacks.

The "old guys" who were established at the club where Siegman got his feet wet adopted him and it soon became his sport of choice. And while he admitted to being less than skillful at cricket, he more than made up for that in lawn bowls. "I got sucked into the sport. I'm still playing it today," he said.

Siegman went on to organize several teams and served in numerous positions for lawn bowls clubs and international competitions. He is a two-time national champion and was inducted into the Bowls USA Hall of Fame in 2002.

He asked the U.S Committee Sports in Israel (the predecessor of Maccabi USA) if they would be interested in putting together a lawn bowls team and they enthusiastically agreed. He persuaded about thirty-five gentlemen—"including the cantor from my temple"—to try out for the sport. Again, it took a year, but they put together a team of about ten players for the 1977 Games. Siegman was a member of the U.S. lawn bowls team for the next three Games as well.

Once again, the American representatives resembled an advertisement for AARP. While the other lawn bowls teams at the Maccabiah were mostly in their twenties and thirties, Siegman said the American team was somewhat older: forties to sixties. "Some of us belonged in the cemetery," he joked.

Along the way, he became more involved in the movement, serving as a vice president for the U.S. Committee Sports for Israel, a group formed, he said, "by four *shtarkers,*" which is Yiddish for "strong men," but also "strong arm," as in having a talent for getting people to fork over money, although not in the Hollywood tough guy sense.

"I said I gotta do something to help promote these Maccabiah Games because they're the biggest secret in the country, particularly among Jews. Maccabiah, isn't that the guy from Chanukah?" he asked rhetorically. "The Maccabiah Games was a way of introducing people to Jewish life," he said. "Sports and music may be the wrong reason to get involved in Judaism, but they connect with people all over the world, particularly young people. And if you can get their attention . . . and they get introduced to Israel, and find out, from whatever country they come from, that there are other people just like them from all over the world. . . ."

Siegman was also among the first *machers* from the West Coast. Heretofore, most of the decision-makers had been in the East, but they recognized that many of the members of the cricket team were "savvy businessmen" who could help raise funds and promote the Games to a wider audience.

"At the time, this was almost an eastern organization. If you lived in New York/New Jersey and you were an athlete, the rumor was you got considered more for a team than you did if you were on the west coast . . . The New Yorkers didn't appreciate the west coast organizers. So some of them came and went. But I got along with people," Siegman said.

Siegman occasionally travelled to New York and would sit in on the committee meetings. "Eventually they asked me to be part of the organization; I was honored."

After the '77 games, with two Maccabiahs under his belt, Sieg-man thought, "I had to do something bigger-than-life for the Maccabiah games." This led to the establishment of the International Jewish Sports Hall of Fame, which eventually moved to Israel's Wingate Institute in Netanya and was formally dedicated at the 1981 Games. He planned the event "as if it was the Oscars, or just a bit short of the Oscars."

"I gave the impression this was a very important affair." He invited personalities he had learned about from *The Encyclopedia of Jews and Sports*, a reference book that was a popular bar mitzvah gift at the time. The honorees constituted a virtual Who's Who of Jew-ish sports royalty: Red Auerbach, Dolph Schayes, Hank Greenberg, and Dick Savitt, among others. Fourteen of the eighteen inductees were represented, either in person, or by the families of those who had passed on.

"I never intended to become an authority on great Jewish athletes," said Siegman. "I just wanted to run a dinner that had a lot of piz-zazz to it. Sometimes you get a little serendipity. Things happen, and it happened in a positive way."

"[The Maccabiah Games have] expanded and perhaps been a little diluted in not all but many of the actual events that take place from a sports standpoint. As far as the pageantry goes, it's expanded. Here in the United States, there's been more people who were not involved who have gotten involved." As an example, Siegman offered Steve Soboroff, a Los Angeles businessman and former mayoral candidate who headed up the "Committee of 18," a group that raised more than $1.5 million for the cause, including the sponsoring of an Indian cricket team in 2009. "He's still devoted to the Maccabiah Games because he sees how it brings so many Jew-ish kids to realize that there's a lot of niceties in being Jewish, that there's a closeness in being Jewish with somebody else. Not [neces-sarily] religious, but just being Jewish.

"Someone came up with the idea ... of having a 'pre-camp,' because the athletes used to arrive maybe two, three days before the opening ceremonies. They would get acclimated to the change in time and climate, but they didn't get a chance to see much of Israel because you had 10, 12 days to pack it all in and you were competing. There were tours, but not very many. So if they could get them there a week ahead of time, they could get acclimated both Jewish-wise, to Israel, as well as practice their sport."

Siegman recalled members of the Jewish Agency speaking with groups of American athletes, talking about the benefits and travails of living in Israel, and having the young people come away with very positive experiences. Most of these young people were brought up in homes that may not have been religiously observant, who did not attend Hebrew school or have a bar or bat mitzvah. "If they had any sporting ability, they would use their down time not to attend Hebrew school, but to hone their sports skills," he said.

He also recalled the 1989 origins of what has come to be a tradition at the Maccabiah: the group bar mitzvah for the athletes, dozens, if not more, gathering together at Masada, or at the Western Wall, or elsewhere, to share in the experience of becoming an official member of the Jewish community. According to Siegman, it began when a member of the Judo team told his coach, who happened to be a rabbi, that he had never had a bar mitzvah and could the coach/rabbi suggest some prayers to say during a visit to Masada. The rabbi agreed and word spread. On the buses carrying the group to the Israeli landmark, the rabbi announced to the group that anyone else who wished to join the young man in prayer was welcome to do so. More than forty agreed to participate.

"That night the kids that were on Masada were walking like they had just seen God earlier in the day. It was ethereal and joyful. This may be the wrong reason for kids to realize their Jewishness, but it's *a* reason, and they are imbued now. How long it will last is another story, but we at least got their attention.

"Each time they go to Israel, most kids come back to the United States and go on with their lives; I'm sure it's the same in other countries, too. But some of them make aliyah. Others get involved with the [Maccabi] organization. It just gets people involved and they do public relations, not so much for the Maccabiah—although it is that [too]—but for Judaism. And not for going to three services a day, which would also be nice, but just an appreciation for Israel."

* * *

Maccabiah Profile: Joseph Garrie, Japan, Judo

California born and raised, Joseph Garrie fell in love with judo at a young age. It's one of the reasons he decided to go to school in Japan, so he could also attend the Kodokan Judo Institute. He studied Far East Area Studies, Japanese and Chinese history, and philosophy at Sophia University, a Jesuit school and one of two accredited schools in the country. He later earned a law degree from Pepperdine University and became a real estate broker and investor.

"Japan actually has a pretty large community," Garrie said. "During World War II, a lot of Jews escaped to China and when the Communists took over, they moved to Tokyo."

Garrie was able to represent Japan at the Maccabiah because of his association with the local synagogue. "They didn't have any problem," he said. "I think they kind of wanted more representation from Jewish communities from around the world, so they encouraged it."

Although he was surrounded by Jews, Garrie's experience would appear to be a fairly lonely one. The only representative from Japan, he had no support crew: no trainer, no coach, nothing. "It was fine," he said. "Judo is pretty much of an individual type of sport. It was just another tournament for me.

"At first the Israeli community thought I was Japanese. I was interviewed by several newspapers. Of course, when they met me, they realized I wasn't." The reporters might have been a little disappointed, he said.

By default, Garrie carried the Japanese flag. "I kind of felt I was representing the Jewish community there," he said, not Japan. He read from an article he had retrieved in advance of our conversation. "'[T]he one-man team from the Land of the Rising Sun will march behind a national flag presented by the Japanese Embassy here.'[9] I actually got the flag from [them] in Tel Aviv."

---

9 "Japan sends judoka to Maccabiah," *Jerusalem Post*, July 1973.

Photo courtesy Joseph Garrie

Joseph Garrie, right, won a silver medal in Judo for Japan at the 1973 Games.

Billionaire businessman Shaul Eisenberg, who fled from Germany shortly after the Nazis came to power and eventually settled in Japan, took an interest in Garrie and became his sponsor while he was in Israel, paying his fees and serving as an advisor. After the ten-hour non-stop flight, Garrie was happy to arrive in the Land of Milk and Honey. "It was very inspirational," he said. "I'll never forget putting my hand on the Wailing Wall. I literally was moved; I could feel movement. It was very special. I never had that experience before."

Garrie's chance to compete came towards the end of the Games in Jerusalem. He spent his down time training with the American team and beat his rivals from Belgium and France in his weight class before losing in the finals to Yona Melnick, an Israeli, whom he recalled as "much older and stronger than me."

* * *

This year's Games also marked the first time that non-Jewish athletes would be allowed to take part in actual events, although their results would not be recorded nor would they win any medals. Non-Jewish athletes had attended previous Maccabiahs, mostly high-profile stars in a particular discipline and/or Olympic champions. However, their appearances extended to them only performing at exhibitions for the crowds at the closing ceremonies and serving as unofficial ambassadors. Among those who would be competing in 1973 was Dutch sprinter Wilma Van Gool, who quit the 1972 Olympics to protest the continuation of the Games after the murder of the Israelis, and four athletes from Kenya.[10]

The Kenyan quartet would be ultimately devastated when politics once again interfered with the Games. They were prohibited from running a post-Maccabiah event because the race contained two individual athletes from Rhodesia. The Nairobi government prohibited their citizens from participating in events that included Rhodesians, even though Maccabi officials had established that the runners in this case were participating under the aegis of a sports club and not as representatives of Rhodesia per se.

"My athletes are disappointed they cannot run...," lamented S.M. Oisebe, the Kenyan's spokesperson and delegation leader. "It's unfortunate that this had to happen. The [Maccabiah] organizers should have known better. We were invited and not told who we were going to meet."[11]

Representatives from South Africa and Rhodesia proposed a revision of the Maccabiah constitution to remove it from the purview of the International Olympic Committee, and thus allow their athletes to participate. "It is high time that the entire present concept of the Maccabiah Games be altered to minimize the effect and the possibility of the present—and let me warn future—pressure from outside the world of sports," said Arthur Goldman, chair of the South African Maccabi Council.[12]

---

10 "13 U.S. swimmers in finals as Maccabiah Games open," *Fairbanks Daily News-Miner* (Alaska), July 10, 1973

11 "Yanks Out To Widen Game Lead," *Ogden Standard-Examiner* (Utah), July 14, 1973

12 "South Africans: Take Maccabiah out of Olympic Frame," *Jerusalem Post*, July 18, 1973

Although the United States had contestants in several events in the swimming finals, there were no marquee performers like a Mark Spitz. While some new Maccabiah records were set, no world records were broken.

As a whole, the American team dominated from the starting gun, winning sixteen total medals on the first day. But it was Anita Zarnowiecki, a nineteen-year-old Swede, who was the human highlight reel at the Galei Gil pool in Ramat Gan. She set new Maccabiah standards in the 100-meter freestyle and 200-meter backstroke and by the time the water settled had come away with seven medals, including five golds, eclipsing Mark Spitz's total for a single Games with five in 1969. Zarnowiecki and her twin brother, Bernt, who won a silver for the men's 200-meter freestyle, were the only swimmers on the Swedish team.

The "Swedish Mermaid" and her brother combined for thirteen medals and were, according to at least some press reports, considered "the star attractions of the Games."[13] Their accomplishments allowed Sweden to finish fourth in the gold medal count behind the United States, Israel, and South Africa.

Another Spitz mark fell when Roy Abramowitz of Princeton, New Jersey, bettered his 400-meter individual medley by almost ten seconds. Bernt Zarnowiecki also eclipsed another Spitz record when he won the 400-meter freestyle in 4:20.9, a two-second improvement. He wrapped up his time in the pool by taking the 1,500-meter freestyle in 17:15.4 for his third gold medal, beating Spitz's time by an amazing thirty-five seconds.[14]

The excitement at the Games was not limited to the action *in* the games. Dr. Max Novich, a team physician for the U.S., belted Shmuel Lakin, the secretary of the Israeli Sports Federation in protest of a referee's decision in a boxing match between Peter Brodsky and his Israeli opponent, Haim Zilberschmidt.

---

13 "Israel drops U.S. cagers," *Winona Daily News* (Minn.), July 18, 1973
14 "Yanks Out To Widen Games Lead," *Ogden Standard-Examiner*, July 14, 1973

After the referee counted Brodsky out after a knockdown and awarded the bout to Zilberschmidt, Novich rushed to ringside. When Lakin—who, had served as the leader of the Israeli delegation at the Munich Olympics—warned him not to interfere, Novich punched him in the face.[15] Outrage, on all sides, was immediate, with calls for suspensions and apologies.

Novich was indeed suspended by the American delegation leaders pending a review by the Maccabiah court of honor, the supreme authority over the Games.

A week later, a column by sportswriter Jim Hubley in the *York Daily Record* put the onus for the fracas on Brodsky for failing to follow the rules by indicating, after he had been knocked down, that he wished to continue the bout by raising his fist. As a result, the referee correctly counted him out and the mayhem ensued.[16]

Novich's suspension was eventually overturned and assault charges dropped after he issued Lakin a written apology. However, he followed that up with a lengthy letter to the editor of the *New York Times*, complaining about the way he had been portrayed in an article about the incident and seeking to exculpate himself from wrongdoing. (The *Times* ran a note from the managing editor of the Associated Press, who stood by the original dispatch.)[17]

This was not by any means the only gripe issued against administrators. An American tennis player complained that the team had been locked out of the practice tennis courts at their hotel. The situation was remedied only after U.S. officials threatened not to pay the bill. On the basketball courts, referees whittled down the Brazilian

15 "Lipman to dive in Maccabiah," *Independent* (Long Beach, Calif.) June 12, 1973

16 "Off the Record," *York Daily Record* (Penn.), July 24, 1973

17 "Mailbox: Boxing Incident at the Maccabiah Games," *New York Times*, Sept. 2, 1973

squad with foul calls until only two players were left in a 63-51 loss to Argentina.[18]

Despite these events, the American mainstream press continued to focus on the popular events: swimming, gymnastics, track and field—pretty much the sports in which the Americans were expected to excel. There was little in the way of "up-close-and-personal" stories to which we have become accustomed from network broadcasts of the Olympics. Nevertheless, their general coverage was better than that of other countries. Allan Jay, one of the premier fencers of his generation, participated in five Olympics (1952-68) and two Maccabiah Games (1953-57). Asked if the Israeli Games were covered in his native England, he replied in an e-mail, "I would be astonished if the British press covered the event."

Ricky Landau, a long-time member of the Venezuelan Maccabi organization who has been to every Maccabiah either as an athlete or official since 1977, said, "Usually the national press has an article and also some TV interviews before we go, some follow-up on some games, and then a report on results. Nothing much but they used to." The interest seems to have dissipated in recent years, as the novelty of a small band of Jews from Venezuela participated in a grand international program wore off. "Now [there's] very little."

The track and field events were held at Ramat Gan Stadium and for once, the American team did not dominate, due most likely to the fact that they did not have a strong women's team. In fact, Lorraine Abramson, described as a "27-year-old housewife and mother," was the sole representative. She had participated in the 1965 Games, a member of the South African team, where she was dubbed "the Golden Girl." It was there she met her husband and moved to the United States.[19]

---

18 "Jewish Olympics Producing A Female Mark Spitz," *Bee* (Danville, Virginia), July 13, 1973
19 "U.S. Wins Two of Top Three Place at Maccabiah Games," *Danville Register* (Virginia), July 15, 1973

The Israeli women took charge of their events, sweeping in the 800 meters race, high jump, long jump, shot put, and discus.

The American men made a good showing, taking first place in six events on July 14, including the 110-meter hurdles (Donald Slevin); shot put (Joseph Gould); 10,000 meters (Gary Cohen); 100 meter (Emanuel Rosenberg); 800 meters (Glenn Harmatz), pole vault (Steve Greenberg); and the 400-meter relay.

"What can we do for an encore tomorrow?" asked the track team's coach, Royal Chernock.[20]

Well, how about a record-setting performance in the 400-meter hurdles by Milton Bressler of Birmingham, Alabama, who bettered the high bar standard he set four years earlier? Or New York's Boris "Dov" Djerassi's hammer throw? Or Jeffrey Freid, of Milford, New Jersey, winner of the high jump?

Despite these successes, the men's medals were widely distributed for a change, with Australia, France, Great Britain, Greece, Israel, Italy, Mexico, and, Switzerland also taking home souvenirs.

The United States was on a mission to return to basketball glory after their upset by Israel four years earlier. They beat Canada in their first game, 68-53, led by eighteen-year-old Ernie Grunfeld, whose family immigrated to America from Rumania in 1965. The future New York Knicks favorite scored 18 points.

In what had become the most anticipated event of the Maccabiah, the Israelis beat the U.S. in the finals, 86-80. Tal Brody, now wearing the colors of Israel instead of Team USA, scored 20 while another former American hoops star, Barry Leibowitz, dropped in six. Grunfeld led his team with 27 points in defeat. The U.S. team committed three turnovers in the last two minutes to seal their fate.[21]

---

20 "Sweep gold medals in Maccabia Games," *Neosho News* (Missouri), July 15, 1973

21 "Israeli cagers defeat U.S. in Tel Aviv games," *Pantograph* (Bloomington, IL), July 18, 1973

Maccabiah Profile: Ernie Grunfeld, United States, Basketball

Ernie Grunfeld was the only high-schooler on the U.S. basketball team but he played like a veteran, leading the team with a 20-point average.

When I interviewed Grunfeld, now president of the NBA's Washington Wizards, and rattled off a list of his accomplishments, including his 1976 Olympic medal, he was quick to point out—good-naturedly—that the medal was gold. Indeed, he is one of a select group who earned such awards in both Olympic and Maccabiah competition.

"I've been very fortunate," he said modestly.

Grunfeld, the son of Holocaust survivors, was born in Romania in 1955. The family moved to New York nine years later.

"I had never played basketball in Europe," he said. "We played soccer, and when I moved to Queens and I went down to the playground, everybody played basketball. I was always a fairly good athlete, that's how I picked up the game."

He doesn't remember exactly how he heard about the Maccabiah Games, but he played basketball in Jewish centers around his neighborhood—"anyplace you can get a game, you would go," he said.

"I got a call after my senior year in Forrest Hills High School and was asked if I would be interested in playing for the [U.S. Maccabiah] team. We had a tryout in Long Island and we had a very famous and great coach in Harry Litwack, which was a great experience. I always felt I was a pretty decent player. There were some good college players on the team at the time and it was a competitive situation and I wanted to prove that I could belong. I ended up being the high scorer on the team."

Unlike many of his new teammates, Grunfeld—who had committed to attending the University of Tennessee—had been to Israel several times prior to the Games. "I had a lot of relatives there. So it was a good opportunity for me to go back there and also to represent my country in an international competition."

Still, the opening ceremonies were "tremendous," Grunfeld said. "That was the first time you walk into the gigantic stadium and you see all the different countries with all the different colors and the different uniforms, it was pretty special.

"It was a great sense of all these Jewish athletes from all over the world coming together and competing against one another, but there was a feeling of real brotherhood.

"Israel obviously had an outstanding team," he said. "We had some injuries to our big guys in the final game. But the competition was solid."

Comparing Maccabiah experience to his other big quadrennial sporting event, Grunfeld said, "The Olympic experience is a little bit different. I was a college player at the time and we were playing against all the best players in the world and I think the competition level [at the Olympics], was higher; it's a more spiritual experience at the Maccabiah Games.

"I still keep in touch with some of [my Maccabiah teammates]. There are great memories. . . . It's something you remember for the rest of your life."

Grunfeld coached the first master's basketball team in 1989. Unfortunately, he was still too young to play himself. "There were only two countries that had teams that time, the U.S. and Israel, and [Israel] had a really good team. That was also a great experience."

More recently, his son, Dan, followed in his Maccabiah footsteps, earning MVP honors for the gold-winning 2009 team under the leadership of Coach Bruce Pearl. Dan made aliyah and played pro basketball in Israel for several years before returning to the States.

* * *

Fittingly, it was Brody—who had opened the Games by lighting the Maccabiah cauldron—who closed the Ninth Maccabiah by extinguishing it. Foreign Minister Abba Eban told the audience of 40,000, "Now that the Maccabiah has closed, may the 10th Maccabiah Games find us sitting on our soil building our state in a state of peace."[22]

---

22 "Maccabiah Games close," *Kingsport News* (Tenn.), July 20, 1973

The Jerusalem Post published an editorial pondering the future of the Games.

"...[T]he Ninth Maccabiah has left its organizers, as well as thoughtful spectators here in Israel, wondering whether a "Jewish Olympics" is really the target to be aimed at. ...

"[T]he Games have shown up Israel's lamentably low standards in so many sports. .... The root of the trouble is in our schools where there is an indifferent and even apathetic attitude to games. The dearth of adequate sports facilities accounts for this in part—and the result is ... that 20 percent of our 18-year-olds joining the army are overweight."[23]

At the final tally, Israel just edged out the United States with total hardware, 163 to 162, although the U.S. was ahead in the precious gold by a sizable margin, 76-60.

The Final Medal Count (Gold/Silver/Bronze):

Israel 166 (60/45.5/60.5)
USA 162 (76/51/35)
South Africa 42 (16/9/17)
Great Britain 26 (5/9/12)
Australia 21 (4/10/7)
Canada 21 (0/10.5/10.5)
France 20 (4/6/10)
Sweden 19 (11/6/2)
Mexico 18 (2/6/10)
Holland 16 (3/8/5)
Italy 11 (2/5/4)
Rhodesia 9 (1/5/3)
Germany 8 (5/3/0)
Brazil 5 (0/2/3)
Austria 4.5 (.5/1/3)
Belgium 3.5 (.5/2/1)
Argentina 3 (0/2/1)
Japan 1 (0/1/0)
Greece 1 (0/0/1)

---

23 Ibid

Chapter 11

The Tenth Games
July 12-21, 1977

"If these governments enable Jewish sportsmen to take part in the games, it will prove that, in spite of ideological differences, there is still something which can unite humanity, and this is the noble spirit of sport. It will be a contribution to understanding between nations and their striving for peace."

Menachem Begin in a letter to Israel Peled, chair of the International Maccabiah Games Committee, regarding the participation of Soviet bloc nations.[1]

---

1 "Begin to help woo athletes from E. bloc to Maccabiah," *Jerusalem Post*, June 15, 1977

"We got olives and tomatoes for breakfast. It's a nice idea, but I'm used to two over easy and grits."

John Citron, American track athlete[2]

After Dolph Schayes, a member of the NBA Hall of Fame, was appointed to coach the U.S. men's basketball team, a fundraiser to help send local athletes to the Games was held in his honor at Temple Adath Yeshurun in Syracuse in May of 1977.[3] Several former teammates, including fellow Hall of Famer Hal Greer, came to show support. Schayes had spent his entire professional career with the Syracuse franchise, the Nationals, from 1949-1963; they moved to Philadelphia and became the 76ers in his last season. As a rookie, he led the team in scoring and continued to do so for the next ten years, during which the Nationals never failed to make it to the playoffs, winning the NBA championship in 1954.

In addition to the NBA Hall of Fame, Schayes was inducted into both the National (1995) and International (1979) Jewish Sports Halls.

A more unusual funding event took place at Beall Stadium in Frostburg, Maryland, where Herb Wilens, a student at Frostburg State College, beat his light-middleweight opponent Charles Tuttle in a five-round boxing match. Profits from the event, which drew 1,000 spectators, were donated to a "sports fund for Israel on behalf of Wilens who will fight in the world-renowned Maccabiah games."[4]

Other prominent figures in their sports included water polo coach Bob Horn of UCLA, whose teams had won more than 200 games and had earned at least a share of the Pac-8 title since 1964; and Phil Cohen, the B'nai B'rith Southern Regional director, who was named to lead the boxing team. Cohen, a retired Marine colonel, had been a Marine Corps heavyweight champion; Adrian Cole, cricket chair for

---

2 "Maccabiah Games a U.S. Gold Rush," *Bridgeport Telegram* (Conn.), July 19, 1977

3 "Cohen, Schayes Maccabiah Picks," *Post-Standard* (Syracuse, NY), May 16, 1977

4 "Wilens Unanimous Winner Over Tuttle," *Cumberland Sunday Times* (MD.), June 26, 1977

U.S. Sports in Israel, was picked to lead the second U.S. cricket team, but the group disbanded after the sudden death of John Martyr, the team's heart and soul, according to 1973 team member Joe Siegman.

Approximately 2,700 athletes from 34 countries attended the opening ceremonies. Prime Minister Menachem Begin once again noted the absence of participants from Soviet bloc and Arab nations and expressed the hopes that they would be able to join in the festivities four years hence.

In addition, Rhodesia which, like South Africa, was banned by various sporting governing bodies for their apartheid politics, decided not to send its delegation of 13 lawn bowlers and three tennis players, breaking a connection to the Games that began in 1953.

Wendy Weinberg, who won a bronze medal as a swimmer in the 1976 Olympic in Montreal, carried the U.S. colors. Track and field star Esther Roth, one of Israel's most famous athletes, served as flag-bearer for the Maccabiah flag, just as she had at the Montreal Olympics, where she became the first Israeli to reach the finals of an Olympic event: Roth finished sixth in the 100-meter hurdles. Four years earlier, in Munich, she set an Israeli record of 11.45 seconds for the 100 meters sprint. Her coach and mentor, Amitzur Shapira, was one of the eleven Israelis murdered by Palestinian terrorists at those ill-fated games.

Mickey Berkowitz, a basketball star on Maccabi Tel Aviv, lit the Maccabiah cauldron.

Another veteran of the '72 Olympics was prominently featured in the opening ceremonies: Bert Kops, a wrestler with the Dutch delegation, who had refused to participate any further after the decision had been made to continue the Games after the slaying of the Israelis.

This time the Americans sent almost 340 athletes, coaches, and officials. One of the difficulties was that the media presented the total numbers of those attending the game as competitors, but in reality, this accounted for everyone: athletes, support staff, and administrators.

Upon her return to the United States, Alice Blue, leading a Wisconsin Israel Study Mission, told the *Wisconsin Jewish Chronicle* about her group's experience at the opening ceremonies.

"It was something like the opening of the Olympics, the kids marching, holding flags from their respective countries. Grade school children did acrobatics on the grass—2,500 of them, making the shapes of the number 10 [signifying the 10th Games], [the word] Shalom, and the Star of David.

"I think the kids were surprised to realize that the athletes were all Jews—not just another delegation of athletes. There were Jews from Ecuador, South Africa, Asia, etc."[5]

For the first time contract bridge was added to the slate of events, leading writers who covered the topic—primarily for the arts and leisure sections—to drift over to into the unfamiliar territory of the sports section.

The swimming competitions were the first to be held and Weinberg was one of the stars of the U.S. team that was once again expected to excel. But the Swedish twins, Anita and Bernt Zarnowiecki—winners of 13 medals between them at the 1973 Games—were back as well, making for an interesting face-off.

Weinberg got off to a fast start, winning a gold medal in the 200-meter butterfly in 2:20.80 on July 13, first day of the swimming events, breaking her own Maccabiah record set four years earlier in the process. It was one of four golds the U.S. won that day (Lance Michaels, 100-meter breaststroke; Mark Heinrich, 100-meter backstroke, and Hillary Bergman, who anchored the men's 800-meter relay). The U.S. also won three silvers and a bronze. The next day Weinberg broke another Games record when she won the 400-meter freestyle in 4:26.14. Bergman won another gold as well, as did Michael Saphir. Overall, the U.S. won three of the five events. Israel's Anat Farkas, just fourteen years old, won the women's 200-meter breaststroke and Gillian Peters of Australia won the 100-meter backstroke.

Overall, the U.S. came away with twenty-two out of twenty-seven gold medals. Weinberg accounted for eight of those with six golds and two bronzes, with Bergman close behind with six golds.

---

5 "Teens Home From Israel Despite Delay," *Wisconsin Jewish Chronicle*, Aug. 18, 1977

The American team also swept the women's gymnastics. Sharon Shapiro, a sixteen-year-old from Arleta, California, won all-around, floor, uneven bars, and vault horse while teammate Marcy Levine won the balance beam. The following day, Shapiro added golds in uneven bars and floor exercises.

In the men's events, Israel's Dov Lupi won the overall with a gold in the horse and several silvers.

Even though they had Dolph Schayes at the helm, the U.S. basketball team was not expected to do well. Their young group included the coach's son Danny, a 6'11" center, and other players unfamiliar with the rough and tumble world of international play.

Israel, on the other hand, was "on the map," as Tal Brody exclaimed after Maccabi Tel Aviv won the European Basketball Championships in April against a much tougher Russian squad.

Both teams went through the preliminary rounds undefeated, and by considerable margins. The U.S. beat Columbia, 106-32, while Israel beat France, 99-75. Israel next crushed their opponents from Belgium by almost 100 points in a 156-60 romp. The Americans had just a slightly tougher time against West Germany, 95-27.

The U.S. beat Argentina in the semifinals 100-53, as Israel defeated the Canadians, 105-65, despite the characterization by Israeli coach Ralph Klein that "In our last game with Canada, we played terribly."[6]

For the seventh time, the U.S. faced their Israeli counterparts in the finals having lost the last two in a row. Willie Sims, an African-American Jew from New York, sank a pair of free throws with three seconds remaining to give the U.S. a gut-wrenching 92-91 victory. A crowd of nearly 5,000 at Yad Eliahu Stadium saw the lead change hands a dozen times in the final minutes. Danny Schayes, who would go on to an eighteen-year career in the NBA, and Brad Magid each scored 18 points.

Sims was drafted by the Denver Nuggets in 1981 but never appeared in the NBA. Instead he played in Israel for several teams from 1981-96 and again briefly for the 1998-99 season.

---

6 "U.S. Cagers Corner Jewish Olympic Gold," *Panama City News-Herald* (Fla.), July 21, 1977

Maccabiah Profile: Danny Schayes, United States, Basketball

"As early as I could play, I was playing," said Danny Schayes in a telephone interview. He was always the biggest kid in his class; by the time he entered high school, he was already 6'8".

"We were fairly more cultural than religious, I'll say. I grew up in a strong Jewish neighborhood. We belonged to synagogue [but] we didn't go weekly. Schayes was involved in Jewish youth organizations and "went to a lot of bar mitzvahs." The Schayes family moved around quite a bit when he was young—five schools in five years—so the disruption prevented him from having his own bar mitzvah when he was thirteen.

Schayes made the Maccabiah team as an eighteen-year-old for the 1977 Games—the only time he played for his father ("He was a bit of a yeller, but we had great guys. It was a lot of fun."). He returned four years later for another gold-medal win over Israel.

"It was interesting. We actually had a great team, loaded with Division One players," he recalled, along with the three-a-day practices, which he was definitely not used to in high school.

The trip to Israel was Schayes's first taste of international competition apart from Canada. "I went to Israel expecting a great basketball trip and it went way beyond my expectations as far a cultural experience and Jewish awakening. It was amazing.

"I didn't really have much of an expectation of any one thing I was looking forward to," said Schayes. "I just really wanted to see and experience the country. I didn't know much about the politics, per se. It was a period of calm when we were there. Going to Jerusalem, the Old City, the Arab quarter was not an issue. While there was a lot of security, there wasn't a lot of tension.

"What really impressed me most was the ancientness of the sites. In America, 100 years old is old. To them, 100 years old is fresh off the assembly line. We would go to some of the sites and you see a city excavated over a city excavated over a city. It was such a different perspective than anything I had experienced growing up in the States."

So was the experience on the court. Schayes said he "had no idea what to expect from the other countries. I knew our team was strong." Strong enough that no team came within 50 points of the U.S. until the last game. Schayes characterized the team as the "600-pound gorilla." That is, until they reached the finals.

"Israel was just coming off their first European Championship. Many of the stars that were on that team were playing [at the Maccabiah Games]. Going to the finals, we were the underdogs by a huge margin."

"The championship game was a huge game, sold out, tons of energy. It was a very, very well-played game."

To hear Schayes tell it, the 1981 Games were almost a bit of a disappointment.

"Very very different," he said. "We didn't have nearly as strong a team. But the Israelis sent mostly their junior players instead of their top players. We won the finals easily. We pretty much walked to the Gold Medal. The experience was us taking care of business." By that time, Schayes had been selected by the Utah Jazz as their number-one pick in the NBA draft.

In 1977, the athletes were housed by country, which he enjoyed for the opportunity to hang out with his fellow Americans from many different disciplines. In 1981, the arrangements change to the current system of housing by sport. Schayes called that "a little dicey. Number one, we were the ones beating up on everybody. Number two was we had the language issue. English wasn't predominant so it was a lot tougher to experience camaraderie. We did get together with some of teams and players but it wasn't nearly as fun as having all the American athletes in one place."

Still, Schayes admitted that being embedded with athletes from other countries had a "coolness" factor to it.

Some things were not as big a deal for Schayes in 1981, although he did have the honor of carrying the American flag for the opening ceremonies, "a thrill to have that responsibility for leading the team into the stadium."

If the first time was a kind of introduction to his Jewish experience, the second time was more of an advanced class, allowing Schayes to go deeper. "They were both special in their own ways.

"It's hard to put into terms comparing it to what you're used to here in the United States because life in Israel is so spectacularly different," he said, looking back on his numerous trips to Israel over the years. "The threats are so close and real, the human connections are so much more intense because of that. The reality that they live in is so much more real than here in the States where it's all video games and pop music and who's wearing what. There's so much more superficiality here.

Schayes has maintained his association with Maccabi USA. He sponsored a position in 1993 and has been on the board for several years. He served as the coach for the Masters team at the 2013 Games and described them as "giddy as kids" when they won the gold. (He considered playing for the Masters, but didn't feel he was in good enough shape.)

"I would imagine going to Israel in the '70s and '80s was more like being here in the States right after World War II where there was this growth excitement and people were hustling and moving and doing and growing. There's a way, way different energy there than here."

By the way, Schayes finally got that chance to celebrate his bar mitzvah, in Israel during the Maccabiahs. "It was at a sunset ceremony in Masada. I organized it around the Games in '93. There's no better place to get bar mitzvahed than at Masada."

* * *

While some of the same things occurred year to year on the court, there were similarly some of the same problems that persisted. One of the early controversies occurred when the U.S. Maccabiah soccer committee ruled that David Freud, a football player at Indiana University, was ineligible to compete on the American soccer team for the upcoming Games because he was actually a citizen of Israel. "Rules require a player to compete only for the country of which he is a citizen."[7]

7 "Sports Shorts: Hoosier Declared Ineligible," *Galesburg Register-Mail* (Ill.), June 21, 1977

Of course, such rules have often been circumvented, as was the case with Joseph Garrie in 1973 who, although a citizen of the United States, was Japan's sole representative and won a silver medal in his judo weight division by dint of his association with the Jewish community center in Tokyo where he was attending college.

In another odd turn, Leo Weiss, a table tennis player from West Germany, was not allowed to compete because he was considered a deserter from the Israeli army. It seems Weiss had lived in Israel long enough to qualify for military service, but never served.[8]

Overall coverage in the American press was somewhat muted compared with previous Maccabiahs. Fortunately, there were no tragedies involving Jewish athletes to memorialize. After the Yom Kippur War in 1973, the situation in the Middle East had stabilized, relatively speaking, and security was not the issue it was, or would be in Games to come.

There was also little in the way of in-Games controversy, no team representatives slugging officials, no overt complaints about Jewish identity or the legitimacy of representation for a country. Sure, there was the usual grousing by young people who were used to the way things were at home and disappointed that the conditions were not ideal, whether it comes to the food made available to them or conditions at the various venues, whether man-made or of natural occurrence, but such aggravations can happen at any competition. Ken and Buddy Kring, a pair of brothers from California, finished first and third in the decathlon, with Israeli Moshe Hirsch sandwiched in the middle. Ken Kring told the media, "It was a very slow track, and we ran with a headwind all day. I probably would have scored over 7,000 in better conditions, but I think this is my best overall result, considering the circumstances."[9] John Citron, who won two golds on the track, said the only time he was served steak, he snuck back to the dining room for extra portions. On the other hand, Danny Schayes might have groused about the beds being too small for his a 6'11" frame. Instead,

---

8 "Athlete Labeled Deserter," *Danville Register* (Virg.), July 13, 1977
9 "Krings 1-3 in decathlon," *Independent* (Long Beach, Calif.), July 20, 1977

he compared it with his days at summer camp. "The accommodations were perfectly fine," he said graciously.

The Israeli men continued to dominate the track events, but the Israeli women as in the previous Games faced little competition, literally and figuratively. As she did four years earlier, Esther Shahamorov-Roth won the 110-meter hurdles, breaking the record she established in 1973. The Israelis also swept the 400-meter race.

The 10th Maccabiah ended at the Western Wall in Jerusalem on July 21, with Mayor Teddy Kollek, acting Prime Minister Simcha Erlich, and other dignitaries in attendance, along with several thousand satisfied fans. As a sendoff, the fireworks display at the end of the ceremonies spelled out "Meet you at the 11th Maccabiah."[10]

The United States finished with a medal count of 83 gold, 65 silver, and 47 bronze (195). Israel garnered 60/70/60 (190), followed by South Africa (32, 16-7-9), Holland (23, 11/9/3), France (33, 10/7/16), Canada (30, 8/8/14), and Australia (29, 6/13/10).

In a wrap-up of the games in the *El Paso Herald-Post*, columnist Bob Ingram noted the strict security measures in place at the opening ceremonies, the residue of the attack in Munich in 1972, in eerily prescient imagery.

"Imagine playing a football game in this country and forcing every fan to be checked at the gate," Ingram wrote. He quoted Bobby Goldfarb, a local tennis player who would be competing in the first-ever masters competitions for athletes over thirty-five, who said, "Soldiers were everywhere. They not only searched your clothes but they went through everything you were carrying."[11]

For better or worse, these anecdotal reports about the Maccabiah were almost all readers around the world had to go by. In an assessment in *The Jerusalem Post*, Paul Kohn enumerated the difficulties he and his colleagues had faced in the course of plying their trade.

---

10 "U.S. Dominates in Maccabiah," *York Daily Record* (Penn.), July 22, 1977
11 "Goldfarb helps U.S. athletes in medal grab," *El Paso Herald-Post* (Texas), Aug. 5, 1977

"For years now, the Games have been officially recognized as regional games by the world's leading sports bodies. And some of this year's achievements were at the highest international level. Yet the foreign press virtually ignored them, and the fault lies squarely with the organizers, the Maccabi leaders who happily boasted that 350 foreign pressmen would be coming to cover the event."[12]

He recounted the poor working conditions, with cramped and smoke-filled rooms and officious Maccabi workers who thwarted journalists who didn't have the proper credentials, not caring that these men and women had jobs to do, jobs that could only help the Maccabi cause. In addition, the organizers didn't provide much in the way of press releases or other handouts that might have made the reporters' jobs easier (including the correct spellings of the athletes' names). When they did, the information was often sketchy. "[E]xaggeration seemed to be a sport of its own," he wrote. Venues were also misstated, causing no small amount of confusion as writers and photographers rushed to various sites, only to discover they were in the wrong place (athletes complained of similar "misdirection").

"[I]t is high time, after all these years and so many Maccabiahs, that the Games' organizers realize that even if a few newsmen do shuffle among them and the athletes, they are doing a job of work *for*, and not *against*, the Maccabiah," wrote Kohn [original emphasis]. And bear in mind this is coming from a local journalist, not some outsider complaining that Israeli standards were less than adequate.

---

12 "Maccabi beats the press," *Jerusalem Post*, July 26, 1977

Chapter 12

The Eleventh Games
July 6-16, 1981

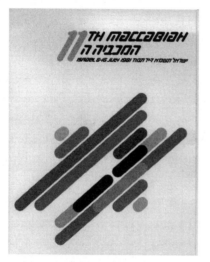

"It's fantastic. It's international competition and a free trip to Israel. The Jews are dispersed all over the world. I think it's exciting we can come together once every four years."

Paul Friedman, United States marathon runner[1]

As if we needed a reminder of the importance of sports in society, the Israeli Knesset ruled that an agreed-upon date of July 7 for a

---

1 "11th Maccabiah Games Begin; Criticism of Games, too," *New York Times*, July 7, 1981

general election might have to be changed because "Cabinet ministers were unaware when they selected it that it would conflict with the opening of the Maccabiah Games."[2]

Other issues came from outside the Jewish state.

Despite the hopes that the Games might supersede the usual international political enmity, it was business as usual in 1981. Fearing economic reprisals from the Arab boycott of Israel, the Danish audio equipment giant Bang and Olufson withdrew their support of the local team. "This late withdrawal of their sponsors has caused serious difficulties to the Danish contingent," said Michael Kevehazi, chair of the Maccabiah Organizing Committee.

West Germany held back a few politicos from accompanying their delegation in retaliation for remarks made by Israel's Prime Minister Menachem Begin when he reproached Chancellor Helmut Schmidt for having expressed a "moral commitment to the Palestinians." Begin accused Schmidt of having served in the German army during World War II, with that such a charge might imply regarding anti-Semitic leanings.

"It seems that the Holocaust had conveniently slipped his memory and he did not make mention of a million and a half small children murdered, of entire families wiped out.

"The German debt to the Jewish people can never end, not in this generation and not in any other," Begin scolded. "The entire nation cheered on the murderers as long as they were victorious. But what do we hear? We hear of a commitment to those who strove to complete what the Germans had started in Europe."[3]

Zimbabwe (formerly Rhodesia) did not respond to an invitation to send a delegation. While it had been "officially" absent from the 1977 Games because of pressure from the international sports community over its apartheid policies, some athletes from the country had participated as individuals or on teams that did not need approval from the various governing organizations, representing the local Maccabi clubs

---

2 "Government Coalition, Alignment Bargaining Over Election Date," *Wisconsin Jewish Chronicle*, Jan. 23, 1981

3 "Begin Rebukes Schmidt for Remark on Palestinians," *New York Times*, May 5, 1981

instead of the country itself. Rhodesia had participated in the Games from 1953 to 1973.

The participation of South Africa in the Games was also criticized. That contentious nation sent about 250 athletes, even though they were banned by the international federations of six sports.

The Maccabi Tel Aviv basketball team—pardon me, the *European championship-winning* Maccabi Tel Aviv basketball team—came to New York in June for an exhibition game with the American squad that would compete in the upcoming Maccabiah. The visitors took the contest, 91-83, thanks in part to 29 points by former ABA player Aulcie Perry's 29 points and 12 rebounds. A JTA story identified Perry as "a veteran of the American Basketball Association and the National Basketball Association," but a trip to Basketball-Reference.com reveals that the 6'10"center out of Bethune-Cookman College in Daytona Beach, Florida, actually played just 21 games in one season (1975) with the Virginia Squires of the ABA.[4]

That's not to say Perry wasn't a great player. He was "discovered" by a scout for the Israeli team during a pickup game in New York City's famous Rucker Park in Harlem. He eventually signed with MTA and played with them for nine seasons, leading them to six Israel Cups and seven league champions. He even converted to Judaism along the way and made aliyah.

Team USA featured Hal Cohen, who scored a game-high 31 points, and Danny Schayes and Willie Sims, both of whom had played for the 1977 gold-winning team.

New Zealand, Puerto Rico, and Singapore were among the nations making their debut at the Games. The U.S. once again would send the largest delegation outside the Jewish state with an announced 400 "sportsmen" (though those numbers would change, as they usually did). South Africa and Brazil would send about 250 each.[5]

---

4 "Israel Basketball Team Beats U.S. Squad in Queens Exhibition," JTA, June 25, 1981

5 "Israel To Hold 11th Maccabiah Games," *Wisconsin Jewish Chronicle*, March 27, 1981

Once again, preparations for the Games came down to the wire, a trademark of the Maccabiahs since its debut almost fifty years earlier. "I do wish Israelis could get out of the habit of finishing things at the last minute," Kevehazi told *The Jerusalem Post,* citing the delay at customs of a bridge flown in from Germany to span the Yarkon River. The structure would allow the athletes to cross over from the staging grounds at Hadar Yosef Athletic Stadium to Ramat Gan Stadium, where the opening ceremonies would be held.

Veterans of the First Maccabiah, including Joseph Yekutieli, Dr. Robert Atlasz, and Mordechai Ben-Dror, led the march of the athletes on July 6. Uri Zohar, a discus thrower, initiated the athletes' oath while the customary display of paratroopers, orchestras, and singers, and thousands of young people performing exhibitions of dance and calisthenics, entertained the crowd. U.S. Congressman Jack Kemp of New York, a strong supporter of Israel, marched with the United States team, whose flag was carried by Danny Schayes, the MVP of the 1977 basketball finals.

Israeli tennis star Shlomo Glickstein ran the Maccabiah torch into the arena. He was the top-seeded player for these Games and would go on to play in the European Zone Davis Cup semifinals—also hosted in Israel that year—against Hungary.

"We don't have too many things to cheer about," said Ilan Rubin, a spokesperson for the Games on behalf of the 50,000-plus supporters who attended the opening ceremonies, referring to the sometimes difficult and violent lives Israelis faced on a day-to-day basis. "A sporting occasion is one. We see these Jewish athletes as our brothers and sisters abroad and hope they'll share their lives with us."

Critics of the Games downplayed such sentiments, which were a staple of the event, especially during the closing ceremonies when Israeli leaders such as David Ben-Gurion and Golda Meir urged the athletes to make aliyah. The level of talent was also an increasing disappointment to some. "The Maccabiah no longer has sports on a high level," said Moshe Lehrer of the Hebrew-language newspaper *Ma'ariv.* "There used to be Olympic champions. Now it's nothing like before."

Lehrer pointed out that one of the underlying purposes of the Maccabiah was convincing the athlete to make aliyah. "Since 1950, only a few people are staying to settle. It's mostly just a Jewish youth festival."[6]

The United States was expected to take most of the gold medals, including—as opposed to the previous Maccabiah—the men's basketball gold. Could this have led to Lehrer's "sour grapes" evaluation?

In the overall relative carefreeness of the Games, there was a portion of sadness: Absent from the Games for the first time since 1973 was Pierre Gildesgame, the president of the World Maccabi Union, who was killed in an automobile accident in London in March. A paid death notice in *The New York Times* on behalf of the U.S. Committee Sports for Israel hailed Gildesgame's accomplishments: "His dedication to Jewish youth around the world has made the dream of the Maccabiah a reality." The Pierre Gildesgame Sports Museum in the Maccabiah Village in Ramat Gan was named in his honor and he was hailed as a "Pillar of Achievement" by the International Jewish Sports Hall of Fame.

In 1982, Yekutieli, considered the creator of the Maccabiah Games concept, died at the age of eighty-two. Like Gildesgame, he was similarly recognized by the IJSHOF as a Pillar of Achievement for his incalculable contributions.

In a continuing effort to minimize national divisions, the athletes were housed by sport rather than by country. "In spite of the problem of language and other technical difficulties, the change has been made to encourage athletes from the overseas countries to mix with each other and with Israelis," said Louis Gecelter, chair of the Maccabiah accommodation department. "In addition to inducing a greater spirit of fellowship among the athletes, we think that participants in the same sport will often have more in common with each other than with compatriots taking part in different events."[7]

Thirteen venues served to house the various groups, including:

---

6 "11th Maccabiah Games Begin," *New York Times*, July 7, 1981

7 "Boycotts, camaraderie expected at Maccabiah," *Jerusalem Post*, May 31, 1981

Tel Aviv University: swimming, soccer, hockey

Beit Berl, a college in Kfar Sava: soccer

The Ramat Aviv Hotel (Tel Aviv): tennis, track and field, rowing

Avia Hotel (Ben Gurion Airport): basketball and chess

Maccabiah Village (Ramat Gan): Judo, karate, wrestling, squash

Dan Caesarea Hotel: golf

Basel Hotel (Tel Aviv): lawn bowls

Wingate Institute (Netanya): gymnastics, fencing

Green Beach (Netanya): volleyball

Marine Center (Kibbutz Sdot Yam): sailing

"The Maccabiah accommodations obviously cannot compare in any way to the Olympic villages in Moscow or Los Angeles. But they are as good as we can afford," said Kevehazi.

As an additional benefit, the new setup would theoretically make it easier to transport the athletes to their venues. Some of the housing was even *at* the location of the event, such as the golfers' site.

Despite the perceived benefits, not everyone was on board with the arrangements. A commentary in *The Jerusalem Post* of July 12 indignantly noted the lack of involvement of Israel's most historical city. "The privilege of being the only athletes to perform in the capital of the Jewish people was reserved for the women volleyball players, who performed at Hebrew University. Without denigrating this excellent sport in any way, it can hardly be called the most popular in the country."

The piece lamented, "It must be admitted, by even the proudest Jerusalemite, that, in the case of the capital, the Maccabiah organizers can argue that the facilities for sport are so appalling that they are too ashamed to invite people from abroad to come here" and worried that "it is doubtful whether we will be any better off in four years time, when the 12th Maccabiah will take place."[8]

For some of the participants, these Games were a bittersweet occasion. Several countries, including the United States, Israel, Canada, South Africa, and Argentina, among others, boycotted the 1980 Olympics held in Moscow. For hundreds of athletes, this might have

---

8 "The Maccabiah Cinderellas," *Jerusalem Post*, July 12, 1981

represented the one chance they had to perform on the ultimate international sports stage.

Jack Abramson, chair of the U.S. Maccabiah team, published a list comparing the size of delegations sent to the 1981 Maccabiah to the number of athletes, presumably gentile *and* Jewish, that competed in the Moscow Olympics. In the case of those nations who did not participate in the 1980 Olympics, he used figures from the 1976 Olympics in Montreal.

Among the larger delegations who attended the Moscow Olympics:

	1980 Olympic Entries	1981 Maccabiah Entries
Australia	182	300
Belgium	105	106
Columbia	34	116
France	213	108
Great Britain	249	114
Mexico	99	144
Spain	115	53
Sweden	122	55
Venezuela	31	221

And those who did not:

	1976 Olympic Entries	1981 Maccabiah Entries
Canada	391	179
United States	368	375
Israel	26	500
Chile	7	48
Uruguay	9	56
South Africa	0	222
Argentina	70	204

You might say you could tell who the United States's and Israel's friends were by who made the decision to go to Russia and who backed the boycott.

* * *

The U.S. hoopsters demolished Uruguay by more than 100 points. Mark Rosenberg scored as many points as the entire opposition in the 128-17 explosion. Danny Schayes commented on the mismatch: "We were up 25-1 after only 3 minutes; what more can you say?"[9] The U.S. had already beaten France 108-44; Argentina, 96-59; and Canada, 83-45 to move into the finals against their Israeli archrivals.

Schayes and Willie Sims scored 28 and 14 points, respectively, to give the Americans their second straight basketball gold, beating the Israelis, 91-71. Although they were up by just a single point at halftime, they opened up a comfortable margin early in the second half. It was much more satisfying than the one-point victory in 1977, even if the drama wasn't there.

"The coach had a few words about our defense in the first half, and that was a key in the second half," said starting guard David Blatt, who scored 17 points.[10] Like Tal Brody and Sims, Blatt—who became the head coach of the Cleveland Cavaliers in 2014—remained in Israel, where he played for several years before becoming coach of Maccabi Tel Aviv, the Israeli basketball equivalent of the New York Yankees in terms of historical success.

The U.S. men continued to dominate in the water, sweeping all the events on the first day of competition, including the 100-meter breaststroke and backstroke. The next day, however, was a different story. The Israelis stormed back with top honors in three of the six events, including the 200-meter butterfly, 1,500-meter freestyle, and

9 "Yanks stage Israel Games show," *Ukiah Daily Journal* (California), July 14, 1981
10 "Americans Top Israeli Squad," *Daily News* (Huntingdon, Penn.), July 16, 1981

200-meter individual medley. They added three more golds the following day with the 400-meter men's freestyle and women's 400-meter freestyle relay.

"We were swimming well today, but sometimes you just get beat," said men's coach Don Gambril, taking a philosophical attitude.[11]

Some non-American, non-Israeli women also had strong showings with Deborah Stone of Australia and Charlotte Hilez of Sweden taking the 400-meter freestyle and 100-meter backstroke, respectively.

The gymnasts vied for attention with Mitch Gaylord, one of the stars of the 1984 Los Angeles Olympics, who picked up all but one of the available gold medals.

Maccabiah Profile: Mitch Gaylord, United States, Gymnastics

Mitch Gaylord grew up in Southern California where he attended UCLA. He won four medals—a gold in the all-around, a silver in vaults, and bronze for rings and parallel bars—at the 1984 Olympics in his native Los Angeles and became the first American gymnast to score a perfect 10.00. As a sign of his accomplishments, two of his maneuvers on the horizontal bar were named for him: the "Gaylord Flip" and "Gaylord II," both of which are still performed and considered among the most difficult gymnastic maneuvers.

Among the accolades for his accomplishments were an appointment to the President's Council for Physical Fitness and induction into the Olympic Hall of Fame in 2006. He was also enshrined in the International Jewish Sports Hall of Fame in 1988 and the National Jewish Sports Hall of Fame seven years later.

But before the Olympics, there were the Maccabiah Games.

---

11 "U.S. Gymnasts, Israeli Swimmers Shine," *Galveston Daily News* (Texas), July 9, 1981

Gaylord experienced a "typical Reform Jewish upbringing" in Los Angeles, which included Hebrew school and a bar mitzvah. "It was a pretty big part of my life in the growing-up years," he said in a phone interview. Although he had learned about Israel in school, he had never been there, which added to the allure of the Maccabiah opportunity for the 11th Games.

Gaylord had previous experience in international competition, participating in the University Games and World Championships in Russia, but this was his first trip to Israel. The entire Gaylord family made their pilgrimage together, including parents Fred and Denise; sister Jeanine; and brother Chuck, who was also a member of the gymnastics team.

"I don't think anything could have prepared me for how powerful that was going to feel," Gaylord said. "It was a really incredible connection to all of that history, that heritage, and our people. It was much more than a sporting event, that's for sure."

The cultural component "was probably some of the most rewarding experiences," Gaylord said. "It was definitely the connection to the historical sites that made is such a wonderful, wonderful trip. Masada was one of the most powerful [sites] for me because it felt like I was stepping back into history. That was pretty incredible."

Israel has traditionally provided the largest team at the Games, mostly due to logistics, but it didn't help them for the gymnastics events this time around. The competition "wasn't on the same level as [the U.S.] at the time. We were pretty far ahead of them . . . , but that's really not what it was all about," Gaylord said. "It was more about the experience of being there and the celebration of sport. It wasn't about who was going to win; we knew we were going to win. It was just about the enjoyment of the competition and the competition of the games."

That turned out to be not just a sense of the athlete's bravado. The men's gymnastics team won 14 out of a possible 21 medals, the women 10 of 15. Gaylord led the way, tying a Maccabiah record with six golds, including the all-around, floor exercises, horizontal bar, parallel bars, pommel horse, and rings. The only second-place finish was to his brother in the vaults. For his performance at those Games and continuing contributions to Maccabi USA, Mitch Gaylord was named a "Legend of the Maccabiah" in 2011.

Gaylord said despite the overall confidence, "We just approached it the same way as any other competition. Even though we felt that we were better than the other teams that were there, we still wanted to do our best; I think all athletes want to do that because it raises the level of competition for everybody.

"I think there's a lot of pride in hosting the Games out there. I think that they do feel it's a big deal and they're proud to do it. I know that we made some incredible relationships."

It served as a great preparation for his turn at the Los Angeles Olympics when he won four medals, including one gold, one silver, and two bronze.

"It was a completely different experience. I think the Olympic Games were very much about the competition and about winning," he said with a chuckle. "It wasn't so much about the cultural experience or interacting with the other athletes. It was very competitive. At the Maccabiah, it was obviously about much more than the competition."

That spirit carried back to the U.S. "When I competed in '84, the Israeli delegation was there and I heard incredible cheers from the crowd when I medaled on rings because they were sitting behind [me], and I looked back and I said, 'Man, who's cheering so loud?' It was the Israeli athletes I had met in 1981. It was kind of cool to have that bond."

Gaylord returned to Israel in 1985. He and fellow Olympic and Maccabiah hero Mark Spitz did several promotional appearances "and that was rewarding, as well."

He was able to parlay his success into a career as an actor and media personality—he appeared as a judge in the reality series *Celebrity Circus* and basically played himself in the 1986 feature film *American Anthem* and served as a stunt double for Chris O'Donnell in *Batman Forever*—and does numerous speaking engagements for groups as diverse as Fortune 500 Companies to students across the country.

Gaylord had been a commentator for the Atlanta Olympics in 1996 as well as for ESPN and FOX programs. Jewish Learning Television CEO Phil Blazer asked him to host a series of "up close and personal" vignettes for the 2009 Maccabiahs. "Anything to help promote the Maccabiah Games, I'm all for that," he said. "My wife had never been to Israel and I thought, what a great time for both of us to experience the country together as well as participate in the Games on the other side of the fence.

"It wasn't like NBC doing the play-by-play and having to be at the venue for hours and hours and hours," he said. "I had a lot of free time so my wife and I took advantage of that and we definitely toured Israel and went to all the cool places and had great experiences."

Gaylord played a similar role in 2013, but this time he introduced the segments on tape from the U.S. He prefers that to play-by-play or analysis, in part because, as he admitted "I haven't kept up with [gymnastics] for years."

"What I like is the human interest stories, that's what fascinates me and that's what I like finding out: what makes athletes tick and what their families are all about and how they got to the levels they got to. That kind of stuff is fun and more interesting to me."

Gaylord was amazed at some of the countries that sent delegations. "That was one of the things that I do remember when I was there: wow, there's Jewish people from all over the world here. That's pretty cool."

Visiting Israel amidst its never-ceasing security issues wasn't a consideration. "I had no concerns about that at all. I think one of the coolest observations when we were out there is how protected we felt, the presence of military and police force around. It felt very protected and very safe. I think prior to that, I don't think I had an understanding of how that all worked."

While he has no formal relationship with Maccabi USA, Gaylord said he's always available to help promote it. He served as an inspiration to young gymnasts when he appeared at the trials in December 2013 in Oklahoma, where he met a lot of the athletes trying to make the team.

"It's all about getting American athletes that have never been to Israel," he said. "They'll remember it for the rest of their life. I think that's super important to make that connection for people to the State of Israel. Jewish people around the world who haven't been there, it's a great time to all go and be together. Also I think the celebration of sport and culture all mixed together, which is what those Games are all about, is just wonderful, and like I said, the Olympics is definitely about the competition and winning and it's rare that you get a huge sporting event like the Maccabiah Games where it's more than that."

* * *

In the track and field events, the Americans won four more gold, with Jason Meislor breaking the high jump mark with 7'2.25" and Gary Williky doing the same with the discus record, raising it by more than 12 feet, from 173'2" to 187'7". More records fell when Boris Djerassi broke his own 1977 mark in the hammer throw with 220.3 and Evan Fox won the 3,000-meter walk in 13:18.27, beating the old standard of 13:35.4. James Espir of Great Britain won one of the few track golds by someone not from the U.S. when he broke the tape in the 1,500 meters.

On the soccer field, there were multiple upsets, starting with the United States defeating Great Britain, 3-1, and South Africa's 2-1 victory over Israel. Unfortunately, the U.S. luck ran out when they failed to win gold with a 3-1 loss in the finals.

Two future tennis pros met in the singles finals, with Israel's Shlomo Glickstein beating the United States' Brad Gilbert, 6-2, 6-3. But Gilbert and his partner John Levine took the doubles crown over another pair of Americans, Rick Meyer and Paul Bernstein, in straight sets, 6-4, 6-3.

The Jerusalem Post ran the customary review of the Games, a combination of praise and regret. The latter suggested that Israel did not put forth its best athletes, primarily in basketball and soccer, who were either otherwise occupied at international events deemed more worthy of their participation, or simply uninterested. According to one summation, Mickey Berkowitz, one of Israel's most prominent basketballers, "made no effort to join [Maccabiah] this year."[12]

On the positive side, the fans had a good time. They were able to attend many events free of charge and the compliments from foreign delegations about the new facilities were rewarding: "The typical 'Anglo-Saxon' sports—badminton, bowls, cricket, golf, softball—went as smoothly as a wood rolling across an immaculate green."[13]

---

12 "Plaudits and lapses in Maccabiah summing-up," *Jerusalem Post*, July 19, 1981

13 Ibid

Chapter 13

The Twelfth Games
July 15-25, 1985

"My lifelong dream was to become a professional baseball player and play in the World Series. I'll never get to see that dream come true, but representing the United States in softball at the Jewish Olympics will more than make up for it. It's such an honor."

Mike Levine[1]

Once again, the Maccabiah Games opened to a packed house at Ramat Gan Stadium. In addition to 50,000 friends and family in

1 "From Baseball to Softball to the Maccabiah Games," *Boston Globe*, June 17, 1985

the stands and 4,000 athletes on the field from seventeen countries—including "juniors" for the first time—more than 1,000 performers wearing costumes danced and sang welcome. In addition to that, another 2,000 members of the Young Maccabi Youth Movement put on a gymnastics display.

Israeli President Chaim Herzog, who had boxed for his native Ireland's Maccabi team in the 1930s, formally opened the Games.

Twenty years after he burst upon the international swimming scene in the Seventh Maccabiah, Mark Spitz returned to Israel to carry the torch, the first American to do so. New Jersey-born Tal Brody had the honor in 1973, but as a member of the Israeli basketball team. Spitz was accompanied by Shirli Shapiro, Anok Spitzer, and Shlomit Romano, children of three of the Israelis slain at the 1972 Munich Olympics.

For Spitz, who went on to record-setting fame at those Olympics, this might have been a consolation prize. He had been embroiled in a controversy surrounding whether he would be among a group to bear the Olympic Flag at the opening ceremonies of the Los Angeles Games the previous year. When that turned out not to be the case, speculation began that he might carry the Olympic Torch instead. At the last minute, the honor went to Rafer Johnson and the granddaughter of Jesse Owens, leaving Spitz and his supporters exasperated. Rumors began to fly about the reasons behind the decision, including a conflict of interest because he was working as a television announcer for the Games, which were broadcast that year by ABC (that theory was refuted, since two of the flag-bearers were similarly engaged by the network), or perhaps it was the lawsuits in which he was engaged against the Olympic Committee, regarding merchandise he was allegedly selling that featured the Olympic logo.

Appointing Spitz the torchbearer for the Maccabiah Games may have been a panacea for what had taken place in Los Angeles, but it was certainly not a substitute.[2]

Not on display at the opening ceremonies? National flags. In March, the International Maccabiah Games Committee had passed a

---

2 "A Slight to Inflame the Heart," *Los Angeles Times*, July 11, 1985

resolution calling for their elimination from future kickoffs for the sake of unity.

"We are getting rid of national flags because they are a symbol of the separation of Israel and our people in the Diaspora," said Michael Kevehazi, chair of the Organizing Committee. The International Olympic Committee had been looking into a similar move, noting that displaying the flags of the individual countries was "part of the negative nationalistic aspect of the contest."[3]

Opening night fashion continued to be a favorite topic. The JTA noted that "the Brazil delegation was led by women in . . . native dress moving to the sound of the samba beat" and that "If medals were being given out on opening night, the 90 Italians would have walked away with the gold as the most nattily attired team, for their white [jackets] and navy blue slacks and ties."[4]

The athletes, representing thirty-five countries,[5] were led by Israel's 800-member team, followed by the United States, with a delegation of more than 500. Three countries—Zaire, Monaco, and Gibraltar—made their debut and Yugoslavia returned after an absence of fifty years, becoming the first Eastern Bloc nation to participate since World War II.

The cost of sending the American team—athletes and support personnel, including coaches, trainers, and medical staff—came to roughly $3,000 per person, or about $6,650 in 2014 dollars.

Despite concerns that a larger field of athletes would dilute the talent pool, each new "generation" seemed to bring superior swimmers, talented track and field stars, and worthy wrestlers and weightlifters. In swimming alone, seven men's and fourteen women's records were broken, with the U.S. team winning all but three of the gold medals.

---

3 "Maccabiah to Drop Flags to Symbolize Unity of Jewish People," JTA, March 6, 1985

4 "Maccabiah Games Get Under Way; Emotion, Pride Mark The Opening," JTA, July 17, 1985

5 It is interesting to note the discrepancies in the number of nations attending which ranges from 35-38 depending on the source.

Twelve new men's records and seven new women's records were set in track and field.

Marina Davidovich, a rhythm gymnastics coach for the 1985 Games, described in great detail on her website the feelings of leading a group from the United States. She discussed the three-day orientation at Rutgers University in New Jersey as well as the ten-hour plane ride and the feeling when they touched down in the Holy Land. "The surge of energy radiating from each member of the US delegation was unmeasurable!"

Once on the ground, she gave a frank and insightful assessment of the housing arrangements and logistics. "Our accommodations were very much military style. Small beds, tiny bedside table and few chairs. But everything was very clean and orderly. We woke up at 7 a.m. for breakfast at the big cafeteria: hard boiled eggs, bread, tomatoes and cucumbers. Training at 8 a.m. Free time until 3 p.m. Training again at 4 p.m. Dinners were wonderful: delicious food, loud and happy people, singing and dancing afterwards. We did have military protection at all times. Soldiers with rifles on the roofs, in the hallways, on the buses. It was so strange at first, but after [a] few days it was part of our lives."

Davidovich, a native of the former Soviet Union, gushed about the opening ceremonies, saying, "All were united by a love of sport and a common heritage. Barriers of language, culture, age melted under the stadium lights."

She closed her entry with a sentiment that represents the vast majority of Maccabiah participants: "I will treasure every moment of these 2 weeks for the rest of my life!"[6]

Once again, a major controversy of the Games involved South Africa's participation: Did the team represent an apartheid nation or the country's Maccabi groups? Complicating the matter: different sports governing bodies have different rules; citizens of that country were banned from competing in International Olympic Committee–sponsored

---

6 "1985, July 15-25, The 12th Maccabiah Games," marinadavidovich. com/2012/08/1985-july-15-25-12th-maccabiah-games.html

events, but several of the programs at the Maccabiah fell outside those restrictions.

As a way of circumventing the problem, the South African athletes who were still allowed to compete were placed in a club designated as "Maccabi Modi'in," basically a catchment for those who had immigrated to Israel but had not quite met the residency requirements. Because the nature of the Games was to provide a competitive atmosphere for Jewish athletes *in toto* as opposed to athletes representing individual countries, they were given this dispensation. More than 180 athletes under the Modi'in umbrella had participated in the 1981 Games, accounting for the third-most medals after the United States and Israel. At the '85 Maccabiah, the Modi'in contingent would finish seventh.

Concerned with the possible ramifications and potential sanctions that might be handed down by international sports federations, Isaac Ofek, chair of Israel's Olympic Committee, ordered an investigation into how the South Africans received the special treatment. In a bit of playing fast and loose with the rules, a spokesperson for the Maccabiah Games said as far as his organization was concerned, "there are no South Africans in the Maccabiah."[7]

That situation, however, was "old news," having been a staple of the Maccabiah for the past several Games. This year's potboiler came on the women's basketball court in what amounted to a battle of the sexes.

Because the men's finals have customarily been the marquee event of the Games, organizers made the decision to switch venues after the Canadian men refused to play Brazil at the Kfar HaMaccabiah Stadium and insisted on moving to the larger facility at Yad Eliahu, where the women's final between Israel and the United States had been scheduled. The Israeli women found this unacceptable and demonstrated their displeasure by boycotting the finale. In a move of solidarity, their American opponents similarly refused to play, stopping their bus en route to the revised site.

---

7 "Participation of South African Olim in Israel causes Flap at Maccabiah," JTA, July 24, 1985

Anat Dreigor, captain of the Israeli squad, said her team refused to play because their supporters had already bought tickets for Yad Eliahu. She accused the Games' organizing committee of making a "very big mistake" in neglecting the women's final in favor of the men.

Zvi Eyal, a spokesperson for the Maccabiah Organizing Committee, told Israel Radio that a disciplinary committee would meet to review the Israeli women's position, and would be asked to "punish the girls with the full force of the regulations." Eventually, that ruling came down as a forfeit, thereby awarding the gold medal to the U.S. team by default.

Maccabiah Profile: Donna Orender, United States, Basketball

Donna Orender was an all-star point guard in the short-lived Women's Professional Basketball League (1978-80), spending single seasons with the New York Stars, New Jersey Gems, and Chicago Hustle. Following her playing career, she spent 17 years working for the Professional Golf Association and served as president of the WNBA from 2005-10, earning numerous awards and accolades for leadership. Currently, she is head of her own marketing and branding company, Orender Unlimited.

She serves on the boards of numerous institutions, including the UJA Sports for Youth Initiative and Maccabi USA/Sports for Israel, among many others.

Orender (née Geils) described her Jewish upbringing as "a very rich one. We belonged to a conservative synagogue which was the center of our life in terms of our youth group, friends, family."

Orender, who grew up in Queens, NY, started playing basketball at the relatively late age of thirteen. She didn't recall how she first heard about the Maccabiah Games, but said it happened after she had been a professional player. In order to qualify, she said, "I had to go get my amateur status back."

Despite her credentials, Orender had to try out for the team in 1985 and was the oldest player selected, based on her experience as much as her skills. Since the women's league folded she had kept up with her game by playing a lot of pickup ball.

"I think what I brought . . . was the sense of presence," she said. "I had been away from the game, in the workplace. I was coming back and every moment felt precious to me. Whereas the 'youngsters,' if you will, didn't have that sense of occasion or an appreciation for what you have. It just meant so much to me."

Recalling the battles between the U.S and Israel at the Games, Orender said "[Israel] beat us once and we beat them once. It's never even competition. It wasn't at a level that I was used to. But I was having a blast," she said. "I just played as hard as I could. I just loved to play. It was such a privilege, such a privilege."

In a classic example of poor planning by the Games' organizers, what should have been an enjoyable and exciting showdown ended in disappointment for Israel's women's basketball team.

"The Israeli women felt they were being disrespected because the men's team was playing for the gold medal in the big arena and the women were playing in [a] small high school," Orender said, still somewhat bitter about the outcome.

"We honored their boycott. In order for us to get the gold medal, we had to take the court," she said. "And we chose not to. Over the years, it's become kind of a badge of honor.

"There were a lot of people who were probably disappointed, but really, it was the right decision to make."

Disappointment aside, Orender loved her first visit to Israel. "I didn't know what to expect," but "It was idyllic. We stayed at Kfar Maccabiah, which I thought was the greatest place on the planet, a beautiful place. We were with the men's basketball team, but we met basketball players from Canada, Australia, from all over the world. It was like a country club. We would go out some nights, we visited with Israeli soldiers; we had the time of our life. Everything I saw . . . was incredibly inspiring and overwhelming and to see it with the group was also very special."

Although she was still single at that point, she was already thinking about her future family. "I just knew that I wanted to get my kids [to Israel] earlier than when I came, because I was just so moved by the whole experience."

Long after Orender participated as an athlete, she remained connected to Maccabi USA and the Maccabiah Games as a volunteer.
"I felt it was a gift, and it was so meaningful" she said of her 1985
experience. "Obviously sports is my avocation and vocation. I'm
proud to be a Jewish athlete and I love the people and I wanted to
stay connected and give back."

At the time of this interview, Orender was a vice president of the
board and a co-chair of the publicity committee for the Maccabi
junior boys' basketball program; her twin sons, Jacob and Zachary, were on the team. She had already fulfilled the promise she had
made to herself in 1985 by bringing them to Israel for their bar
mitzvahs.

"Sports is an international language and it has a way of bringing
people together. It's a common thread and that common thread
provides the impetus for awareness, for growth, for unity, for building support and understanding of our heritage and also reminding us of our responsibility to pay it forward," said Orender. "The
number of participants has grown and I think that's great. The
more people you can touch in this magical period of time, that's so
impactful."

* * *

As for the men's game, Team USA edged Israel, 95-94, in a dramatic
finish before a crowd of 7,000.

The Americans led by 53-37 at halftime, but Israel rallied early in
the second half to tie the game at 63-63.

The U.S. team took a 95-90 lead with 53 seconds to go. Israel's Jamchi Giamsci narrowed the deficit to 95-94 with a free throw with 18
seconds left. Then, with three ticks remaining, teammate Adi Rosenberg drove for a layup that tauntingly hung on the rim before falling
out.

U.S. coach Gerry Gimelstob praised his team's victory as a "great
job against Israel," which was playing with three national-team players
in its lineup.

Canada defeated Brazil, 74-55, to win the bronze medal.[8]

Despite the feel-good attitude engendered by the Games, outside events continued to have an impact. There seemed to be no respite from the tense situation in the Middle East.

Writing in the *Toronto Globe and Mail*, Lorne Rubenstein observed that life in the Jewish State was not exactly conducive to the types of leisure activities enjoyed in places like Canada and the United States, or pretty much anywhere else in the free world. His melancholy story focused on an unnamed kid, perhaps seven or eight, who looked like he had a natural talent as a student in the golf school in Caesarea.

"Twelve years from now, he might compete for the Israeli team. But circumstances will intrude upon his life that cannot intrude upon that of a young Canadian golfer," Rubenstein ruefully offered, calling to mind Sandy Lyle, a Scotsman who had recently won the British Open.

"When Lyle was seventeen, he lost in a match-play tournament to David Marriott, an Englishman who played in the Maccabiah Games this year. But Lyle didn't have to go into the army the next year. He continued to develop his golf.

"That won't be the case with the young lad at Caesarea. He is more likely to serve in the army before he golfs for his country. . . ."

Rubenstein warned that young Israelis who showed any real skills would most likely leave the country, seeking opportunities to craft their game, and thereby depriving Israel of producing champion-level golfers.

"One cannot envy the choices or obligations these golfers face," Rubenstein concluded. "For them, talent is a burden and source of frustration."[9]

On a more uplifting note, in the heat of this competitive atmosphere, more than a few budding romances resulted in weddings.

---

8 "U.S. Women Refuse Maccabiah Games Gold," *Philadelphia Inquirer*, July 25, 1985

9 "Israeli golfers torn by choices," *Globe and Mail* (Toronto), July 26, 1985

As Steve Lippman reported in the *New York Jewish Week*, "Sprinter Lorraine Lotzof went to the Maccabiah Games from South Africa in 1965 and caught the eye of Richard Abramson, an American swimmer.

"She returned to Israel in 1973 as Mrs. Abramson, a Boston house-wife, an American team member, and "the only mother on the track."

Both husband and wife were medal-winners in their sports: Lorraine won two golds and a silver at the 1961 Games, with three more golds in 1965 when she was named South Africa's female athlete of the year. Richard won a gold and a silver in 1961 and failed to medal in his lone 1965 event.

They both had Maccabiah pedigrees as well: Lorraine's uncle, David Shaya, competed for Poland in 1935 and was one of the hundreds of eastern Europeans who remained in Palestine following the "Aliyah Games." Richard's brothers, Allan and David, also won medals in swimming in 1957 and 1961, respectively. The family's patriarch, Jack, served as vice president of the U.S. Committee Sports for Israel.

The Maccabiah "is important because of the terrible stress the Israelis are under," said Richard Abramson. "Things that are involved with the body and the mind are critical for a country. It makes a healthy country."

Lorraine made the team for the U.S. in 1969 but dropped out upon learning that she was pregnant. Four years later, she was back in form, winning silver and a bronze.[10]

Like many former athletes, Lorraine and Richard Abramson kept a connection with the Games, working to give back through fundraising efforts.

* * *

American athletes at the 12th Maccabiah Games brought home the most medals, with a total of 246, followed by Israel, with 217. Other countries were left in the dust, with only Canada breaking the 50-mark.

---

10 "'Jewish Olympics' played cupid for '65 competitors," *New York Jewish Week*, June 28, 1985

The Final Medal Count (Gold/Silver/Bronze):
USA 246 (109/90/47)
Israel 214 (62/67/85)
Canada 51 (12/15/24)
Brazil 32 (10/11/11)
Maccabi Modi'in 28 (6/12/10)
Great Britain 22 (7/6/9)
Australia 19 (6/5/8)
Mexico 16 (1/3/12)
Holland 13 (7/5/1)
France 11 (6/4/1)
Argentina 11 (0/5/6)
Sweden 5 (1/2/2)
West Germany 4 (1/2/1)
Denmark 2 (1/0/1)
Other countries 11 (0/4/7)

Chapter 14

The Thirteenth Games
July 3-13, 1989

[I]n these Maccabiah Games, look to the athletes not for victories of this or that tribe or nation. Watch instead for that graceful moment under pressure when a young mind makes its body reach out to grasp at that which for us mere mortals, is beyond our reach.

Robert Rosenberg, *Jerusalem Post*[1]

As early as January 29, *The New York Times* ran an item in its travel section advising those interested in taking in the Maccabiah Games in Israel six months hence to book early. "While tickets to many

---

1 "The Pursuit of Glory," *Jerusalem Post*, June 4, 1989

events are still available, travelers interested in attending the Games, especially the opening ceremony and the basketball finals, should make arrangements soon, according to the Israel Tourist Office." Tickets for most events were priced at $10-40, with the Opening Ceremonies going for $45-90 and at least one travel agency offering a package deal that included airfare, accommodations, and tickets to various events.[2]

One of the highest profile fundraising events had to have been the "Jokes for Jocks," hosted by Budd Freidman at his famous Improv comedy club in Santa Monica, California on June 4. In reviewing the evening, which cost $100 for dinner and the show, an article in the Torrance *Daily Breeze* noted the impending departure of the 450-person U.S. delegation from New York to Israel.

"But the U.S. team can't return from Tel Aviv if it doesn't have the plane fare. In fact, it can't even leave if it doesn't have the plane fare."

Don Segall, chair for the event, announced the cost to send each athlete was $3,500. "That includes everything: training, room, board, air fare, you name it," he added. "But it's worth every penny."

It was only logical that one of the biggest names at the soiree was Leonard Nimoy, who was brought up in an observant Jewish household in Boston. Everyone knows him for his role as Mr. Spock in the *Star Trek* franchise, but few remember he received an Emmy nomination for his portrayal of Morris Meyerson, husband to Golda Meir, in the 1982 TV biopic, *A Woman Called Golda*. Nimoy introduced a twelve-minute film about the history of the Games. Ellen DeGeneres, Larry Miller, Kevin Pollack, Jeff Altman, and Charles Fleischer were among those lending their comedic talents to the affair that night.[3]

"There were actually five 'Jokes For Jocks' comedy nights staged in Southern California," said Los Angeles premier publicist Joe Siegman in an email. He was on hand for that June 4 event along with other members of the lawn bowls team. "The one in '89 was the third.

---

2 "Travel Advisory," *New York Times*, Jan. 29, 1989

3 "Food and fun for funds - La Scala, Improv host 2 benefits," *Daily Breeze* (Torrance, CA), June 6, 1989

"In 1984, with a Southern California committee of Maccabiah veteran competitors and enthusiastic supporters, and two entertainment industry friends who wanted to do something off the beaten path to raise awareness and funds for the Games, specifically the '85 Games, so with Segall and game show producer Ronnie Greenberg, we came up with the idea of staging a super comedy night. Mort Greenberg was the West Coast director of the U.S. Committee Sports for Israel, and I was a VP of the organization at the time. We came up with the 'Jokes For Jocks' concept and got Budd Friedman on board.

"Budd collared most of the performing comics [including] Jerry Seinfeld, Bill Maher, Dick Shawn, I think Roseanne Barr. Other names escape me. Billy Crystal was the night's host. Norm Crosby and L.A. Raiders star lineman Lyle Alzado were event co-chairs and lent their names to advertising and promotion. Ronnie Greenberg (no relation to Mort) and Segall handled the details of running the evening. [Women's basketball legend] Nancy Lieberman somehow showed up to serve on the details committee. Needless to say, the event was a hit."

"The last two 'Jokes For Jocks' were held at the L.A. Skirball Cultural Center, a larger venue than the Improvs, each with a pallet of comics, young and veteran."

Siegman was proud that the comedians donated their services to the cause. "All the comics were either regulars at the Improv, did Improv tours, or worked on my various live comedy concert shows I produced at colleges and casinos. The younger comics were doing favors for the people who got them paying work. The veteran comics did favors for their friends."

Siegman termed the money raised at the 1984 event as "modest but nice."

The 13th Maccabiah—the "Bar Mitzvah" Games—brought 4,500 athletes to Israel from forty-five nations. Among those making their debuts were Portugal, Panama, and a one-man "delegation" from Hong Kong.

Earlier in the year, there had been hope and speculation that this might finally be the year to see landsmen from the Soviet Union marching in the opening ceremonies.

"Michel Green, chairman of European Maccabi, noted that Soviet Jews have been partaking quietly in their own kind of Maccabiah in a suburb of Moscow every four years but this time it is hoped the authorities will not bar them coming to the real event. His branch of Maccabi has issued an invitation for 50 athletes to make the trip."[4]

Sure enough, Russia made its Maccabiah debut, a most welcome guest at this milestone celebration. Hungary, Yugoslavia, and Lithuania, all of which had participated in the first Games in the 1930s and had been absent since the dropping of the Iron Curtain, also returned to the athletic fold.

Almost 850 Israelis participated in the 13th Games, with the United States, as usual, providing the largest delegation of any Diaspora nation with more than 500 competitors. Canada and Australia were next on the list with 267 and 237, respectively, according to reports.

The tennis courts at Ramat Hasharon were the busiest venues, with more than 400 entrants. By contrast, there were 169 track-and-field athletes running around Hadara Yosef Stadium. The rugby and hockey tournaments took place at the Wingate Institute, badminton in Rishon Lezion, and squash at the Herzliya club with the lawn bowls spread out on pitches in Kfar Hamaccabiah, Savyon, Ramat Gan, Ra'anana, Wingate, and Haifa.

The Israeli media separated out "Anglo sports" from those presumably more demanding and traditional activities such as martial arts, shooting, gymnastics, swimming, and track and field. These "English-speaking" sports included softball, which would be played on fields at Kibbutz Gezer; basketball, at various sites from Carmel to Beersheba; rowing, at the lake in Kinneret; golf, at the world-class course in Caesarea; and sailing off the Nahariya coast. Two cricket fields in Ashdod would accommodate teams from Israel, England, India, and the defending gold-medalists, Australia, plus a team comprised of athletes from the "Rest of the World."

The Maccabiah's newest sport—tenpin bowling—was played at the Kolbo Shalom Bowling Centre.

---

4 "Soviet Maccabeans hoping to join Bar Mitzvah Games," *Jerusalem Post*, Feb. 11, 1989

The Games are known for having some infrastructural problems that provide a certain amount of angst. This time there were no such reports. The opening ceremony began on schedule as enthusiastic spectators packed the stadium. The athletes marched in, sang Hebrew folk songs along with some of Israel's most popular performers, and marvelled at brilliant overhead laser and firework displays.

"Ramat Gan Stadium's playing field suddenly became a *shtetl*, featuring every type of Eastern European Jew, as hundreds of men and women in Hassidic garb danced to the evocative sounds of *Fiddler on the Roof* led by singer Dudu Fisher in the guise of Tuvia [sic] the Milkman. Fisher had previously presented a heart-warming rendition of the Games' official song 'I Belong'. . . ."[5]

President Chaim Herzog, Prime Minister Yitzhak Shamir, members of the Knesset, and foreign dignitaries watched as the Austrian delegation led the parade of athletes, once again in alphabetical order according to the Hebrew language. They were followed by the large green-and-gold bedecked Australian contingent, moving to the tune of "Waltzing Matilda."

The Ecuadorean team consisted of three members, all from the same family, while solitary athletes represented Paraguay, Costa Rica, Hong Kong, and South Korea. An especially sentimental response was reserved for these smaller delegations, proof of the strong desire of Jews from all corners of the world to stay connected. Pockets of fans, now immigrants settled in Israel, could be heard loudly cheering their former countryfolk.

The U.S. team was so large that its flag bearer was well down the processional by the time the last of the red, white and blue-clad athletes, "half of them as busy with their video cameras as the press photographers to capture the moment" entered from the far end.

Members of several delegations caught up in the excitement endeared themselves to the fans tossing souvenirs, some potentially dangerous, including umbrellas from the Dutch group.

Following the traditional moment of silence for the fallen Israeli soldiers, Hanoch Budin, a twenty-seven-year-old amputee and former

---

5 "Tears and laughter launch Maccabiah," *Jerusalem Post*, July 11, 1989

solider, ran the Maccabiah Torch into the stadium and lit the cauldron. Budin was a two-time gold medalist at the Seoul Paralympics in 1988. The torch had been lit early in the morning in Modi'in and was carried to the stadium via a relay of 500 runners.

Herzog officially opened the Games, with an extra *"baruch haba"*— "Blessed is he who comes"—to the groups from Hungary, Lithuania, and Yugoslavia. Olympic marksman Eddie Papirov invoked the athletes oath, while veteran international basketball referee David Dagan performed the same duty for the Games' officials.

Maccabiah Profile: Ron Kaplan, Israel, Gymnast[6]

Ron Kaplan got his first taste for gymnastics when he was just five years old. "My father was the head coach of Hapoel Beersheva and he took me to have fun at the gym. I think I was born into it. I believe that as I became a real 'professional' gymnast at the age of 14 or 15, it was more relevant to me."

Although his dad was a professional coach, Kaplan said he didn't need any encouragement. "The Maccabiah Games is the Jews Olympics. If you are a[n] . . . athlete and a Jew, it's one of your goals."

"Before the competition, we had ordinary training days, with maybe more of an audience in the gym and some journalists asking questions and taking pictures. I remember it as very happy and 'good vibe' days."

During his competitions, however, that feel-good demeanor changed.

"I remember it as a very tense day," said Kaplan, who was nineteen at the time. "The competition, as far as I was concerned, was difficult. I was too excited because people were expecting me to win. And in the last round I almost lost the Games. But eventually I was the 13th Maccabiah champion in gymnastics."

---

6 Not the author

Being a Sabra (native-born Israeli), Kaplan did not participate in the extracurricular activities of touring Israel that have become a staple of the Maccabiah experience for athletes from other nations. "We were happy to host the gymnasts, as I remember it," he wrote in his email. "We had a good time in the gym and outside the gym with the guys from abroad."

Three years later, Kaplan took his talents to Barcelona.

"The Olympic Games in 1992 were the highest and most important event for me as an athlete and as an Israeli gymnast representing my country."

* * *

While Jews from Communist nations were at long last welcomed to the Maccabiah, athletes from South Africa continued to pose their quadrennial problem.

"No South African flags will be flown anywhere during the Maccabiah," said Michael Kevehazi, chair of the International Maccabiah Committee. Prior to the Games, he held a press conference to lay out procedure: Since the Israeli Games followed the same rules as set for the Olympics, South Africa would not be allowed to participate as a national entity, nor would teams from that apartheid state be allowed to participate. Individual athletes, on the other hand, would compete as part of a "Rest of the World" category which allowed countries that were unable to muster enough of their own troops to fill out a full team for a sport.

"Athletes' registration was carried out on an individual basis. The Games are for Jews, no matter from where they come," said Kevehazi.

Nevertheless, "In many sports—including track and field, swimming, water polo, judo, karate, and wrestling—the relevant governing body has decreed that no South Africans may participate, a ruling to which we have adhered. The IMC will always honour the decisions of any individual sport's governing body. In other sports, such as tennis, golf and squash, South African players compete regularly as individuals in the international arena, so there is no problem."

For example, because water polo's international governing body barred South Africans, such athletes could not be added to the "rest of the world" group. The only exception: FIFA granted special permission to Jewish soccer players from South Africa to participate at the Maccabiah.[7] But the eight-member organizing committee, fearing penalties from the International Football Federation, nevertheless banned the nation from the soccer competition. A representative from the team was critical of the decision. "We feel we have been turned away as Jews," he told the media.[8]

With the exception of the swimming and track and field events, medals were relatively evenly distributed. The United States dominated in the water, with the men winning twenty-five events (including a sweep of all the relay races) while the women took twenty-two. Ruth Grodsky won five individual titles while Joanna Zeiger grabbed four; Rick Aronberg led the men with four individual medals.

On dry land, however, Israel won the bulk of the track and field events with a combined fifty-eight medals between the men and women.

Maccabiah Profile: Steve March-Tormé, United States, Softball

Like that of his father Mel, Steve March-Tormé's day job—or perhaps more appropriately, night job—is that of a singer. He also hosts a couple of radio shows in Wisconsin.

His parents divorced when he was a toddler, his mother marrying Hal March, host of the popular TV show, *The $64,000 Question*.

"[Hal] taught me how to play baseball and football. When I was a little boy, I wanted to play for the Yankees," he said, but he came to

7 "The position of South Africans," *Jerusalem Post*, July 2, 1989
8 "South Africa Athletes Barred from Competing in Maccabiah," JTA, July 6, 1989

realize he had a better shot of making the "big leagues" as a singer. He transitioned to softball as he got older, figuring he would have more opportunities to play as an adult. He began with the slow-pitch version when he was seventeen, before moving on to modified fast-pitch a couple years later. He taught himself how to pitch in his late twenties.

March-Tormé said he didn't have anything of a Jewish upbringing; his father came from Russian-Jewish stock (in his autobiography, *It Wasn't All Velvet*, Mel Tormé wrote, "I have always believed [my father] could have been a great cantor."[9])

"My Jewish background is I was brought up around Borscht Belt comedians my whole life," he joked. "I didn't really start exploring the Jewish side of me until I got involved in the Maccabiah.

"A friend saw an ad in the *LA Times* for a tryout and I was already pitching in a bunch of fast pitch leagues." He had heard about the Maccabiah Games, known that Mark Spitz had made his international debut there, and figured he had nothing to lose. "I went to

Steve March-Tormé, second from right, with the 1989 USA softball team at the Western Wall.

the tryout, did well, and was told to stay ready and keep in shape."

At that point, March-Tormé started doing more research. "I knew some of the athletes who played. I knew Danny Schayes, I knew his dad, Dolph, [and] Brad Gilbert. There have been quite a few legitimate professional athletes that came out of the Games."

9 Tormé, Mel. *It Wasn't All Velvet*. New York: Penguin, 1988. Page 1.

He estimated that more than a hundred hopefuls attended tryouts in Los Angeles and Chicago. "It's such a unique combination," he said. "You can find lots of fastpitch players but not that many of them are Jewish. And you can find a lot of Jewish athletes who can't play fastpitch softball. So you're only going to find so many who fit into this niche category."

Although he wasn't initially selected for the team, he did earn a spot as a first alternate. "I just wrote it off," he said. "I thought there must be fifteen guys across the country who are better than I am. I have no problem with that and if they don't call, they don't call."

Three weeks later, March-Tormé received a call informing him that one of the players selected for the team had to back out, so he was in. "It was Walter Mitty-ish for me to make a national sports team. I've played on a lot of tennis teams and baseball teams, but to make a national team was something special."

He also thought it special because he accomplished this as an older player, relatively speaking, at the age of thirty-two; most of the other players were in their early twenties.

March-Tormé came along at a propitious moment. The Maccabi organization had changed the requirements, accepting those who had Jewish blood from either parent, not just the maternal side, as a strict adherence to Jewish law dictates.

"You and I both know, they're going to do what they can to get athletes," he said with a touch of cynicism. "This is a hard slot to fill. I was asked to throw last year [2013]." But he declined. "I live in Wisconsin, so it's not like we have nine months of sunshine like in Southern California."

Travelling to Israel for the first time in 1985 was "an overwhelming experience," he said. "Even if you are not from a religious household, you have to be a blind idiot to get there and not soak in where you are. It's a pretty humbling experience, where civilization started and to be taken to the Old City and to see all the different spots they took us to. I thought it was a very enriching experience.

"There were guys who were much more religious than I was, but there were also guys like myself, guys that had Jewish heritage and blood by birth that tried out for the team that were very similar to myself. But there were also guys who had been absolutely bar mitzvahed, that had come up in a much more kosher household, and I'm sure it held a different perspective for them.

"I didn't spend all of my time listening to rock music and being an idiot, which I'm sure some did. I had a pretty decent knowledge of what was going on there from reading the news. I knew basically what was going on as far as how hard it's been for them to hold onto their land, to be constantly surrounded by people on all sides who don't necessarily want them to be there."

He thought back to the opening ceremonies for his first Games. "Not a big secret: it's a little warm in Israel. They had us in these ridiculously ugly button-down sweaters. We were just *shvitzing* [sweating]. It was ridiculous."

March-Tormé offered a scouting report on the opposition:

"The Venezuelan team was pretty good. The Panamanian team was not. How many Panamanian Jews play fastpitch softball? Mexico had an okay team, Israel had an okay team. We knew once we got there, there was only one team that even had a shot and it was Canada." In fact, he thought they were even "a little better than the U.S. squad."

As for his own squad, he was surprised "everybody got along as well as we did. It's not like when you're fourteen or fifteen years old and the coach tells you, 'Stay on line and if you're all good we'll go to Wendy's.' These are adults, some with kids, so your personality has been established and if you're this good in a sport, you have an ego. . . . Everybody has quirks, but the fact that we were as close-knit. . . . Not that I expected us *not* to be, but it was a pleasant surprise that we pulled together that well and all these years later, I'm still in touch with some of these guys and we're still buddies. That's pretty cool."

March-Tormé was the starting centerfielder for the game in which Team USA clinched the gold medal against Canada. "The game came down to one or two pitches," he said. "Otherwise we could still be playing today."

He made the team again for the following Maccabiah. "Same thing. We went back with a little different team. Now I'm thirty-six and I make the team again? Talent-wise, our team was a little deeper [but] I don't know if we were as close. The '85 team was an experiment.

We were the first ones; it was new to all of us. The second time, a little more disparate, personality-wise. We beat Canada again."

In 1989, March-Tormé was the second starting pitcher behind the legendary Dave Blackburn. He drew starting assignments against Panama and Venezuela. "My job was to take a lot of the pressure off Dave so he wouldn't have to pitch every day. I tried to be as helpful as I could. I loved going the second time."

March-Tormé still remembered the disarray at the closing ceremonies in 1985. "We got tear-gassed. . . . People panicked. Some people jumped out of the [reviewing] stands."

He also remembered the rugged security at JFK airport in New York for the 1985 trip, with armed guards and luggage checks. "And this was way before 9/11. There's always going to be some incident. You're an American Jewish athlete over there; you have a little bit of a bulls-eye on your back, in my opinion."

But overall, "It was great. We were just this bunch of schmucks playing softball in Southern California, and now we're walking into a stadium with parachutists. It was great. It may not be the Olympic Games, but it's as close as we're going to get."

* * *

Results aside, it's quite possible Israel's Ultra-Orthodox community was never pleased by the spectacle of the Maccabiah Games; if they were, it never received widespread attention. The fact that the Maccabiah Committee used the Western Wall, Judaism's holiest site, was their main bone of contention and was denounced as a "desecration of the Temple's honor." They also objected to male and female athletes competing at the same event.

In fact, considering how much the idea of concentrating on the physical over the spiritual that had long been a philosophy in Judaism, and how much ancient Jews objected to the Greeks and their mania for the perfect physical form, it seemed a bit ironic that Israel was now the site of such a huge gathering of athletes. But that was one of the things that separated cultural Zionists from the "religious" Jewish community.

The closing ceremonies were interrupted by a smoke bomb. After initial concerns over terrorist attacks, the Ultra-Orthodox community was suspected as the troublemakers, but an investigation determined the incident was "probably accidental" and set off by the police themselves.[10]

The incident led to what was arguably the most impressive performance of the Games. Charlie Faulkner, the coach of the British rugby team, probably saved the life of a baby whose stroller had been overturned as frenzied fans and athletes scampered in all directions. Faulkner pushed his way through the crowd, grabbed the child in its carriage, and carried it to safety. "I've never been so frightened," he told the press. "It was a real stampede and that poor baby could have been trampled to death."[11]

There had already been a tragedy during the Games. On July 6, a suicide terrorist wrested control of a passenger bus in Abu Gosh, some 33 miles southeast of Ramat Gan, sending the vehicle into a 400-foot ravine. Fourteen people were killed with another twenty-seven injured, including the mother of an American athlete participating in the Maccabiah. News of the incident was widespread and provided the Games with its biggest, if not the most welcome, publicity.

Israel led all participants with ninety-seven gold medals followed by the United States' seventy-four.

The Final Medal Count (Gold/Silver/Bronze):[12]

Israel 258 (97/82/79)

USA 199 (74/73/52)

Canada 70 (16/21/33)

Brazil 31 (15/9/7)

Britain 26 (details unavailable)

---

10 "Smoke Bomb Mars Festive Closing of 13th Games in Jerusalem," JTA, July 14, 1989

11 "Lifesaving run by a former British Lion prop," *London Times*, July 17, 1989

12 "Smoke Bomb Mars Festive Closing of 13th Games in Jerusalem," JTA, July 14, 1989

Mexico 20 (2/5/13)
Australia 19 (10/8/1)
World Team A 18 (10/4/4)
Hungary 15 (4/5/6)
Argentina 14 (0/7/7)
France 10 (4/3/3)
Holland 6 (1/1/4)
Venezuela 5 (4/0/1)
Austria 4 (0/2/2)
Italy 4 (0/1/3)
Panama 4 (0/4/0)
Belgium 3 (1/0/2)
Sweden 3 (2/1/0)
West Germany 3 (0/1/2)
World Team B 3 (0/2/1)
Chile 2 (1/0/1)
Denmark 2 (1/0/1)
Lithuania 2 (0/1/1)
Ireland 1 (0/1/0)

Chapter 15

The Fourteenth Games
July 5-15 1993

"When we were coming down Masada, somehow I found myself in the front of the line. At some point, I glanced behind me and saw a group of athletes picking up the kids in wheelchairs and carrying them down the ramp. We'd made provisions for the disabled athletes to take elevators to the bottom, but that turned out not to be necessary. It was such a beautiful thing to witness that it just took my breath away. I'm not sure I can think of a more telling illustration of what the Maccabiah movement is all about."

Bob Spivak, president of Maccabi USA/Sports for Israel, recalling the 1993 Games[1]

---

1 "Maccabiah Man: Businessman gives his all for Jewish Olympics," *Jewish Exponent* (Philadelphia), July 10, 1997

The 14th Maccabiah Games represented a new beginning: new nations, new sports, new controversies, and new stories to tell.

President Ezer Weizman opened the Games at Ramat Gan Stadium, welcoming 45,000 spectators and 5,500 delegation members from 57 countries. The march of athletes this year took the order of the Latin alphabet, rather than Hebrew, and had them flying the flags of their countries, they only time such nationalism would be on display according to the July 6 *Jerusalem Post*.[2] Once again, Israel supplied the largest team with 800 participants, but the United States wasn't that far behind with 650. The media toned down its rapt descriptions of the teams' attire, reducing the usual "red carpet" analysis to a simple acknowledgment that the athletes were "dressed in festive costumes representing their countries."

After a memorial service for the victims of two World Wars, Israelis lost to the violence of defending their country, and a tribute to the eleven athletes murdered at Munich more than twenty years earlier, Yael Arad, recipient of Israel's first gold medal at the "real" Olympics in Barcelona in 1992, entered the stadium with the Maccabiah torch, ran up the equivalent of a five-story building, and lit the fifteen-foot cauldron (recognized at the time as the largest at any sporting event by the *Guinness Book of Records*). Estimates put the cost of these festivities, which featured the traditional performance by thousands of young Israeli gymnasts, a "folklore" presentation, and fireworks, at $1 million, ($1.6 million in 2014). The entire Games would come in at about $8.5 million (almost $14 million).

In his greetings to athletes, which was published prior to the opening ceremonies, Aryeh Rozensweig, chair of the 14th Maccabiah Organizing Committee, noted, "Political realities have changed since we last hosted the Maccabiah, four years ago. Jews from the former communist bloc can now attend the event, and we welcome the return of Poland, Bulgaria, and a joint Czech Republic-Slovakia delegation, who will be appearing for the first time since the Second World War. The collapse of the Soviet Union spawned the formation of dozens of

2 "President Weizman Opens 14th Maccabiah," *Jerusalem Post*, July 6, 1993

new Maccabi clubs, whose representatives will be competing under the CIS banner."

Rozensweig also welcomed debuting delegations from Croatia, Zimbabwe, Costa Rica, and Hong Kong, and embraced the return of South Africa which "returns as a full delegation, following the lifting of the international sporting boycott which previously forced its sports-crazy Jewish community to appear under the banner 'Rest of the World.'"[3]

With South African participation no longer an issue, what would take its place as the next big controversy? Racism. But in this case, it was the Jews who were being accused.

An article in the newsweekly magazine *Jerusalem Report* by Peter Hirschberg, quoted an "'anonymous leading Israeli sports official' who feared that 'there is a touch of racism in the Maccabiah.'" Michael Kevehazi answered this veiled accusation: "If bringing thousands of young sports people together every four years is racism, then I have no problem being called a racist. As if we do not have enough bad press from outside the country, the last thing we need is this kind of self-hatred from one of our own journalists."[4]

This was all part of the larger criticism by the local press about the value of the Games as a whole for contemporary Israel. Some complained about the quality of the athletics, that the vast majority of the swimmer and runners and soccer players, et al, were not Olympic material. Conversely, more and more Jews were participating in the Olympics and other international competitions. That would be a valid point if the Maccabiah was only about sports, but organizers would tell you that sport was the "carrot" to attract people to come to Israel.

A more practical consideration: the Games were increasingly expensive to stage on the part of Israel, where perhaps the funds could be better spent, as well as for the national Maccabi organizations and the athletes, who had to come up with major funds, either on their own or through exhaustive fundraising efforts.

---

3 "14ᵗʰ Maccabiah Greetings," *Jerusalem Post*, July 2, 1993
4 "MWU Boss fumes over "Racist" Remark," *Jerusalem Post*, July 4, 1993

Despite these concerns, the consensus was that the Games still represented the founders' philosophy that the now-quadrennial event was a gathering of family.

"The reason the Games continue is because the athletes want it to," said Aryeh Rozensweig. "All of them feel that it's important to come to Israel."[5]

The article cited Jennifer Frank, an eighteen-year-old track-and-field athlete from Oak Park, California. Although she said her family did not follow many religious practices, "This visit has made me realize I'm Jewish and that it's important not to let my Jewishness go."

One of the unique aspects of the Maccabiah Games is its fluidity. Sports—and races and events within each sport—are added and subtracted as more or fewer athletes are available to participate. This can make planning quite challenging when it comes to making up schedules.

One of the new events for 1993 was netball, a British creation dating back to the late 19th century and played at these games, at least, by women only. *The Jerusalem Post* published a brief primer to educate its readers to this strange import.

While it may not have been the national pastime—professional baseball in Israel would get a very brief run in another decade or so—the first event of the Maccabiah games was a Fourth of July softball game, which the American squad won over Team Israel, 10-1. William Brown, the U.S. ambassador to Israel, threw out the ceremonial first pitch. There's no report whether he made his delivery overhand or underhand.

As a reminder of the precariousness of the region, Katyusha rockets exploded in the northern town of Metulla hours before the July 6 basketball game between Israel and Mexico was to begin. There was no impact on the game, in which Israel defeated their rival, 99-50.

---

5 "Maccabiah Games Instills Jewish Pride in Athletes from Around the World," JTA, July 8, 1993

Maccabiah Profile: Daniel Greyber, United States, Swimming

Daniel Greyber participated in two Maccabiah Games, twenty years apart and in very different capacities.

In 1993, as a member of the U.S. swim team, Greyber won a gold medal for the 100-meter backstroke. He also won a bronze medal for the 200-meter race.

In 2013, *Rabbi* Greyber served as the spiritual consultant for the American team.

Greyber was twenty-one when he competed, following a "convoluted" academic career in which he swam only one year at the University of California at Berkeley before transferring to Northwestern University. He still had three years of eligibility left, which allowed him to continue swimming after he received his bachelor's degree and was working on his masters.

Greyber thought the talent level at his events was "pretty high."

Photos courtesy Rabbi Daniel Greyber

Daniel Greyber won gold in the 100-meter backstroke and bronze in the 200-meter backstroke at the 1993 Games. He returned to the Maccabiah in 2013 as rabbi for the U.S. delegation.

"It's not the Olympics, but it's also not a backwater for athletic competition," he said. "We had people on the team from Stanford and Michigan, some of the top swimming programs in the country.

The top two Jewish athletes in the U.S. were on our team. I don't think we had people who were Olympians, but we did have people who were competitive in the NCAA on a high level, national and internationally." He expressed some gratitude that he didn't have to face Olympic gold-medal winner Lenny Krayzelburg. "I was lucky to precede him by four years," he said with a laugh. "I certainly wouldn't have won the gold medal if he had been there."

For any athlete, regardless of how gifted he or she might be in their respective event, walking into the opening ceremonies is goose bumps time. But not all memories are based on spectacle or pomp. The thing Greyber remembered most was the heat. "[In those days] the U.S. team had these [heavy] rugby shirts. Now the U.S. team has these lightweight jackets." He pointed out that the ceremonies for the 2013 Games were held in Jerusalem, which he estimated was "about twenty degrees cooler" than Ramat Gan. It was a minor inconvenience in light of the overall picture.

"It's an extraordinary experience. There are thousands and thousands of Jews from around the world as athletes, tens of thousands of fans who have come out. It's all on Israeli television. The leaders of the state are there." There was also a "home factor."

"The rabbi from my synagogue growing up happened to be in Israel with a mission and when they heard that I was going, they purchased tickets and made that part of their trip." In addition, Greyber had an uncle who had made aliyah. "I felt this extraordinary connection to the entire Jewish people and at the same time to family both at home and in Israel as well."

Greyber remains in touch with Dan Kutler, his roommate at the Games, who also made aliyah, taking a path that Greyber still wonders about: Kutler competed for Israel in the Atlanta Olympics in 1992, swimming in the finals of the 4x100 meter backstroke relay, the first time an Israel swim team had advanced that far.

The feeling of winning a medal might offer wonderful memories, but those can be fleeting when you get back to the real world. The Maccabiahs gave Greyber something that was life-changing.

He had never been to Israel prior to his 1993 excursion. And he definitely did not yet have any notion of a profession in the clergy.

"If I hadn't gone to the Maccabiah Games I would not be a rabbi today," he said. "I was fairly-to-moderately affiliated with the Jewish community and I was beginning to become interested in questions around Judaism and religion. But the moment I won the gold medal was a bridge moment. It was a moment I could put a cap on my swimming career, even though I would go on to swim for another year at Northwestern."

Given this epiphany, Greyber began to explore his Jewish identity. He had majored in communications and was working at an advertising agency, but that soon changed after his adventures in Israel.

"I felt very at home. I was obviously at home in the pool, but to also be at home in a place where I was competing against Jews from around the world in the Jewish homeland . . . all of those experiences was very powerful. It became the impetus for me coming back to Israel the following year, learning Hebrew, and becoming more interested in Judaism."

This all led to his decision to return to the United States and study for the rabbinate. He received his degree at Ziegler School for Rabbinic Studies at American Jewish University in Los Angeles.

Greyber was asked to serve as team rabbi for the United States delegation for 2013. It was a position that did not exist when he competed twenty years earlier and the United States was the only country to have it.

Greyber took his responsibilities very seriously. "The most important thing I could do was form relationships and get to know as many of those kids as possible . . . to make sure when they had a question there was someone there to explore that [with]. Informal but sometimes very life-changing conversations as you're walking on the top of Masada or riding on a bus or just sitting up late at night."

Having had the experience of participating in the Maccabiah Games as an athlete gave Greyber special insight, an additional credibility. He befriended members of the U.S. swim team and joined them for some of their workouts. Having been in their shoes, so to speak, put him in a special stead.

"There's a little bit of them being able to identify with me and me being able to identify with them just in terms of the unspoken language of sports and the understanding of the intensity of the experience. I do think that that helped."

Greyber also led several memorial services at Yad Vashem, Israel's memorial to the Holocaust, and a Sabbath celebration. But even more extraordinary was the group bar and bat mitzvah service Grebyer conducted, which he described as "the quintessential part" of the non-competitive experience at the Maccabiah Games. This "neo-tradition" was popular with those who wanted to have the spiritual experience of celebrating that Jewish rite of passage in the Holy Land. A large number of U.S. team members had never had a "formal" bar mitzvah, nor had athletes growing up in nations where worshipping was difficult for one reason or another.

Liturgical materials had been sent out beforehand to those Americans who had expressed an interest and Greyber studied with those who requested additional instruction.

"We had group aliyots as part of the service in the afternoon and it was just a pretty wonderful thing," he said, using the Hebrew word for being called up to bless the Torah before each reading. This is usually done singularly, but in certain cases, when many people are being honored, it can range anywhere from two to twenty people or more.

"The first [aliyot] was for people who had been to Israel and who had had a bar or bat mitzvah before," Greyber explained. "The second was for one or the other, but not both. The third was for those who had had neither experience."

For many, this ceremony "was their first aliyah to the Torah," Greyber said. "There were probably 125 kids who came up for that and it was just a lot of joy and it was a tremendously meaningful moment."

"For me it was an excellent dream. I can't imagine being able to do something more meaningful than spend so much time helping more than 1,100 athletes—many of whom are young adults—to fall in love with the *land* of Israel, the *State* of Israel, and Jewish identity through athletics. That's pretty much my story, and to be able to share it with so many other people is wonderful.

"The Maccabi movement and especially Maccabi USA have come to understand what a powerful experience this is in terms of Jewish identity and the exploration of a connection with the Jewish people. I commend them highly, not only because I got a chance to go, but for understanding the significance of the work that they're doing in a different way."

Greyber is currently the spiritual leader of Beth El Synagogue, a Conservative and Orthodox synagogue in Durham, North Carolina. Just as Greyber himself has tended to Jews from many different levels of faith and identity, Beth El is known for welcoming intermarried and gay and lesbian families. He still has ties to swimming; it's a component of his website—rabbigreyber.com—which features his writings on a variety of subjects, including an extension of his book, *Faith Unravels: A Rabbi's Struggle with Grief and God.*

* * *

Even though South Africans had been participating in Maccabiah Games all along, it must have been a huge relief to be welcome en masse. No longer would they be under the stigma of their country's unpopular racial policies. Now they were allowed to be embraced by the sporting community and praised for their accomplishments without the awkwardness that such affirmation would be construed as approving of apartheid. They collected almost forty team and individual medals, ranging in sports from cricket to track and field. This added to a global event that was expanding to more countries, attracing even more athletes of increasingly disparate age, and fulfilling the mission of the Games' founders in creating a giant celebration of Jewish fellowship.

Maccabiah Profile: Bob Spivak, United States, Chair

Bob Spivak, now seventy-eight, has been involved in Maccabi USA since 1977.

"I knew about the Games through a childhood friend and tried to make the team in the '50s in track, and didn't make it. He did and went to Israel and won a gold medal. If I would see him now, he would give me a little *zetz* about it, too."

Bob Spivak of the United States, left, and Roy Salomon of Canada, have been associated with the Maccabiah Games for more than 70 years combined.

Spivak attend Muhlenberg College. He modestly attributes his sports career there to the fact that the school needed athletes to fill out the teams. In addition to track, Spivak played soccer and football; "anything where you could get a free meal."

Tryouts depend on the sport; those that relied on objective statistics and rankings, such as fencing, swimming, and track relied on data submitted by coaches to the individual committees. Team sports such as basketball and soccer held formal tryouts. Talent wasn't necessarily enough to make the team. As Spivak explained, "A lot had to do, very honestly—I'm told in the sixties and seventies—with who could afford to come up with some money."

Spivak became more involved in the organizing committee the following year, becoming president, a role he retained for twenty years. Now he serves as chair of Maccabi USA.

The president runs the organization, with the executive committee, which makes overall decisions, Spivak explained; the chair is more of ceremonial position with some fundraising and promotional duties.

Spivak made the decision to move the headquarters to his hometown of Philadelphia from New York because it was the only way he could "put the time and energy that was needed into it," which he estimated at "probably thirty to forty hours a week," a fulltime job in itself.

A profile in the July 4, 1993 *Jerusalem Post* said "Spivak spends two-thirds of his time on Maccabiah business . . . . Within that two-thirds is over 60,000 miles of travel per year attending training camps, overseeing selection procedures, lecturing, and a host of other activities which make nonsense of the volunteer concept. Spivak's repayment comes from the satisfaction of the work he does."[6]

"It became a real labor of love and it was a passion. Look, I love sports and a lot of kids love sports, but I really saw this as a way to take kids to Israel, similar to . . . Birthright."

It was during Spivak's early years that Maccabi USA developed what is now known as the "Israel Connect" program, a cultural component bringing the teams over prior to the start of the athletic competitions to give them a chance to soak up Israel's rich heritage.

Spivak was also at the helm when the master athlete program, which allows older athletes the thrill of competing in Israel, was expanded in the late 1980s. That dramatically increased the size of the American delegation. Nevertheless, he says, that doesn't necessarily translate to more medals. "I don't think we'll ever win more medals than the Israelis because they're in many more sports than us, sports that we don't participate in like men's field hockey, things of that nature."

Spivak has been to each of the Games since 1977, as well as the other competitions the organization holds such as the Pan American Games, which also take place every four years and "a few European Games."

"This became a real way of life for me," he said. "I've just enjoyed it, it's a great passion."

"It's been a basic program of trying to take kids to Israel and give them a cultural and education component with it. This is our modus operandi."

---

6 "Bob Spivak, hands on Jewish Sports World," Jerusalem Post, July 4, 1993

Spivak stressed the financial changes that have taken place within the program. "We were very lucky," he said. Funding from major companies to donate equipment or uniforms "was pretty easy. It's a little rougher today than it was then. Whatever we needed, we got."

Despite the more recent difficulties of a stalled economy, the most rewarding part of Spivak's work is demonstrated by something that took place three nights prior to our conversation.

Spivak was attending a meeting of international Maccabi organizations in Israel in December of 2014. "A young woman who was at the hotel came over to us, recognized who we were by our shirts. She was on a basketball team. She was from Sioux City, Iowa, had tried out for the U.S. team about eight or nine years ago, didn't make it, waited four years, made the team, went to Israel for the [2013] Games, and was recruited to play professional basketball in Israel. She said it really changed her life. . . .

"It really impacts kids' lives, the very unique experience of going to Israel and being part of it and maybe, who knows, professionally where this may lead for her?"

Chapter 16

The Fifteenth Games
July 14-24, 1997

"I want to go and represent American Judaism. I am looking at it basketball-wise [that it will] get me in shape and ready for Oklahoma State. And culturally, it is a great learning experience. Where can you learn more about history than in Israel and Jerusalem?"

Doug Gottleib, member of the United States men's basketball team[1]

"The event is not a Jewish Olympics but an ingathering of Jewish sportspeople of all ages and all abilities who come to compete, not to

---

1 "U.S. Maccabiah Team Mixes Diverse Ages, Stages," *Washington Post*, April 28, 1997

break records. Every four years, the Maccabiah grows in size by up to 25 percent. We must be doing something right."

Yoram Eyal, Chair of the 15th Maccabiah Games[2]

A story in the *Jerusalem Post* published just as the 15th Maccabiah was about to begin noted that there were still those in Israel (and elsewhere, no doubt) who thought the idea of a Jewish competition was wrong on many levels. Among the reasons: a discernable lack of high-quality athletes; the cost was only affordable to those with means, thereby cutting off other, perhaps superior, candidates; and, the capper: a so-called "Jewish Olympics" by its nature excludes gentiles, which would seem anathema to a people who had been ostracized for millennia.

Yoram Eyal, chair of the 1997 event, understood the concerns, but noted that, "The term Jewish Olympics was once relevant because Jews were barred from many international teams. One has only to look through the names of the athletes in the first few Maccabiahs to realize that the event did once constitute a who's who of Jewish sport. Nobody needs to be reminded that as late as the 1960s both Mark Spitz and Tal Brody took part in the Maccabiah."

As for the cost of sending the teams, he said, "It's true that the athletes must pay their own way to the event. However, in all countries the community helps those in need."

Though the concern had been heard before, there was much that was new about the 1997 Games. For the U.S., one notable difference was the leadership on the men's basketball team. Herb Brown, an assistant coach for the Indiana Pacers, was tabbed to lead the U.S. men. In thirty-six years, his teams won more than 700 games and championships on the professional, international, and college levels.

"It's a great honor and I'm very proud to have been selected," said Brown, no relation to the Naismith Hall of Famer Larry Brown, who

---

2 "Who Needs It?", *Jerusalem Post*, July 11, 1997

played on the1961 Maccabiah team and went on to a gold-standard career as an NBA player and college and professional coach.[3]

Several events made their debut at the '97 Games, including beach volleyball. Given the climate, such an addition made sense. But ice hockey? Four teams competed in this anomalous choice: Canada, which was led by former Stanley Cup-winning coach Jacques Demers and would snag the gold medal; the U.S. (silver); Ukraine (bronze); and . . . Israel.

The cost of getting to the Games was a bit higher for the U.S. hockey athletes, since so much equipment is involved. The total was listed at $100,000, about $5,000 per player. Fundraising events included raffles sold by team members.

Overall, with some 4,000 participants from 50 countries[4]— including 1,500 from Israel—the budget was set by Israel at $11 million (more than $16 million in 2014). One again, the U.S. sent the largest foreign contingent of some 600 athletes and support staff. About 350 Canadians made the trip as well.

Despite operating under the continual threat of violence from without, the 1997 Games suffered a devastating catastrophe from within. A force of 800 Tel Aviv policemen, including mounted police, bomb-disposal experts, and helicopter patrols, oversaw the July 14 opening ceremonies. Traffic patterns around Ramat Gan Stadium were altered to maintain free passage.

After the usual round of dignitaries opened the Maccabiah Games with speeches of welcome, praise, and invitations to make aliyah, the procession of athletes began, returning to the custom of alphabetical order according to the Hebrew. The small delegation from Australia made it over the 45-foot footbridge meant to convey the athletes from the staging area, across the Yarkon River, and into the stadium.

The weight of the much larger Australian team proved too much for the structure and it began to collapse, plunging scores of what had

3 "Pacer assistant to lead U.S. team," *South Bend Tribune* (IN), Jan. 29, 1997
4 Depending on source, the number of participants range from 4,000 to 6,000-plus. Similarly the number of countries attending varies from 50 to 58.

just moments earlier been ecstatic revelers into the toxic waters nearly fifty feet below. Looking at videotape of the river and the bridge that is now in place, it's hard to imagine how the destruction could be so serious, especially the injuries sustained, from being in the narrow strip of water for such a brief period.

Suspicions immediately suggested sabotage at the hands of terrorists. Those notions were put to rest when it was discovered that the wood-and-aluminum structure was simply not up to the task of holding so many people at once. Media that would not cover the Games under normal circumstances ran front-page stories.

It was as a long-time leader of Maccabi Australia Inc. that Bernie Gold found himself towards the front of the delegation when the bridge collapsed. "As I am a MAI Life Member, I was invited to be in the leading bunch of officials and was in the second or third row," Gold said in an e-mail interview. "I suffered badly bruised ribs and spent one night in the hospital. I was one of the lucky ones as I did not fall in the water; I slid down the broken bridge and hit other members; that stopped me from falling in."

Following the calamity, many delegation members—including Gold—could not conceive of continuing with their participation. "We held a team meeting the next morning; I arrived straight from the hospital. My feeling was that Australia should withdraw . . . however the majority wanted to compete. This decision came after a plea from one of the ten-pin bowlers that had lost a member to stay and compete."

As thousands of athletes waited to make their entrance, Roy Salomon, a leader of Maccabi Canada, had been milling around with his delegation, chatting with friends he'd made during his many years with the movement.

As North American chair, Solomon was among a small group of executives that was to meet privately with the Israeli president on the infield. When the ceremonies began, he crossed the bridge.

After a time inside the stadium, however, he realized something was amiss.

"There's huge delays," he recalled. "And finally we see helicopters going over the stadium." No one inside the stadium had any idea of the carnage that had ensued.

"And then we're told: there's been a tragedy. The bridge collapsed.

"We all gathered together and had to make a decision: does the ceremony go on? We determined that there was one road leading to the place where the bridge collapsed. If we announced that everything was off or that anything was going on, everybody would have exited the stadium at the same time. The emergency cars could not have gotten through and it was critical that they did. The ambulances traveled down that road to get to the people. And we made a decision that we would continue with the opening ceremony."

Despite this logical consideration, told with the benefit of almost twenty years of hindsight to dull the pain, the decision did not sit well with everyone in the immediate aftermath. Isi Liebler, World Jewish Congress lay leader and former president of the Australian Jewish community, told the media, "I am shocked, outraged, and for the first time in Israel, embarrassed at the extraordinary lack of sensitivity by those who decided to proceed with the artistic and dancing program . . . at the same time they were looking for survivors.

"I believe this is one of the most horrible examples of lack of sensitivity that I've ever experienced, and to hear the mayor of Ramat Gan describe this as Zionism suggests that the man is a primitive person, without any sensitivity," said Liebler, no doubt expressing the opinion of countless others.[5]

While Salomon was inside the stadium, Joe Siegman, another Maccabiah veteran as well as founder of the International Jewish Sports Hall of Fame in Netanya, was in the staging area, waiting to cross over the bridge.

"We had just had Hall of Fame inductions, as we normally do within the Maccabiah Games framework, and I was the flag bearer of the year's honorees. For reasons unknown, our group was slated to march in in front of the U.S. Maccabiah team, situated as America—not USA—making us third in line over the bridge and into the stadium. Since we fronted the American team, our small group of Hall of Famers followed Australia. In other words, we were in the front of most other marchers.

---

5 "Controversy rages over decision to proceed with opening ceremony," *Jerusalem Post*, July 15, 1997.

"The athletes always march in after the hoopla that goes on inside the stadium, which [they] don't get to see. When march-in time came, we sharpened up and started to move forward, then suddenly stopped. No reason was given. We stood in position for some time, but [there was] no explanation."

It was at that point Siegman and the others learned what had just happened.

"Eventually, TV coverage was reporting what was going on and family and friends of marchers contacted the few Israeli marchers who had cellphones to get word into the holding area about the bridge," Siegman said.

"After several hours of speculation, security staff established a plan of evacuation from the holding area. Spectators had already emptied the stadium. The evacuation inconvenienced and annoyed everyone, especially since they didn't know what had happened.

"The Games schedule did continue, but there were nightly memorial ceremonies, including a couple of major rallies. The Australian team leadership thought that competitions should have been cancelled, but sending home 5-6,000 people, plus several thousand relatives and friends, was not considered prudent by leadership.

"As the days and weeks went on, when it was learned that the construction of the bridge was flawed and had been built with little expertise or supervision, some of the Australians went ballistic."

At that point, all anyone knew was that the bridge had collapsed, but no one seemed to fully grasp the dire scope of the situation. Gregory Small, age thirty-seven, and Yetty Bennett, age fifty, both 10-pin bowlers from Sydney, died at the scene; an additional sixty-four were injured, some critically. Elizabeth Sawicki, a forty-seven-year-old bridge player from Melbourne and Warren Zines, fifty-six, a lawn bowler from Sydney, died on July 26 and August 10, respectively, as a result of being submerged in the polluted waters. In some cases, illness took several weeks to manifest.

Investigations would detail environmental disasters that were common to almost all the waters in Israel. In this case, one of the problems was that the area had been spread with an insecticide, ostensibly to kill mosquitos and provide the athletes to cross over the bridge relatively unscathed.

The media roundly condemned the decision to continue the opening ceremony in particular, and some the Games in general. An editorial in the *Jerusalem Post* cited the organizers' "stone-hearted insensitivity."

"Ramat Gan Mayor Zvi Bar, who backed the organizers' decision to proceed with the celebrations, argued last night that since Israel is now celebrating 100 years of Zionism and its 50th year of independence, there was no choice but to continue and mix, in his words, joy with sorrow. Israel and the Ramat Gan Municipality will have plenty of opportunities to celebrate 100 years of Zionism and 50 years of independence; last night was not one of them," the editorial stated.[6]

A news report in the same publication noted "The only tasteful moment in a totally miserable evening came with Kerri Strug ran into the stadium with the torch and handed it to a solemn-looking Mickey Berkowitz who bounded up the steps to light the Maccabiah flame."[7]

Strug had been the darling of the 1996 Olympics in Atlanta when, despite a badly injured ankle, she won a gold medal in the vault and helped the U.S women's team capture their gold as well. She did not compete in these Maccabiah Games. Berkowitz, the Michael Jordan of Israeli basketball, could have been the first Israeli to play in the NBA, thirty years before Omri Casspi made his debut with the Sacramento Kings.

In the end, the organizers postponed the sporting events by one day, a decision that was compared with the decision to postpone, but still move forward with, the 1972 Munich Olympics following the massacre of eleven members of the Israeli team.

"The initial, knee-jerk reaction was that we made a mistake," said Salomon. "Still looking back now, I think we did the right thing."

"I was close to the Australians. We were *all* close; we were a family," he said. "The next day the Australian team gathered in one of the main meeting halls and I'm seeing some of my friends with bandages. There

---

6 "An insensitive ceremony," *Jerusalem Post*, July 15, 1997
7 "The opening ceremony goes on," *Jerusalem Post*, July 15, 1997

but for the sake of God go I. You never know. It could have happened to anybody.

"By then we knew of two deaths . . . . And they had to make a decision whether they were going to stay at the Games. I had met early in the morning with four Australian leaders, and I said, 'would you mind if I had a rabbi come and speak to your team?'" Salomon had an old rabbi friend from Montreal who was now living in Jerusalem and agreed to come by. The Australian leaders consented and several people ended up addressing the disheartened team.

The rabbi's message, according to Salomon: "Don't go home. I know how hard it is for you. But honor the people who died by participating."

The president of the Australian delegation called for a vote to see what the team wanted to do. "Almost every person stood up and started applauding," Salomon said. "That was their signal that they were staying."

That decision, obviously, was not universally well received. "Then there was plenty of trouble after that," Salomon said.

Salomon was also a member of a small delegation to address the Australian Jewish community in Melbourne and Sydney. "It was very tough. By then the Israeli press had come out soundly against [the Maccabi] movement and people in our movement, blaming us for things we weren't responsible for. We tried to explain the things they were talking about were not factual. We said, look, Israel is always telling us to be on the lookout around the world to make sure we correct all the wrong things that are being said about Israel, and here you're doing the same thing to us. I appeared before a committee before the Knesset along with three or four other people, and we spoke about what was going on. It took a long time, but ultimately Australia did not leave the movement. They were getting a lot of pressure from home that they should leave and not be part of Maccabi.

"We were never able to straighten out all the stories because sometimes . . . once things get out into the press, it's very hard to turn around. When they first come out, people start believing the stories as factual, and they weren't all factual. Stories about the bridge, why didn't you hire this one, why didn't you hire that one."

Bob Spivak, president of USA Maccabi, said the incident was the most troubling of his nearly fifty-year association with the Games.

"There [were] a lot of issues about blame, a lot of issues about not taking care of it and no matter what we did, we could not satisfy the Australian delegations for years. In fact, some people now are probably still bitter about it. And I cannot help [but] believe that I would have been the same. We lost lives there. It was very, very tragic."

The contractors and, more generally, a laissez-faire way of handling things that had become part of the Israeli culture, quickly took the blame. More editorial called for the virtual heads of those responsible and both Israel and Australia launched investigations. Micha Bar-Ilan, the engineer who approved the materials for the project, said he had warned authorities the bridge only accommodate 100 people at a time and that a monitor was to have been put in place to make sure the bridge wasn't overburdened.

Was this a case of penny-wise and pound-foolish? According to reports, the Israeli army had said they could build the bridge for under $90,000, but the contract was awarded to a private company for $20,000.[8]

The government agreed to advance a total of $500,000 to the athletes injured as temporary compensation for the disaster until various insurance policies kicked in.

The Prime Minister's Office announced the athletes would return the sum once insurance companies, at odds over who was responsible, paid out claims to those hurt.

Demands for an inquiry were swift. Less than two weeks later, a public commission found that Bar-Ilan was remiss for not submitting an actual plan for the bridge as well as failing to design an adequate structure and not overseeing the work. The contractor for the project was also charged with shoddy work, using substandard materials and being unauthorized to build such a structure.

---

8 "Engineer: bridge approved for just 100," *St. Petersburg Times*, July 16, 1997

The commission did not have the power to take further action, instead submitting their findings to the Israeli Attorney General's office.

In November, a group of forty Australians announced their plans to sue the Maccabi World Union, the bridge's builders and contractors, and Israeli municipal authorities. The following month five Israelis—including Bar-Ilan and Yoram Eyal, the head of the organizing committee—were indicted by an Israeli court.

Eyal resigned shortly before the proceedings were announced.

The trial opened on Jan. 20, 1997, and dragged on for months. In Jan. 1999, three Israeli athletes returned the medals as a sign of solidarity with the Australians at a Knesset committee meeting investigating the incident. Anat Hoffman (swimmer), Debbie Marcus (a track athlete in the 1961 and 1965 games), and her son, Boaz Marcus (lawn bowls, 1977), dumped the medals out on a desk as their protest.

On April 17, 2000, the five Israelis were convicted of causing the deaths of the Australians. Two months later they were sentenced: Bar-Ilan received twenty-one months in prison, and a like amount of suspended sentence. Yoram Eyal was ordered to do six months of community service. The remaining defendants were sentenced to combinations of jail time and community service. The Australians were generally outraged with the lenient punishments.

In July 2000, nearly three years after the accident, the Knesset Committee recommended the resignation of Maccabi World Union president Ronald Bakalarz, and further suggested if he did not step down, the government might not finance the 2001 games. Bakalarz left a month later.

An editorial in the *Jerusalem Post* seemed to speak for a sports world, as well as a country, thankful the issue had been officially laid to rest, if nothing else: "While nothing will heal the pain caused by the bridge disaster, it is time to look to the future, and to build a new bridge of reconciliation."[9]

With the distance of almost twenty years of hindsight, Salomon stood by the decision to hire Bar-Ilan. "He was a noted builder for the

---

9 "Time to look to the future," *Jerusalem* Post, Aug. 7, 2000.

government of Israel," Salomon said. "They were not a small outfit. The people they subcontracted out to for certain supports, *they* were the ones responsible for the bridge collapsing. They didn't do *their* job."

While the MWU hired the contractor, they did not hire the subcontractors.

"It was a long rebuilding process with Australia. And ultimately now they're a major part of the Maccabi movement. It would have been a major loss not to have them in the Maccabiah Games. They participate as well as any organization in the world."

Once the 1997 Games continued, it was difficult to temper the joys of victories with the horrors that had transpired.

Two days after the tragedy, the Australian basketball team, wearing black ribbons as a sign of mourning, lost to Israel, 71-59.

In the face of such utter heartbreak, the team performed amazingly well in their events. They beat a heavily-favored South Africa to win gold in the cricket tournament, in an exciting, last-gasp effort. In lawn bowls, one of their best sports, the Australians won five medals, including a silver for men's pairs and rinks (quartet) to go with a bronze in trios. The women's team took gold for trios and a bronze for rinks. This was especially remarkable since they lost five members of the team to injury because of the bridge collapse.

On the first day of softball events, Team USA's stalwart pitcher Dave Blackburn tossed a no-hitter against Israel, claiming a 10-0 victory. But that wasn't even the best performance of the day, from a team standpoint: Panama shut out Great Britain, 26-0. Allowances might be made, since this was England's first appearance in softball.

Other than Israel's Mickey Halika, who won six medals in swimming, matching the total set by Mark Spitz and repeated by Seth Cohen in 1985, there were no standout performers in the pool. Halika's teammate Anya Gostomelsky won gold for the 100- and 200-meter freestyle and a silver in the 50-meter free, while the United States' Rachel Johnson, Sarah Solomon, and Arianne Cohen each won two medals.

In another anomaly of the Maccabiah set-up, three Israelis accounted for each of the twelve medals awarded for the new sport of water skiing.

In the marquee event, Canada beat Great Britain, 76-70, to win the gold in basketball.

Few would have thought these would be the last teams standing. Each had to upset their opponent in the semifinals to reach the ultimate game. England, which lost to Team USA by a disheartening fifty points in round-robin play, got their revenge for the War of Independence in 1776 by ousting the Americans, 83-76. Canada, under five-time Maccabiah coach John Dore, outlasted Israel in overtime, 63-60.

The U.S. hoopsters could do no better than the bronze, beating Israel, 75-55, in the "consolation" game.

The closing ceremonies have traditionally been a bittersweet time. The excitement of the events has ended and it's time to return home, leaving behind a lot of new-found friends. These Games had a particularly hard meaning this time around.

Bob Spivak described to the press his feelings about the failed promise of these Games.

"[The delegations are] about to march into the . . . stadium, which is filled to capacity, for the opening ceremony. In a lot of cases, their parents have come to Israel to witness this moment. It's going to be something truly incredible. And, just like that, it's taken away.

"The celebration is about to begin," he said, "but instead, what happens is so devastating, it's still almost impossible to comprehend."[10]

When athletes return home after the Games, it's not unusual for their local community newspapers to write up a little story about their experiences. While it's understandable that the participants express joy at having been there and a tinge of sadness at having to leaving such a life-altering event, the fact that many such stories made no mention of the Australian tragedy can perhaps be seen as a surprise.

It was an unfortunate blight against the record and purpose of the Maccabiah, and unfortunate for those whose dedication and training had to be placed on the back burner for what should have been a joyous experience.

---

10 "Tragedy's aftermath: For athletes, Maccabiah games remain shrouded in sadness," *Jewish Exponent* (Philadelphia), July 24, 1997.

Difficulty in finding accurate results was a problem as usual. One father of a certain age—his daughter competed in 50-and-over tennis events—wrote an angry letter to *The New York Times*, complaining about an article that mentioned people who had *not* won medals, whereas his daughter was a multiple medalist. A response from the *Times'* writer indicated that he had tried to confirm the claims of victory, but that a Maccabi USA spokesperson had basically told him they did not keep track of results as scrupulously as they might have.[11]

And as if things hadn't been difficult enough, Israel suffered a one-day strike by state-owned companies in the communications, transportation, and utilities sectors just as the Games were coming to an end. Fortunately order was restored before it seriously affected the athletes making their way home. Had the strike lasted longer, special dispensation had been put in place to allow the El Al flight carrying the members of the Australian team to leave the country.[12]

The closing ceremonies were understandably staid. The two Australians who had lost their lives were in the minds and hearts of the audience and speakers, including Yoram Eyal, chair of the organizing committee, who said, "We will forever remember Greg Small and Yetti Bennett, blessed be their memories, who died tragically during the opening ceremony of the Maccabiah Games."

Maccabi World Union chair Uzi Netanel said, "This Maccabiah has been one of pain, blood and tears. In the name of the movement and myself, I want to apologize to all of you for the portion of your dream that has been destroyed."

The ceremony concluded with the playing of the Maccabiah theme "and the crowd, on their feet, broke into a lively dance, the only real show of boisterous energy throughout the entire evening," summed up the *Jerusalem Post* story under the incongruous headline "Bridge tragedy dampens festive Maccabiah closing ceremony."

---

11 "Letter to the Editor: Other Athletes won in Maccabiah Games," *New York Times*, Aug. 31, 1997

12 "One day strike cripples economy, Jerusalem Post, July 25, 1997

The media wrap-up had plenty to complain about. On top of the bridge debacle, there were the standard annoyances that paled in comparison: poor organization, conflicting schedules, medals that weren't distributed to event winners because their sports were not recognized in the Maccabiah's constitution (shouldn't someone have checked that when the events were scheduled in the first place?).

"Yet, despite the organizational gremlins and the questionable levels of sport, we should not forget what lies behind these games," stated Heather Chait's commentary piece in the *Jerusalem Post*. "Is it the Israeli goalkeeper who stood in for the Australian team member injured in the bridge accident? Or the crowds who turned out to encourage the shocked and hurting Australian teams? Is it champion swimmer Yoav Bruck who, after winning the 4x100 meter freestyle event, said, 'What a great feeling! It's the first time we've beaten the Americans in the Maccabiah.' It's all this but much more.

"Sabras may view it as merely another source of traffic snarls or a wasted ten minutes nightly on Channel One, while the games may evoke wistful memories for Anglo-Saxon immigrants of Saturday afternoon rugby matches in their native countries, but for the thousands of visitors, the Maccabiah is an emotional high."[13]

---

13 "Maccabiah defies mediocrity, the Games will go on," *Jerusalem Post*, July 24, 1997

Chapter 17

The Sixteenth Games
July 16-23, 2001

"Cancelling the Maccabiah or postponing it is like granting Yasser Arafat the gold medal."

Knesset member Eliezer Sandberg[1]

"The very fact that the 16th Maccabiah was held, against all odds, is a tribute to the Jewish people of the world."

Oudi Recanati, chair of the Maccabi World Union[2]

---

1 "Solidarity gives Way to Caution As Diaspora Jews Cancel Israel trips," JTA, June 12, 2001

2 "16th Maccabiah Games come to a close," JTA, July 24, 2001

Perhaps no other Games presented the challenges of the 16th Maccabiah.

Israel was in the midst of the Second Intifada, a period of Palestinian violence which began in September, 2000, when Ariel Sharon, then the Prime Minister of Israel, made a controversial trip to the Temple Mount, starting a demonstration by Palestinian protestors that ended in casualties on both sides. The violence continued until the death of PLO leader Yasser Arafat in 2004.

In the interim, Israel was the constant target of terrorist attacks, including the suicide bombing of the Dolphinarium discotheque in Tel Aviv on June 1 by a member of Hamas. Twenty young people were killed in the strike, which was condemned, at least outwardly, by Arafat.

Throughout the violence, international Maccabi groups debated the best, if not most prudent, course of action. The organizers of the United States team were among those who decided they would not jeopardize their citizens by sending them to the Games, a philosophy that did not sit well with Israel and its strongest supporters.

As late as a month before the opening ceremonies, the leadership considered postponing the event for a year. This would have been the first cancellation of the Maccabiah since before World War II.

Other Jewish groups were cancelling their regular trips, including the U.S. Reform movement's summer youth camps. A survey of European delegations showed that many would also drop out. Israeli officials characterized these decisions as "disgraceful." Ephraim Sneh, Israel's minister of transportation, called out fair-weather friends "who for all these years have talked to us about the unity of the Jewish people over mounds of bagels and lox." Such action would represent a "slap in Israel's face from world Jewry.[3]

An editorial in the June 15 issue of *The Jerusalem Post* addressed the general consensus:

> Today, the children of those who [volunteered during the 1967 war] are reacting differently, as many of them, most notably the

---

3 Ibid

US reform movement, are canceling previously scheduled trips to Israel.

Perhaps most sadly the organizers of the Maccabiah . . . are being pressured to join that defeatist trend.

Though it did occasionally benefit from the performance of athletes like US swimmer Mark Spitz, the Maccabiah never purported to be a world-class sporting event. Instead, it thought to display the new Jews' embrace of the athleticism that their ghetto ancestors shunned, and to rally behind the Zionist idea and the State of Israel.

Now the organization's US wing is reportedly seeking to postpone the games until the violence subsides. Such a request must be rejected outright.

Few things could give terrorism a sweeter sense of victory than such a disruption of Israel-Diaspora relations.

Fortunately, a last-minute agreement by the U.S. delegation—appeased to a degree by a U.S.-brokered cease-fire—to attend led to a decision to hold the Games as planned. With the U.S. on board, Canada and South Africa announced they would also be sending delegations. Great Britain, which initially declined even after the U.S. agreed to go, changed its collective mind. A letter was sent to the British athletes, stating that there would be a delegation and asking who was still interested in going to Israel. John Barnett, a masters tennis player who was also the co-chair of Britain's organizing committee, insisted there would be a national presence at the Games, even if he was the sole representative.[4]

Bob Spivak was in his last term as president of Maccabi USA. He still considers the decision to go to Israel in the face of uncertainty one of his most rewarding moments with the organization.

"Everybody in the world canceled," he said, speaking of the other organizations that routinely hosted large-scale trips to Israel, "and we

---

4 "Britain will send team to Maccabiah after all," JTA, June 20, 2001

took the team. And it really meant a lot. The Israeli people knew we were there at this really desperate time.

"We all attended with probably half to a third of what we would have liked to bring. We were young, we were not professionals, we may not have handled it right, but I believe firmly we made the right decision."

In a video produced by Maccabi USA in 2012 honoring Robert E. Spivak as a "Legend of the Maccabiah," he suggested that this was the defining moment for the U.S. organization.

"The leadership was strong enough and brave enough to send a team to Israel during the time of the Intifada. We felt comfortable enough to say 'We want to support Israel, we want to support our Jewish brethren.' That was a very, very strong and difficult time for the organization to stand up and be there, but they did it. And we're very proud that we were part of that."

Roy Salomon, a long-time leader of Maccabi Canada, spoke about the decision for his own national organization.

"There was a lot of controversy at the time because what we all agreed upon is that if there was any danger, we would not be going to Israel, we would not hold the Maccabiah Games in 2001."

Once the United States decided to go, however, Salomon said other countries followed their lead. The bottom line: It was important for Israel to hold the Games.

"It was a very difficult time. You had half the parents calling up and yelling at you, 'How could you *not* go to Israel at a time like this? You're Maccabi and you're supposed to be standing for strength and sports.' Then you have the other half [who say] 'Are you out of your mind? How could you possibly bring our kids to Israel like this?'

"So we eventually made everybody aware . . . that there were dangers in going over there. And we were assured by the Israelis that the security would be unbelievable; It would be the best that you've ever seen."

Israeli officials ramped up measures, including at least one armed guard assigned to each busload of athletes and an additional force of more than 600 police officers at the opening ceremony. A 24-hour hotline was also set up for athletes to call with problems or questions.[5]

"At that point we were all set," Salomon said. "We were going to have the Games in Teddy [Kollek] Stadium in Jerusalem, the first time the Games would ever be held [there]."

The reason for the relocation from the traditional site in Ramat Gan was possibly that security was more or less concentrated in Jerusalem, according to Salomon. "It was their way of saying that this is the capital of Israel and it was giving a message as well."

Members of the 120-person delegation from Russia also voiced its support. As with most nations, the Russians were dealing with financial difficulties. But since the Maccabiah Games are a joint effort, shared by Jews from all over the world, the concept of helping out those who were your competitors wasn't much of an issue; other countries came to the aid of Russia. Irina Koval, a champion runner, told the Jewish Telegraphic Agency she didn't understand the concern over Mideast violence preventing the Games. "Israel is my land," she said, "and nobody can persuade me that I have to be scared to go there.[6]

One team that had a particularly difficult time of it was Australia, still feeling the pain of the tragedy that started the previous Maccabiah on a sorrowful note. That, compounded by the current circumstances, reduced their delegation from 374 to just 67.

Bernie Gold, a veteran organizer of Maccabi Australia Inc. who was injured in the Yarkon River Bridge collapse, said, "The main reason was because of the Intifada. The Games were to be cancelled, but at the last moment it was decided to hold them. By then it was too late to organize a proper sized team."

The Australian survivors had to deal with posttraumatic stress, even as they struggled to keep on with their sports. Zac Ashkanasy, a track athlete, was a flag-bearer on the bridge. Although he was physically

---

5 "The 2001 Jewish Olympics: As athletes train and unwind, they're ready for Maccabiah to begin," JTA, July 10, 2001

6 "Russian athletes psyched for Maccabiah Games," JTA, July 9, 2001

unharmed, it took him several years to recover psychically and emotionally. He returned for the 2001 Games, believing it would be part of the healing process. "If you don't go, the resentment you've built up will take longer to resolve," he told reporters.[7]

Golfer Robbie McGore agreed with his teammate.

"Not going back is not going to help anyone," he said. "We have to go forward. We can best honor their memory by continuing to attend the event in which they obviously believed strongly enough to be there in the first place."[8]

The evening before the opening ceremonies, the Australian delegation held a memorial for their fallen comrades at the site where the bridge had stood.

* * *

The smaller turnout had far-reaching financial implications as well. According to a Maccabiah organizer, "It is a big problem. Two to three million dollars will be lacking in the budget," in terms of ticket sales, and other income generated by thousands of potential visitors to Israel.[9]

Those who came were enthusiastic in their situation, claiming they had no qualms about stepping into a precarious situation.

Sure enough, the ceasefire did not last. Just hours before the opening ceremony, a suicide bomber killed two people and injured at least eleven more in the coastal town of Binyamina, some 120 kilometers to the north. Early the same morning, two Palestinians were killed when the bomb they were trying to place blew up prematurely in a field about a mile away from Teddy Stadium. The Israeli authorities believed the bomb was meant to be set off during the ceremonies.

None of this dampened the joy that finally came for the 2,000 athletes who attended the Games, about half of what had been expected.

---

7 "Australian athletes deal with memory of disaster," JTA, July 10, 2001
8 Ibid
9 "Maccabiah organizers upbeat on downsized Games," *Jerusalem Post*, June 28, 2001

Security at the stadium was similarly heightened, with more than 1,000 guards checking identification of workers and an estimated 20,000 tickets-holders, who were subjected to searches by civil defense guards and women soldiers; even cameras were inspected.

Despite the obvious inconvenience, athletes and sports fans alike were grateful for the opportunity to be there at all. Hometown newspapers around the world sent off their local athletes with best wishes, proclaiming them fearless and heroes, even if they didn't bring back any medals.

All this coming together in a time of extreme duress made the 2001 Maccabiah all the more memorable. "When we marched into Teddy Stadium, everybody had a little flashlight and everybody went to their seats and the lights went out and we all sang 'Hatikvah.' That was the most emotional 'Hatikvah' I ever heard," Spivak said. "The fact [was] that we might not have held the Games, and here we were in Jerusalem."

With the carnage from the two attack sites still being investigated and cleaned up, Prime Minister Ariel Sharon addressed the markedly reduced audience in Teddy Stadium.

"On a day of happiness and solidarity, we have experienced yet another horrible crime of Palestinian terrorism," he said. "Your coming here is proof of the victory of the spirit of the ancient Maccabees, the victory of determination and our just cause."[10]

Maccabiah Profile: Jeff Bukantz, United States, Fencing/Chairperson

Jeff Bukantz started fencing in his mid-teens but admitted he wasn't the most talented athlete. "Candidly, I was a middle range fencer, a 'C-range' fencer."

"The first time I heard about the Maccabiah Games I was leaving the New York Fencers Club after practice in 1977. I was walking to

---

10 "Suicide Bomber Kills 2 Israeli," *Los Angeles Times*, July 17, 2001

the train with one of my teammates . . . and he mentioned that he had just made [the Maccabi] team. I had never heard of this team and I thought this was something to shoot for because I wanted to make the Olympic team, like my dad, but this was a more makeable step. So from that moment, walking to the train station on 38th Street—and I'll never forget this moment as long as I live—I said, 'I have to make this team.'"

Bukantz was twenty at the time.

Although he wouldn't say it was as a direct result, that goal might well have been the impetus for his amazing improvement.

"The fact is, in 1977, something else happened to me: I had gone from 235 pounds to 185 pounds, so I went from a fat tub of lard to a pretty good athlete."

His father, Dr. Daniel Bukantz, had been a member of the U.S. Olympic fencing team for four consecutive Games, from 1948-60; he won the gold medal in foil in 1950. He served as a referee in four more Olympics after that (1964-1976). The boycott of the 1980 Russian Olympics broke the streak, but he returned in 1984 as a bout (head) referee.

He also participated in the third Maccabiah Games, the first after World War Two, winning gold for foil.

"One of my goals was not just making the Maccabiah team, but I really wanted that gold medal that my dad got," said Jeff Bukantz.

He made the team for the 1981 Maccabiah but he ran into a road-block. Battling for the bronze against a French opponent, Bukantz was just one point from victory. Alas, it was not to be, and he finished out of the medal contention.

"Taking fourth in these types of events when you have aspirations, it's the worst. . . . It would have been better if I didn't make the team. I was devastated," he said.

Bukantz returned for the 1985 Games, again one of the top ten ranked fencers in the U.S. "I lost in the semifinals to an Israeli fencer who had just taken second at a French World Cup. He was light years ahead of me." This time, he won the bronze. "At least it wasn't fourth."

In a surprising turn of events, Bukantz won the gold medal for epee, not his weapon of choice. "[I]t wasn't my specialty," he said. "They had an open spot [on the team] and I won."

Still, he didn't feel he had quite achieved what he set out to do. "It was a gold medal, but it wasn't my father's goal," he said. "It was nice, but . . . it wasn't the real thing."

By 1989, Bukantz was the Number Two fencer in the United States, the highest rating he would achieve. That brought about an important decision. "The World Championships were held in Denver the same time as the Maccabiah. When you're Number Two in the country, you're supposed to go to the World Championships and represent U.S. Fencing." But Bukantz realized he probably wouldn't do that well and, still seeking that elusive Maccabiah foil gold, decided to go to Israel instead for one last try.

This time he advanced to the final match. Once again, an Israeli stood between him and his objective.

"I'm up against an Israeli kid who's half my age (Bukantz was thirty-two at the time), twice as fast, and probably half my weight. I mean, this guy was just running me ragged." Bukantz was trailing, 7-5, in a ten-touch bout. And all of a sudden, "I just pulled it together and ran off the next five touches."

A teammate took a video of the match. "When I got the last touch, I just threw the mask up in the air and I just exploded, crying instantly because it was such a journey of trying to follow in my dad's footsteps. It just hit me."

"I had a lot of highlights in my life, [but] that had to be it."

The Maccabi fencing team is fairly easy to try out for because it's based on an objective point system. The same goes for swimming and track. Basketball and soccer are more subjective when it comes to assessing candidates.

"We try to be fair and bring out independent selectors. . . . At the end of the day, I think we get most of the selections right, and that's all you can ask. . . . There's always going to be some people upset they didn't make it; it's not a perfect science."

Bukantz also went to the 1993 Games as a substitute, even though there is, ostensibly, a 'three-time rule,' followed by most, but not all, teams in the U.S Maccabi system. "I call it the *dayenu* rule," Bukantz said, using the Hebrew word for "enough." "If you go three times and not four, *dayenu*; it's enough already. We want other people to have the experience."

It was for this event that he became active in the administrative part of the organization as a volunteer, helping to raise funds for athletes.

"It's a very expensive trip. There's no getting around it," he said. "We have a huge scholarship component. It's very important. Not everyone can afford it and we don't want to leave anyone behind in the open level. In many cases, there were multiple thousands [of dollars in] gifts given to many, many, many of the team. We didn't leave anyone home because [they couldn't pay]."

For the 2013 Games, the junior and youth divisions (eighteen and under) have to pay the entire amount. The open athletes are subsidized by Maccabi for $3,000, meaning they had to put up the balance. "Some people wrote a check, some people got money from their grandmother, some raised the money by e-mails blasts, which were incredibly effective."

Then there are the masters athletes, ranging in age from thirty-five to more than seventy years.

"The mission statement we have is to bring Jewish *youth* to Israel," Bukantz said. "It's not to provide for a summer camp experience for elder statesmen . . . . However, they do have it in the Games and it's great."

The Masters athletes are responsible of paying their entire way. In addition, they agree to sponsor an open athlete to the tune of $6,000. Expensive, yes, but Bukantz sees it as a way of giving back. Someone helped them at one point, he said, now it's their turn to help someone else. "Circle of life," he said. In 2013, Bukantz estimated there were 250 masters athletes. "It helped subsidized a big part of our program."

The Israel precamp component of the Maccabiah started in 1989. "It's really the most touching part of the [Games]," he said. "That's what separates us from the Olympics Games because the Olympics are a one-dimensional sporting event; it is what it is. Ours is multidimensional. We have the sports—yes, it's still about the sports and winning medals—but it's also about our heritage and our culture and seeing Israel."

In recalling his initial trip to Israel in 1981, Bukantz said, "I think at the time it was a bit of a blur. It was the first team I had made and

I was just interested in hanging out with the team and just soaking in the whole experience. I just don't remember all that much."

He did remember his first thoughts upon arriving in his ancestral "homeland. "How do these people survive in the midst of all these enemies? How can they be this vibrant country in the middle of the desert with all these people that hate them? That was the first thing that hit me. But it hits a lot of people differently. We've had a lot of people make aliyah, we have some athletes who were not really raised even quasi-Jewishly and the 'lightning bolt' hit them."

Like many of those who participate in the Maccabiah Games, Bukantz was not raised in a religiously observant home. "In fact, the major part of my involvement with Judaism right now is with Maccabi USA."

"We use the slogan, 'It changes lives,' and it has changed a lot of people's lives."

In 2001, during the Second Intifada, Bukantz was the chair for the junior sports division. "We had a vote of our executive committee and we decided not to go; it was just too dangerous. And then a couple of our leaders went to Israel and they changed their minds, because the feeling was that if the U.S. didn't come, the Games would not go on and that might be the end of the Maccabiah Games."

The decision split the organization, with Bukantz holding to his position that the situation was too unstable. "I was getting calls from parents crying about their kids . . . . . Plus I was getting a lot of pressure from my own family not to go. But I will say this: In May [2001], when my son, Michael, had his bar mitzvah, I had a table of Maccabi USA friends. In June, after I was on the side that said we should not go, these people wouldn't even talk to me. We had a complete schism within our organization. It was a very, very touchy time for us. I'm really even surprised that a lot of people who were on my side were excommunicated from the organization."

Bukantz, however, remained, serving as chair of the 2013 Games, and as first vice president of Maccabi USA. "It was amazing that I was resurrected because very few people were."

Serving as overall chair, "was a mammoth project," said Bukantz. "It was a year and a half-plus of work. It was much more than I thought I was getting into. As we approached the Games, I couldn't wait for [them] to come and be over because it had just taken over my life.

"But looking back at it, I will say that other than raising my children, it was the most gratifying and satisfying experiences I've ever been involved with.

"The lightning bolt has hit me," he said. "I love the people, I love the country, and I certainly take great pride in sending some of our Jewish kids over there; it really means a lot to me. Whatever my involvement will be in fencing, I don't know. But I hope my involvement with Maccabi USA will be for a long, long time."

Ultimately, the Games were reduced from ten days to seven. The pre-camp for the U.S. team—with trips to Yad Vashem, the Dead Sea, the Western Wall, and other sites of historical and cultural importance—went on as originally planned. The demeanor of the team was described as "cautious but upbeat."[11]

Unlike the Olympic Village system of housing, athletes at the Maccabiah Games were spread out all over the country, exacerbating what was an already challenging security situation. "Maccabi World Union and the people in charge of security did an outstanding job," Salomon said. "There's always security at every Maccabiah Games; it has to be. But this was very special. You couldn't afford to have a situation where someone got hurt or someone was killed."

The number of athletes and support staff that came was still substantial, given the circumstances. The rules were relaxed in order to accommodate those who had made the difficult decision to attend.

"We had about half of the [total number] that was supposed to go," said Spivak. "It wasn't easy. There had to be a lot of last-minute changes. There were events where one country wouldn't be sending a team, so you had to be flexible. The rules that are there throughout all the Maccabiah Games didn't hold true at that point. [Normally], you have to have four teams, four countries, to hold an event."

---

11 "Americans going to Maccabiah eager to compete," JTA, June 27, 2001

In some cases, every team won a medal simply because there were only three teams available to play, such as in softball, where there was Israel and Venezuela. Israel ended up splitting into two teams and won the gold and bronze medals.

"Obviously, we would have liked to have more teams," said Goose Gillett, head of the Israel Softball Association. "The Maccabiah's been a bit of a disappointment this year."[12]

The U.S. men's and women's volleyball teams had to borrow players from Israel to fill out their rosters. Both squads won the silver medal, losing to the host Israeli teams.

Only four runners took part in the 10,000-meter race, an event officials had considered cancelling were it not for the importuning of Lenny Ferman, a thirty-seven-year-old U.S. runner who won the bronze medal.

"I'm wearing it proudly," he said of his prize, "And tonight I'm drinking Maccabi beer to celebrate."[13]

One of the big stories of the Games was the participation of Olympic champion swimmer Lenny Krayzelburg. It is difficult to overstate the influence an athlete of that stature has on younger folks and it might not be an exaggeration to say his decision to attend the Games, especially under these conditions, was on a level similar to that of Sandy Koufax, who famously decided to skip his start in the first game of the 1965 World Series because it fell on Yom Kippur.

Even a star performer like Krayzelburg had parents who worry about him; his father supported the swimmer's decision to go to Israel while his mother was against it.

"I feel that at this point of my career, people are looking to me for leadership," he said. "I think we must support Israel during hard times and continue the spirit of the Maccabees."[14]

---

12 "16th Maccabiah Games Teams Scrape to Fill Rosters, but Maccabiah Games Go on," JTA, July 24, 2001

13 "Few competitors or spectators for Maccabiah," JTA, July 19, 2001

14 "Olympic gold medalist goes to summer camp," JTA, July 2, 2001

Roy Salomon had met Krayzelburg when the champion swimmer visited Montreal several years earlier. He heaped praise upon him for another difficult choice: skipping the World Champions for the opportunity to compete at the Maccabiah. "I don't know how many would have done that," said Salomon. "I thought that was a tremendous sign of great character. There are not that many great Jewish athletes in the world, but he was one of hem. And when others see him doing something like that, it's very special."

Maccabiah Profile: Lenny Krayzelburg, United States, Swimming

Krayzelburg and his family left Odessa when he was thirteen. "A very big cultural change," he said in a phone interview. "Obviously coming at that time, it was very conservative in society [in Odessa], going to America and a lot of freedom, especially with a Jewish background. In the former Soviet Union everything was on the hush-hush. You really didn't talk about your Jewish roots. And then coming to L.A., it was very wide open and proud that you're a Jew and associating yourself with the JCC is definitely an interesting transition for sure."

Krayzelburg began swimming when he was just five years old. Recognition of his talent was almost immediate. By the time he left at thirteen, he was training seriously, up to five hours a day.

"[In] the old Soviet sports system, around the age of nine they were already selecting potential star athletes and sending them to training sports schools, equivalent to boarding schools here," he said. Krayzelburg was lucky; his program was based in his hometown, so he would spend the day taking classes and practicing with his team and sleep in his own bed at night.

Once the family found sponsors in the United States, it took them three months to make the move, spending three months in Vienna and Rome before making the last leg of their journey. Krayzelburg's father, Oleg, wanted to make sure there wasn't too much of a drop-off in the transition period and asked friends in L.A. to find a swimming program for Lenny. Within two weeks of settling into their West Hollywood home, the prodigy had found a place on a local team in Santa Monica, about an hour away. It was when he switched to the Westside JCC that he received his introduction to the Maccabi phenomena when he competed in the JCC Maccabi Games in Detroit as a fourteen-year-old, then two years later in Baltimore.

"Just to be part of a very large sporting event that wasn't just [about] swimming was a very unique and special event for me," Krayzelburg said. "Especially just getting acquainted with this country and settling in. Then during those games I heard about the Maccabiah in Israel and it was appealing and interesting to me.

"There was a period of time in '97 that I was considering it, but just the way things played out with my career—I was really ascending to the top—[I] had an opportunity to make a world championship team. So I made that decision that at the time, to do that versus going to Israel. But my dream, my goal, was always to go and take part in it. After a success [the Sydney Olympics], I felt I had accomplished everything I wanted to do in a swimming career at a world-class level. Now I wanted to do something that was more special for myself and experience the [Maccabiah] Games, so 2001 was when I ended up going and competing."

Krayzelburg received a lot of praise for bypassing the World Championship that year to fulfill his dream. It was, to say the least, a significant gesture, though to him it appeared to be a no-brainer. As he explained, "To be honest with you, it wasn't a hard decision for me. I had wanted to go to Israel and experience the Games, and at that time I was starting to get closer to my Jewish roots. Part of it was just maturity, more experience living in this country. Obviously, there was a lot of support I received from the Jewish community, not just in the States but all over the world in the Sydney Games. It was the right thing to do and I really wanted to take part in Maccabiah."

He thought a moment to consider the difference between the two iconic sporting events. "What's so unique about the [Maccabiah] Games is that you're getting such an intimate exposure to Israel and to Jewish culture in general. [And] what the U.S. does with their cultural trip before the Games is incredible." Although scheduling conflicts hindered his participation in many of those opportunities, he did hit the big spots, including Jerusalem and the Western

Wall. "That's a huge part of this whole experience; I'm not sure if it gets talked about enough."

One of the traditional events is a group Bar/Bat Mitzvah at the Wall, either as a first-time rite of passage, or a supplemental excursion, with the holiest of Jewish sites as the backdrop. Krayzelburg, who had never had a Bar Mitzvah ceremony, declined the opportunity. Since his parents had not made the trip, he did not want to attend without their presence. "It would have been important for my parents to be there."

"At the Olympic Games, everything is a lot more sequestered; everything is happening inside the Village. You're just taking buses to your competition."

Despite the risk, Krayzelburg stood by his decision to make the trip to the Maccabiah. Krayzelburg recalled an attack at the Dolphinarium discotheque in June 2001 in which a suicide bomber linked to the Palestinian group Hamas, blew himself up outside the Tel Aviv night spot, killing twenty-one Israeli teenagers and injuring 132.

"There was a reluctance by a lot of delegations to even go to Israel because the situation was so hot then," he said. "There was a lot of talk about cancelling the Games."

But the situation did not deter him from wanting to participate. "I made it clear that I made a decision to go to Israel and I would be there. It was important to support Israel at this tough time. Because the Games are a big part of the country and there were rallies behind it. It gives an opportunity to really put Israel on display. I understood how important the Games were for Israel and also for our U.S. delegation, with me on the team and not being detoured by the conflict made a big statement for U.S. athletes to go. By me going and being vocal about this [and] supporting the U.S. . . . as well as Israel, that made the experience I got in Israel even greater."

That was Krayzelburg's first trip to Israel. "There's a saying, 'To see it once is better than to hear it 1,000 times.' This was a perfect example of that. It was special; it was certainly a life-changing experience for me. It brought me closer to Judaism. Just to see the old country and the Jewish roots, where Jewish people have lived throughout generations. And obviously today's culture. It was definitely very special, a humbling, proud moment for me, during those eight-to-nine days."

Krayzelburg had the additional honor of carrying the American flag in to the opening ceremonies. "It wasn't too much of a surprise, but certainly a tremendous honor. Any time you have the opportunity to lift the American flag and carry it with honor, it's a special moment. For me to carry it and lead the delegation into the stadium with all the dignitaries that were there . . . . Even today stands [it] out as one of the highlights of my life and the experiences I've had."

Krayzelburg returned to Israel for the 2005 Games, although he did not compete. He and Mark Spitz carried the U.S. flag. In 2013, he was one of eight athletes to carry the Maccabiah banner at the opening ceremonies. "Standing in the stadium last year and singing 'Hatikvah' was an incredible moment for me," he said of the most recent Games.

Although he has no official role with Maccabi USA, Krayzelburg, who owns a franchise of swimming academies across the country, is always willing to appear at an event to promote the organization and the Games. It's his way of giving back. He was named a Maccabiah Legend in 2011, along with Spitz, gymnast Mitch Gaylord, tennis star Brad Gilbert, and fellow swimmer Jason Lezak, among others.

"The level of competition is obviously a little bit different, but I think it has gotten so much better even from 2001 to 2013, I can tell that just by looking at the quality of the swimmers just these past Games versus 2001. Tremendous."

Krayzelburg doesn't want to take credit, but no doubt his participation has had an impact and may have influenced other Olympians such as Lezak and Garrett Weber-Gale to participate at Maccabiah. "I assume that the rest of the kids and young adults are looking up to those Jewish athletes at the Olympic level. We're excited and honored to be a part of the Maccabiah."

As to why he continues to be a voice for the Games, Krayzelburg said, "I'm a great believer that we as Jews need to stick together. There aren't many of us . . . compared to the world population. Supporting Israel within their situation . . . . It's very unfortunate and sometimes we take it for granted here in this country. So to show support and to come out for Jewish people to have an experience to go to Israel to take part in an incredibly put-together athletic competition and be able to complement that with the cultural opportunity where you get kind of a 'Cliff Notes' on Israel in five days you really expose yourself to some of the historical places the country has, it is incredible and I think more and more people should know about this. And if they are able to take part in it, [they] *must* take part in it. It would make them better, more well-rounded people and they would experience something not many in this world do."

The activities performed under this cloud of potential violence were still cause for joy and celebration. Krayzelburg won his gold for the 100-meter backstroke, but two other American swimmers did their best to upstage their teammate. Bryan Goldberg won top individual honors for the 200-meter backstroke and the 100-, 200-, and 400-meter freestyle, while Benjamin Weston also medaled in the 100-, 200-, and 400-meter freestyle races along with taking gold in the 1500-meter freestyle and the 400-meter individual medley.

Both the men's and women's basketball finals were held on July 22, and in both cases, the American teams beat their Israeli opponents to secure gold.

The women played to a 67-67 tie at the end of regulation before eking out a 79-76 win. The men had somewhat of an easier time of it, taking the effort by eleven points, 82-71. Australia beat France, 73-64 for the bronze medal.

Not surprisingly, Israel, with far and away the most athletes won the most medals—244, including 96 gold, 74 silver, and 74 bronze medals. The United States was a distant second, with 74 (21 gold, 23 silver, and 30 bronze).

The Games closed as they had opened, with a lot of joy and a lot of security. Hundreds of policemen stood watch over the relieved athletes and spectators, who gladly subjected themselves to x-ray scanners and metal detectors at the Sultan's Pool, a former reservoir that now served as a venue for concerts and festivals.

The general consensus held that every delegation was glad it had taken the bold step to attend in the face on ongoing strife in the region, but that they wouldn't be truly relaxed until they touched down in their respective countries.

The theme of the closing ceremonies was *Am Echad*—One Nation.

This time around, however, the "kumbaya" sentiment that it's "not just about sports," as Bob Spivak said as the 16th Maccabiah came to a close, rang especially true. The 2001 Games had put the Diaspora's support of Israel to the test, and, when push came to shove, the Diaspora came through.

Chapter 18

The Seventeenth Games
July 11-21, 2005

"The Maccabiah is not just for all Jews, it is for all Israelis as well, and I am a proud Israeli."

Asala Shehadeh, seventeen, an Arab-Israeli who won the first gold medal of the 2005 Games[1]

Depending on the source, the Second Intifada ended with the death of PLO leader Yasser Arafat in the fall of 2004 or at the Sharm el-Sheikh Summit at which Israeli Prime Minister Ariel Sharon and Mahmoud Abbas, the new Palestinian president, agreed to end overt hostilities.

Amidst this relative tranquility, participants could look forward to an uneventful time away at the pool or track or other venues for the first time since 1993.

---

1 "Sharon calls Jewish athletes to immigrate to Israel at Maccabiah," Xinhau News Agency, July 12, 2005

That calm did not last.

Eight years after the Yarkon Bridge collapse that resulted in the death of four members of the Australian delegation, with scores more injured, the media was still running stories about the aftermath, interviewing those who had either been injured themselves or watched in horror the events that unfolded before them. Although these stories demonstrated courage and perseverance of the young men and women who carried on in honor of their fallen comrades, they also expressed the lingering anger at those responsible for the incident, primarily Yoram Eyal.

Eyal was chair of the organizing committee for the 1997 Games and had commissioned the construction of the footbridge that collapsed at the outset of the opening ceremonies. He was convicted of criminal negligence and sentenced to six months of community service. He did not, however, lose his $120,000-a-year job as head of Kfar Hamaccabiah, home to Maccabi Israel and Maccabi World Union.

The animosity against Eyal returned in force when he was elected to represent Maccabi Israel on the Israel Olympic Committee.

Colin Elterman, an attorney for the families of the deceased Australians, told the press, "it was highly insensitive of Maccabi to allow him to retain his position, as Australia sends a huge team to the Maccabiah, and the last thing they need to see is Eyal taking an official position in the games. What next—will they make him prime minister? Can you imagine that the members of the massive Australian team may well be expected to march past and salute him?"[2]

The opening ceremonies featured more than 7,000 athletes from fifty-five countries. Some 1,200 came from the United States.

Lenny Krayzelburg, who showed uncommon selflessness when he passed up the World Swimming Championships to compete in the 2001 Games, was back as captain of the American team and its flag bearer for the opening ceremonies. Jordan Weinstein, chair of the U.S. Maccabiah Committee, described Krayzelburg's decision as "the

---

2 "Despite Maccabiah disaster, Yoram Eyal appointed to IOC," JTA, Jan. 6, 2005

watershed mark which revitalized the Games . . . . I can think of no one more fitting than Lenny to lead Team USA at the 17th Maccabiah."[3]

Krayzelburg was inducted into the International Jewish Sports Hall of Fame during his 2005 visit to Israel. Mark Spitz, making his first trip to Israel since 1985 when he carried the Maccabiah Torch into the Stadium, joined him at the head of the U.S. delegation.

Gal Fridman, the first Israeli to win a gold medal at the Olympics, received the flame from Spitz and lit the Maccabiah cauldron, following speeches by Ariel Sharon and Israeli President Moshe Katsav, who made the standard request for the visitors to make the Jewish State their permanent home.

After the parade of athletes made their tour of the track oval, the traditional memorial services recalled those lost to defending Israel as well as the eleven Israelis killed at the 1972 Olympics and the Australians who died in the bridge collapse; the Australian delegation received the most prolonged applause from the crowd of 40,000 fans.

Amongst those parading were several high-profile sportsmen and women who participated in the 2005 Games, including Russian sabre champion-turned-Maccabiah coach Sergei Sharikov, who earned four medals spread out over the Atlanta, Sydney, and Athens Olympics; five-time world fencing champion and Olympic gold medalist, Maria Mazina, also from Russia; Israel-born basketball star Shay Doron, who was a member of the U.S. women's squad; track and field coach Mel Rosen, who led the 1992 U.S. men's team Olympic success in 1992; fourteen-year-old Canadian tennis prodigy Sharon Fichman; and Israeli Olympians Alex Averbukh (pole vault) and Arik Ze'evi (judoka).

If the 1989 Maccabiah was considered the "Bar Mitzvah Games" and the 2001 event the "Intifada Games," the 2005 might be described as the "Raucous Games." During the ceremonies, Brazil's over-excited delegation broke from the parade of athletes and climbed to the top of the podium at the middle of the field. After security guards dispersed them, they ran in zigzag lines, grasping their country's flag.[4]

---

3 "Krayzelburg heads US Team," *Jerusalem Post*, May 25, 2005
4 "The Games Begin With Gusto," Jewish Exponent (Philadelphia), July 14, 2005

Regardless of the lull in overt hostilities in the Mideast, security was still all-important. The stadium was surrounded by more than 2,500 policemen, civil guard volunteers, and private security guards.

Despite the heightened security, the high spirits of the Games' launch shattered two days after the opening ceremonies, when a suicide bomber detonated off his charge in Netanya, some 22 miles away from Ramat Gan, killing at least three and injuring dozens more. Miriam Fierberg, the mayor of Netanya—home to the International Jewish Sports Hall of Fame—got a too-up-close experience as she was driving to the Games. The explosives went off just yards from her car. "I was just dialing the telephone when I heard the boom," she told reporters. "I felt the car jump in the air and the mirror fell off. I looked up and saw the air filled with smoke and body parts flying everywhere."[5]

Maccabiah profile: Ashley Kochman, Canada, Basketball

Ashley Kochman was a member of Canada's first girls' junior basketball team in 2001. She described it as "an interesting time to go."

"That was an amazing introduction to the Maccabiah world and I guess you could say I caught the bug from that." She was so vigorously "infected" that she played on the women's open teams in 2005, 2009, and 2013.

Kochman attended Jewish day schools in Toronto, where she received a better education about Israel than most of her teammates did. She played on recreational teams through the Ontario Basketball Association, her league out of the Bathurst Jewish Center in Toronto. Trying out for the Maccabiah team was a social activity, too; Kochman auditioned with three of her best friends.

"I remember sitting on my bed the day we were supposed to hear whether we made the team or not and being very anxious. It was

---

5 "Israel says suicide attack will not put end to withdrawal," *Times of London*, July 13, 2005

not a casual thing." Kochman saw making the team as the natural progression of her basketball "career," "so it was really important to make [it]."

Her parents had planned on traveling with her on her first trip to Israel, but changed their plans because of the Intifada. Kochman believes they still allowed her to go because of "the assurances Maccabi Canada was giving in terms safety and security in combination with Maccabi World Union in Israel. From the moment we stepped off the plane I never felt we were unsafe."

Going to Israel after already having had such a substantial Jewish education was revelatory.

"We didn't sleep the entire ride; we were just too excited. You hear about it; it's your 'second home,' the Jewish homeland. But I think at that age it's hard to understand what it means.

"I don't know why, but when we got off the plane, me and my closest friends looked at each other [and] we looked at our feet on the ground and we all kind of just felt at home. It was just a huge sigh of relief." The first picture Kochman took was of her and her friends touching the Israeli soil.

"The experience for me was less about the country at that point and more about meeting other athletes from around the world and being proud to be Jewish, proud to be Canadian, and proud to be in Israel competing in a sport that I loved," Kochman said. "We didn't get to tour the country as much as I'm sure we otherwise would have [had it not been for the circumstances with the Intifada]. We were really in our hotel a lot of the time.

"We would go for runs in the morning as a team and the soldiers would have to run with us because we were leaving the hotel grounds. And we thought it was great to have these cute men coming with us. You don't really appreciate they're there for your safety."

She described the surreal experience of sitting in an outdoor amphitheater in Caesarea hearing the familiar Hebrew songs she had learned in school, just two weeks after attending a Backstreet Boys concert at the Rodgers Centre in her hometown.

Her parents did get to accompany her to the 2005 Games. For her father, it was his inaugural trip; for her mother, the first in almost thirty years. "Having my parents there made the Maccabiah experience much more emotional."

Photo Courtesy Ashley Kochman

Ashley Kochman (number 8), defends against Israel at the 2013 Games.

The 2009 Games provided an extra challenge, as Canada struggled to assemble a women's team. "That's when I started getting more involved in the organization as a volunteer." She helped recruit a coach as well as players across the country. "To me [those Games] were more satisfying because of the hard work it took to get the team together." They didn't win a medal, which she found disappointing, but Kochman said "The girls that came enjoyed their experience and being able to watch that . . . was refreshing for me."

Finding Jewish female basketball players these days is a challenge, the result of a vicious cycle as institutions close down for one reason or another, so there are no places to develop female players. Kochman also pointed out another situation that is gender-driven.

"When [women] get married and have a kid, it's usually harder to come back, versus the men who can keep playing and they never really have that real-life event."

As someone who has grown up with the Maccabiah, Kochman has seen a lot of change over the years. "The differences between 2001 and 2013 as a competitor are staggering. In 2001, we didn't have cell phones," she recalled. "In order to phone home, we had to go to the pay phone in the hotel with a long distance calling card. In 2013, here I am with my iPhone. I can take a picture and send it instantly.

"[The Maccabiahs] definitely lived up to the hype. I say that because from that point on I have been back to Israel almost every year. My experience in 2001 definitely shaped the person I became, however it did that, why-ever it did that."

The rising cost of fielding a delegation remains an issue. They include a lot of "below the line" items that are frequently overlooked, such as venue rentals, referees, and transportation to and from events and ceremonies. In 2009, Kochman secured a $100,000 sponsorship from a foundation that paid almost all of the expenses of the women's basketball team. The same circumstances did not happen in 2013, so the athletes had to find the means themselves.

These days, Kochman works in business development for a pharmaceutical company. When she signed her contract in 2012, she worked in the time off needed to attend the 19th Games.

"The novelty never wears off. Forget the Games. The opening ceremonies: walking into the stadium as an athlete representing your country, but also being Jewish. For me, based on my background, with grandparents who were Holocaust survivors, it never gets old, and it will never get old."

* * *

In such a context, the 2005 Games took place.

In women's basketball, Shay Doron, who two years later signed with the New York Liberty of the WNBA, led the USA to a perfect 5–0 run, beating Israel, 78-53, for the gold medal. Just the week before, Doron—chosen as the tournament MVP—had been a vital component for her native Israel in their Under-20 European Championships.

The Australian ladies picked up the bronze by holding off Canada, 64-62. The Canadians had staged a fierce comeback, down by double digits in the second period, but came up agonizingly short.

Among the other highlights in the playing arenas:

In the ever-popular basketball program, the U.S men got off to a fast start by beating Canada in the first round of play, 88-76. Israel, in the meantime, almost doubled Germany's score with a 106-54 victory.

America's Bryan Goldberg earned the honorific of world's fastest Jewish swimmer, wresting it away from his Maccabiah teammate and 2004 Olympian Scott Goldblatt. Goldberg, twenty-two, knocked almost a full second off the previous 100-meter freestyle mark with his time of 51.06 seconds, setting the new Maccabiah record.

In squash, Brian L. Roberts, the chair and CEO of Comcast Corporation, won a gold medal with the U.S. team in his fourth Maccabiah.

In soccer, Jonathan Bornstein, Benny Feilhaber, and Leo Krupnik led the U.S. men's soccer team to their best finish ever with a silver medal. All three went on to play professionally. The U.S. lost the gold medal to Israel, who played with their Under-20 National Team.

In women's tennis, Fichman became the new darling of the courts, sweeping her events with a gold in singles, bronze in women's doubles, and silver in mixed doubles.

Maccabiah Profile: Matt Halpern, United States, Tenpin Bowling

Matt Halpern began bowling when he was around five years old. He first heard about the Maccabiahs in the mid-1990s. "This was pre-email," he said. "We got something at the house about it."

Halpern attended the tryouts in 1997 but came up just short. He passed up the next opportunity because of a scheduling conflict, but the Games remained on his radar. Ultimately, the third time was the charm and he was selected for the 2005 team, where he won a gold medal for the All-Event category. In 2009, he was a member of the silver-winning men's triple team as well as the doubles and team events, both of which earned him bronze. He was a member of the 2013 squad as well.

Photos courtesy Matthew Halpern

Tenpin medalist Matt Halpern (left with teammate Jared Goldschen) appeared in three Maccabiah Games.

"It is a fairly competitive environment. The bowlers all come with strong resumes from their home countries.

"It's different from other sports; when we're in a different environment, whether it's a different bowling facility or a different state or a different country, there's a lot of elements that change. Just the way that bowling centers maintain their facilities, there are different standards."

One of the challenges he and his teammates faced was "bowling in much hotter weather than any of us were used to. That's not to say that we're spoiled necessarily, but when I go into a bowling facility even during the summer, it's kept at a cool temperature. That may not be the case in Israel or another country where air conditioning is more of a premium." That might not seem like a big deal to the recreational bowler, but it can be for someone at Halpern's level. "Every movement you're making, every time you're putting your hands on the ball, that feel, that grip, are all affected by those outside elements," he said.

"The standard that I may use to judge how a tournament is run could differ from somebody else. There's always challenges when you bring people together from different backgrounds. Even though the playing rules by and large are the same, there are variations and differences.

"The management that each country brings with them—the tournament staff and directors—by and large are all volunteers, so that comes into play as well," Halpern said. "They're not professionally running tournaments for a living. Most of them are in other industries. This is something they do because they have an affinity, a passion for whatever sport they're engaged in. It could always be run better."

Unlike some of the other teams, the bowling team traveled without the benefit of support staff, which puts extra burdens on the athletes. "The organization decided a while ago that we did not need to bring a coach and/or manager to accompany us, meaning [we are] responsible for doing whatever administrative stuff, coaching one another, helping, that sort of thing. The higher team management would usually designate someone to be the team leader, usually somebody who has competed previously so they have the experience, not only that but being in Israel, being at the Games, and knowing what could happen in terms of the questions that may come up, or issues."

That's not to say that there the bowlers are totally alone. "For any given team, different family members would come to be cheerleaders.

These past Games, one of the athletes who competed twenty years ago was in Israel with his family and came to see us. There is a camaraderie that stands over time, that's not judged on individual games," said Halpern.

He explained the expectations placed on every athlete who represents the United States at the Maccabiah Games.

"It's fairly specific that when you accept your appointment, you will be in Israel with the team for roughly three weeks. Of that time, there's a two-week competition period where all the events take place. You're not actually competing every day, but during the two weeks all the events are going on. The week prior to that is what we call the 'Israel Connects' program, the sightseeing and educational and cultural component of the experience that really allow athletes to see Israel and learn about Israel and understand what the country is about prior to their competition.

"Basically every morning you would have training, your practice, for us we'd get to go to an area bowling center and work on some things, start to get used to the environment, get used to the conditions, shake off any jet lag. For other sports, going to track, going to the baseball field, whatever it is."

Unlike many of his fellow Maccabeans, Halpern had been to Israel several times previously. "My sense is that for most of the people participating [in the Games] their connection to Judaism in a religious sense is very, very small. And that's not a judgment, it's just what I've observed. For many people, it's their first time going to Israel, but it's also their first time *considering* going to Israel; it was never on their radar. For a lot of people, when we have our Shabbat dinner in our Israel Connect program, it may be the first time where a prayer is being said, maybe since their bar or bat mitzvah, or maybe earlier," said Halpern, the executive director of a conservative synagogue in New Jersey.

"For me, it is a challenge at times, finding a balance between the ritual and the observant and everything else going on in the world. It's making sure that I'm comfortable where I'm at and what I'm doing. During Israel Connects, for example, there are activities that go on during Shabbat. We have the option of not participating for religious reasons. For most people, I don't think that the religious component is a consideration for them, which is fine."

"One of the major parts of the experience is going with your team-mates, bonding together, bonding with other athletes as well, and you don't want to separate from each other. For the most part, in our case, we may not meet each other in person until we get to Israel," said Halpern, who enjoys the closeness afforded by housing the ath-letes according to their specialty. "I don't know what it was like for other sports, but when we're competing, we all want to win, we all want to do well. When we're off the lanes, we're all friends, we're all comrades, and we spend time together, hang out together. So for us as bowlers, it's the icing on top of the cake. I know for other sports that camaraderie does not exist, and that's fine. For us, we thrive on that [closeness]."

Many of them keep in touch throughout the year. Halpern had recently returned from Australia, where he attended the wedding of a fellow bowler. "That is how close we are. I have developed some of my closest friendships with people who are around the world, people that I can stay in touch with on a very constant basis. It's given me the chance to meet people I would never meet, see things I would never see, and really expand my horizons in a way I never thought possible. The friends that I've made through my Maccabi experience are people that I will keep in touch with forever."

* * *

One of the little publicized secrets of the Games is the fraternizing among happy and healthy young people. The *Jerusalem Post* put an end to that discretion when it published "Sportsmen 'just wanna have fun,' undeterred by nearby terror attack."

The article was a mix of the sacred and the profane, coming on the heels of the bombing attack in Netanya and speaking of the Israeli atti-tude that regardless of the difficulties of living in such a volatile region, life goes on. Some women might have found the tone of the *Post* piece offensive, as when one male athlete from Italy told the writer, "The terrorism is, of course, scary. Some of the girls are finding it very scary. Maybe they need a big strong man to protect them. You have to look at the bright side sometimes. Maybe the terrorism will make the girls more friendly."[6]

One of the early missteps of the Games involved a ceremony during the first round of the karate event, which delayed some of the matches so much they had to be postponed until the following day. The Dutch team vehemently criticized the decision because they had arranged with a television station in Holland to air the competition live. Family members and other supporters had similarly taken great pains to attend according to the original schedule.

Their coach scolded event planners. "We have to blame the organization that had ten speakers, and girls dancing for at least forty-five minutes," he said. "We definitely could have gotten the fights in."[7]

The sensitive issue of "Who is a Jew at the Maccabiah Games?" was covered in a fascinating article from *Ha'aretz*, describing the requirements of different countries. While the United States maintained that either parent may be Jewish, other nations, such as Australia, adhered to the strict tradition of matrilineal descent. Ironically, Israel, as the "Jewish State," had no such religious stricture as a condition for participation: *all* Israeli citizens were eligible to compete.[8]

Another controversy that seemed to come out of a Marx Brothers movie was the case of the Swedish wrestling team, which included two athletes who definitely were not Jewish by anyone's standards.

They had discovered the event through an "invitation" for the Maccabiah Games posted on the International Federation of Associated Wrestling website. They maintained that they did not know it was ostensibly for Jewish athletes only.

None of the parties involved in the sport—IFAW, the International Wrestling Federation, or the Maccabiah organizers—would take responsibility for the mix-up. The use of the word "invitation" was evidently open to interpretation. Dr. Solomon Stolar, president of the

---

6 July 14, 2005
7 "Controversy Mars Karate Opening," *Jerusalem Post*, July 14, 2005
8 July 19, 2005

IWF, told reporters, "Everyone can interpret it as they want. I'm not responsible for that."[9]

This laughable incident might have gone under the radar if Mohammad Babulfath—born in Iran, but representing Sweden—hadn't finished at the head of his 84-kg weight class in the Greco-Roman event. The smiles wore off when the event organizers refused to award him the gold medal. It went instead to Israel's Denis Nikolaev.

Or maybe not. Three different sources reveal three different gold medalists for this event. This problematic record-keeping—and overall management in general—finally made its way into the press in another critical report about the questionable methods used to increase the number of countries participating in the Games.

The spirit of the Games might be "alive and well" according to one British participant, but the mechanics seemed to be wearing down.

Perhaps it was because there was little in the way of outside distraction that made the 2005 Games so introspective. Complaints of mismanagement were mostly muted in previous Maccabiahs, including the question in recent years about the necessity to continue hosting the expensive gatherings at all. In an effort to increase the reach of the Games to farther parts of the globe, Maccabiah organizers circumvented some rules to allow for the inclusion of athletes that either went against the "Jewish" requirements or the eligibility as set forth by myriad sports agencies, with their own dizzying array of prerequisites. The rationale that this was more than a sporting event only goes so far before the legitimacy of the accomplishments comes into question.

On the other hand, in a case of the pot calling the kettle black, the *Jerusalem Post* reported that "Gymnast Daniel Gould [a resident of Australia] was excited to be Japan's first-ever participant."[10] In fact, in 1973, Joseph Garrie, an American, won a silver medal in judo for Japan. Garrie was a student at Tokyo's Sophia University at the time.

---

9 "Maccabiah wrestles with its Iranian-born Muslim winner," *Jerusalem Post*, July 18, 2005

10 "Maccabiah rules bent to increase number of delegations," *Jerusalem Post*, July 22, 2005

"According to Maccabiah rules, [Gould] is technically qualified to represent Japan, having lived there over the past six months,
but his inclusion is misleading," noted the *Post* piece, as if such
methods had not being going on for years by numerous countries, including Israel, who push through the red tape to accommodate
talented athletes.

The *Post* ran several opinion pieces and letters to the editor on this
general theme. One Canadian writer who had made aliyah addressed
some of the incompetence in a commentary that read, in part:

> I have been hearing from family members participating in the
> event (at the cost of $6,000 per person) that the Maccabiah
> organizers are incompetent tightwads. Transportation to and from
> events is sporadic. Food is limited—if available at all.
>
> How is it possible for an athlete who has just completed an
> event and returns to his or her hotel for lunch to be told that the
> dining room is closed? How can there be no doctor or physical
> therapist on site at the sport venues in case of injury?[11]

Another *Post* review raised some damning issues:

> The Maccabiah participants handbook lists more than eighty-five
> people with different titles in charge of the events. The organiza-
> tion boasted that it had over 1,000 volunteers this year.
>
> So why was no one available to keep official statistics at the
> basketball game? Why were fencers served spoiled food, causing
> several competitors to fall ill? Several venues reported that they
> were short on water. Last-minute schedule changes frustrated
> many competitors (not to mention fans and members of the
> press). And the "official" results from competitions, as reported
> by the Maccabiah press center, sometimes had little connection to
> what actually took place on the fields.
>
> At the gymnastics, a list of competitors was not made avail-
> able (although it now seems that this may have been deliberate,

---

11 "Why Can't We Be Better Sports?" *Jerusalem Post*, July 19, 2005

to cover up the fact that Ukrainian Valeriia Maksiuta, who won three medals, was not actually eligible to compete in the Maccabiah because she is not Jewish.)[12]

One could only hope that these issues would be addressed and fixed for the 2009 Games.

---

12 "Fair Play?" *Jerusalem Post*, July 22, 2005

Chapter 19

The Eighteenth Games
July 12-23, 2009

Maccabiah
מכביה חי
המכביה ה-18 ישראל תשס"ט
18th MACCABIAH ISRAEL 2009

"I always said I'd keep going to the Maccabiah Games provided I was chosen, and unless I was dead or bankrupt."

Australian golfer Roy Vandersluis on competing in his ninth Games, beginning in 1977[1]

"I hope some of you fell in love with us, because we love all of you without exception."

Israeli President Shimon Peres[2]

---

1 "Lezak strikes gold in Maccabiah debut," July 20, 2009
2 "Peres hopes Israel can attract foreign Jewish athletes," Xinhau News Agency, July 24, 2009

If the 1989 Maccabiah was considered the "Bar Mitzvah" Games, would you say the ever-expanding event reached maturity in 2009?

The number of athletes continued to grow, as did the number of nations and events. Israel would welcome 8,000 participants from sixty nations to compete in twenty-eight sports. The Israeli contingent was so large—2,000-plus—that only half of the delegation was able to march in the parade at the opening ceremonies.

Countries making their Maccabiah debut included Ethiopia, Grenada, Palua, Slovenia, and Thailand.

Coming off his three-medal performance at the 2008 Olympics in Beijing, U.S. swimmer Jason Lezak was chosen to light the Maccabiah cauldron. Like Lenny Krazyburg in 2001, the thirty-three-year-old Lezak passed up the opportunity to compete at the World Championships to fulfill a dream. "It came to a point where if I'm going to do it, now is the time," he told reporters.

Maccabi USA/Sports enlisted Lezak to help promote the Games to young athletes. "It's something for me to get in touch more with Jewish kids and hopefully inspire them. I really didn't have anyone like that growing up," said Lezak, who was conveniently on hand for his July 15 induction into the International Jewish Hall of Fame at the Wingate Institute in Netanya.[3]

Not all parties continued to be so supportive of the Games. Every four years, you could find reports and commentaries suggesting public support was waning from a increasing number of Israelis who believed there might be more appropriate ways for the government to use its resources than hosting a gigantic party for two weeks.

Ori Lewis, a blogger for Reuters, wrote, "Participants may be offended to hear that many ordinary Israelis care so little about the Maccabiah and that they ask why so much money need be spent on it. But those critics are also largely ignorant of the fact that the participants pay their own way to the tune of thousands of dollars per person.

---

3 "Olympics hero Lezak finally opts for Maccabiah," JTA, July 7, 2009

Indeed, the *Jerusalem Post* said . . . that many potential participants could not afford to join their counterparts and were 'priced out' of the games."[4]

Fortunately for a band of Jewish cricket players from India, a group of Los Angeles businessmen ponied up $125,000 to allow them to compete at the Games. "This is our answer to the murderous rampage against Indian and Israeli citizens," declared Steve Soboroff, founder of the Committee of 18, referring to a series of terrorist attacks in Mumbai the previous November. An assault on the local Chabad house resulted in the deaths of Rabbi Gavriel Holtzberg and his pregnant wife, Rikva, who were killed along with four others in a hostage taking that went tragically wrong.

Once again Israel's leader took the opportunity to invite the athletes to relocate to Israel.

"I thank you for coming. I thank you for participating, but I ask you to do one more thing," said Prime Minister Benjamin Netanyahu. "I ask that you make aliyah, not just for the Maccabiah. Come and be one of us, every day of the year."[5]

To assist in the quadrennial appeal, some fifty volunteer rabbis from Tzohar, a nonprofit organization working to "bridge the gap between religious and secular Jews," were on hand to educate younger athletes from around the world.

The leaders of the group visited with the athletes at hotels and other venues with the aim of "reinforcing Jewish identity and reaffirming the link to Israel," according to Rabbi Ronen Neuwirth, Tzohar's overseas department director.

"According to what Maccabiah organizers are telling us, many participants have no real link to Judaism besides the event, which is less than desirable to us," said Neuwirth.

---

4 "Israel opens 'Jewish Olympics' but interest at home is minimal," July 14, 2009

5 "Lezak lights torch at Maccabiah opening," JTA, July 13, 2009

Tzohar, an organization of some 600 volunteers that was formed in 1995, following the assassination of Yitzhak Rabin, also sent the wives of rabbis to engage youths. Besides English speakers, there were rabbis fluent in Russian, French, Spanish and Portuguese to engage as many visiting athletes as possible.

The biggest question mark hovering over the pilot program, according to Neuwirth, is "whether young, competitive, and medal-oriented athletes will make themselves available emotionally or otherwise to the content that Tzohar's rabbis have to offer."

The message received mixed results. "I will make time for this sort of thing," said fourteen-year-old gymnast Doron Beuns from Holland. Judoka Gili Cohen, seventeen, from Ra'anana said she was open to it "as long as it didn't clash with training."[6]

* * *

You can always count on the real world to subvert the joy of the Games. Just weeks before the Games were to begin, Israeli health officials considered requiring all Maccabiah participants to get tested for swine flu, which was reaching pandemic levels around the world. More than 270 Israelis had been diagnosed with mild cases.

In another troubling situation, international supporters of Gilad Shalit, a young Israeli soldier who had been kidnapped three years earlier and was still held captive by the terrorist organization Hamas, came up with the notion that athletes should wear yellow ribbons as a symbol of solidarity. The U.S. and Great Britain were on board with the idea, but the Maccabiah organizing committee ultimately rejected it.

"With all due respect, we can't take a ceremony that we've worked on for the past two weeks and change it to fit what the Shalit forum wants," said a spokesperson for the committee.[7]

---

6 "Rabbis take act to Maccabiah Games," *Ha'aretz*, June 19, 2009
7 Ibid

Closer to the Maccabiah heart, 400 people attended a memorial service for four Australian athletes who were killed in the bridge collapse during the opening ceremonies in 1997.

Josh Small, like his late father Greg, was a 10-pin bowler. Competing in his first Maccabiah Games, Small spoke at the ceremony.

"I am here, in this place, at this time," he said. "I will finish what you started all those years ago. And I will do my best to win your pride and maybe a medal—further evidence that not even a tragedy of monster proportions can break the bond that will forever exist between us."[8]

Small did not earn a medal for his event, but he did receive an "honorary" gold from the Israeli Bowling Federation engraved with the words, "For the courage to accomplish your father's dream. You deserve the gold." He also received the 18th Maccabiah Games ten-pin bowling sportsman award, dedicated in his father's memory and voted on by the male bowlers.[9]

In another shocking story, Australian table tennis player David Zalcberg was just sixteen when he was among those injured in the bridge accident, breaking both legs. He battled back from those wounds and others he sustained in the intervening years—a prolapsed disc suffered during the 2006 Commonwealth Games and a bicycle accident in 2007 in which he broke his arm in two places—to compete in the Beijing Olympics as well as the 2009 Maccabiah.

Unfortunately, another tragedy cast a pall over these Games when the wife of a Russian judoka athlete fell to her death while hiking in a remote area of Israel. Their teenage daughter was also injured in the incident but was able to recover from her physical injuries.

Little glitches of administrative red tape conspired to make life difficult among the athletes. In one case, the softball games at fields at the Baptist Village near Petach Tikva were cancelled due to improper licensing.[10] After a frenzy of paperwork, the schedule was restored two days later.

---

8 "Memorial held for Australian Maccabiah dead," JTA, July 12, 2009
9 "Bridge victim's son gets honorary Maccabiah Gold," JTA, Aug. 5, 2009
10 "Police shut down Maccabiah softball," JTA, July 14, 2009

Maccabiah Profile: Bruce Pearl, United States, Men's Basketball Coach

In addition to Jason Lezak, Bruce Pearl, the effervescent coach of the Tennessee Volunteers men's basketball program, was another high-profile sports personality lending his expertise to the Games for Team USA.

Though Pearl has been one of the most recognizable names in college basketball over the last twenty years, his was a career that almost never happened.

"I grew up thinking that I would graduate from high school, go to Israel, serve in the army, and get my life started that way," he said. "But when push came to shove, I didn't do it."

Pearl said he first heard about the Maccabiah Games as a high school basketball player in his hometown of Sharon, Massachusetts, "but I probably didn't think I was good enough to make the team, so I didn't try out."

Nevertheless, the Games kept a place in his heart and mind. "I wrote the [Maccabi] leadership, whoever that was back in the day, and introduced myself as either a Stanford assistant [coach] or an Iowa assistant. But I had not accomplished enough to be considered as a coach until I got to Tennessee. Then I finally got through."

Before that, though, Pearl went to Boston College. He toyed with the idea of making aliyah after graduation, but once again, something else came along that he couldn't pass up: the opportunity to work at Stanford. Pearl had been recruited before his senior year to work as an assistant coach to Dr. Tom Davis, under whom he had worked as a student assistant at Boston. Pearl remained with Davis until stepping out on his own, beginning in 1992 with the University of Southern Indiana, a Division II school, where as head coach he posted a record of 231–46 in nine seasons. Subsequently, his Division I teams—the Milwaukee Panthers and the Tennessee Volunteers—won 70 percent of their games and made a combined seven trips to the NCAA tournament in ten years.

Pearl's career hit a bump when he was fired by Tennessee for a number of NCAA infractions. But America is a country of second chances, and he was hired to lead the Auburn Tigers for the 2014 season.

"The idea of going to Israel and representing my country and being able to give the young Jewish men I was able to coach and assemble was the experience of a lifetime," Pearl said. "I was fortunate to grow up with a fairly Conservative religious household. My parents were first-generation [American]; my grandparents were all born in Europe and probably spoke Yiddish better than they spoke English. I had a good, strong foundation of who I was and where I came from.

"One of the things I recognized in our younger people—and I'm probably as much at fault as anybody in our generation—is that we may not wear it on our sleeves as much as we should, we may not go to synagogue as often as we should. My grandparents grew up in a Jewish ghetto. My parents did [too], on Blue Hill Avenue in Dorchester. So the entire time I was coaching, I was so trying to either introduce or reinforce a Jewish life. When [Jewish] student athletes in tryouts came to Knoxville, they went to Shabbat services. At the service, I read from the Torah. I wanted them to see that it was cool to be able to be at the Jewish service and read from the Torah and be a basketball player, a basketball coach . . . I wanted them to be better Jewish men, and someday to be better Jewish fathers."

Altruism aside, Pearl's competitive side burned as brightly as his heritage and he freely admitted that he wanted to win a Maccabiah Gold Medal.

Photo courtesy Bruce Pearl

Bruce Pearl, far right, led the 2009 USA basketball team to a Gold Medal.

"It had been a number of years since the men's open team had won a gold," he said. "I had a couple of guys that had graduated from college and were playing overseas professionally, and some guys that were going to be on the Israeli national team against great coaches as well."

One player in particular stood out for Pearl. "I had a chance to coach Danny Grunfeld." Danny is the son of Ernie Grunfeld, who competed at the 1973 Maccabiah before going on to a career as an NBA player and executive.

"Danny was our best player, our most accomplished player. He was playing professionally overseas but because of his experience in the Maccabiah Games, got great visibility and exposure and got to play in Israel."

Team USA faced the reigning Maccabiah champion Israelis once again in the basketball finals, a tooth-and-claw affair that wound up 79-79 in regulation play, thanks to a basket and a foul shot by Grunfeld with less than 20 seconds left. A missed shot at the buzzer by Avi Ben-Shimol, Israel's leading scorer for the game, resulted in a thrilling overtime with the Americans eventually running away with a nine-point victory, 95-86. Grunfeld scored a team-high 25 points and was named tournament MVP. "Ernie won silver [in the 1970s]," Pearl pointed out. "Danny won gold."

Pearl was used to playing with some of the best college athletes in the United States, if not the world. Nevertheless, he had no illusions that the Maccabiah Games would be a cakewalk, even if the final showdown had been all but preordained by the media. "While the American players are unflinching in their stance to not take any opponent for granted, a final pairing which includes any clubs but the U.S. and Israel would be a monumental upset," wrote Uriel Strum in the *Jerusalem Post* after the Americans obliterated Mexico in the hoops opener, 112-13. The winners chucked in 22 points before their opponent scored their first points.[11]

Pearl was diplomatic. "The level of competition was as tough as I expected it to be. Danny could have played for [the Volunteers]. Todd Golden probably could have played point guard. Zach Rosen could have been a backup. I would say the rest of us were hard-playing, physical over-achievers. My son, Steven, was the sixth man for me on the Maccabiah and he was the eighth man on my roster at Tennessee. So I think they all could have played a role, but the Tennessee teams would have been more physically talented for the most part."

Despite the generally convivial atmosphere and common bonds, Pearl noted, "We competed, once we stepped on the floor. When

---

11 "U.S. destroys Mexico to open hoops campaign," Jerusalem Post, July 15, 2009

we played the team from the Soviet Union, it was a battle. When we played Israel, we were clearly brothers, but we were brothers from another mother on that day. In Israel, their lives are basketball."

Asked to pick which he would rather have, a Maccabiah gold medal or an NCAA championship, Pearl was fairly sensitive. "Competing at the 18th Maccabiah was as meaningful to me as any Elite Eight run in the NCAA tournament. And I've had a few. I would probably trade an NCAA *win* in the tournament for the gold medal. I probably would trade a *league* championship for a gold medal. But a national championship in the NCAA would probably be too much to pass up."

Pearl's first trip was an affair for the whole *mishpucha* (family). "I got to share it with my wife, Brandy, and two of my children, Steven and Jacqui." Steven was on the team and Jacqui was the team manager. Pearl's parents, Bernie and Barbara, also joined in the excitement.

The long-delayed trip to Israel was incredibly emotional for Pearl. "I kissed the ground when I got off the plane. I wanted to go find the trees that I planted every year through Hebrew School." (But of course he couldn't: "There were a lot of trees.")

"I spent four years in California, and Israel—the way it looked, because how hilly it was and next to the Mediterranean—reminded me of California. Living on hillsides and it was obviously beautiful."

At this point in the conversation, Pearl turned from the frivolity and etherealness of sports to the real world. "There were so many families, there, so many children, and young people. What bothered me was [that] Christians, Jews, and Muslims—everybody was just there trying to live and enjoy life and take care of the families, so why can't we all get along? You walk through the marketplace and right now everything is fine, but the minute something happens politically, we become enemies so quickly. It bothered me that somehow, someway we just can't figure out a way to love one another, respect one another, [if] just for the sake of the kids, for the families. Let the children grow up."

Pearl did not hesitate when asked if he feared for his safety while there. "No, never," he said. "They did discourage us from going to Bethlehem. They thought it would be a little bit too dangerous. There was just a little concern for my visibility and exposure," as one of the more-high profile personalities there that year. "But I never felt unsafe at all."

In 2008, Pearl took his Tennessee team on an overseas trip and visited the Terezin concentration camp near Prague. "It's my job as a teacher and a leader to expose our student-athletes, and therefore the rest of the world, to what happened in our lifetime. It was obviously educational and it's important that we never forget. Some were surprisingly less-informed than others and for the life of them couldn't quite grasp why [the Holocaust happened].

"Being a basketball coach, I spent a lot of time fighting for racial equality, and [the trip] allowed me to show some of the African-American players that if they thought they were the only ones affected by discrimination, welcome to *our* world."

Pearl was hit by a strange feeling when they arrived at Dachau. "It was way too clean, way too white, the barracks smelled of fresh wood like when I was in summer camp. When we had been in some work camps in Belgium with my Milwaukee team, they were dirty, they were smelly, they were old, they were original, and that's what I wanted to see; I didn't want to see flowers on windowsills.

"The last thing was when you read the list of the names of the memorial that were on a wall, it just so happens that my family surnames are Rosenberg, Schneider, and Pearlmutter and for some reason, the "p's" and the "r's" and the "s's overlapped on one of the plaques that had three of those four surnames on the wall. They weren't necessarily my relatives, but I bear their name, and it was very emotional."

Maccabiah Profile: Dan Grunfeld, United States, Basketball

Dan Grunfeld already had an extensive resume as a professional before joining the U.S. basketball team in 2009. He was a star at Stanford University and had played professionally in Germany and Spain. He was briefly with the Romanian National Team, but never actually played for them. That was something of an ancestral homecoming: his paternal grandparents emigrated from Romania following World War II.

"I wanted to be a professional basketball player. I would have preferred to play in the NBA, of course." But he suffered a knee injury while in college, which set back his timetable and made NBA clubs a bit wary. Grunfeld was invited to training camp with the New York Knicks, with whom his father had played for four seasons in the 1980s, but was cut before the season started and returned to Europe.

"When I graduated, my best option was to go over to Germany and I had never been to Europe . . . I just found it to be not only a great place to play basketball but a great place to live. I really grew as a person, being overseas."

"My parents were very supportive of me whatever I wanted to do," he said. Although his father never pushed, young Dan gravitated towards the game. "He never coached any of my teams, but on the weekend we would play each other." Father and son would shoot around on a side court at Madison Square Garden, where Dan would absorb the information after regular practice.

"I was that kid rebounding before the game, buzzing around the locker room, slapping five with the players . . . . It was a fun experience for a kid, but also just being around the game so much, I learned a ton, seeing things at a young age. A lot of kids didn't have that opportunity, so I'm grateful and I cherish those times."

Dan Grunfeld knew his father had played in the Maccabiah in 1973. "He loved his time spent there and spoke very highly of it," Dan said. "It's nice for us to be able to share that kind of experience of playing in the Maccabiah Games.

"It was something that was always on my radar screen," he said. His first opportunity could have been in 2005, but the knee injury put that off as he concentrated on the college experience and trying to make it to the next level.

By 2009, Grunfeld already had three years as a professional under his belt. "I was pretty much in the heart of my career and then came a call from Bruce Pearl." The family had a personal relationship with Pearl, stemming back to Milwaukee, where Ernie Grunfeld began his NBA career and Dan attended school with Pearl's kids, including Steve, who would also be a member on that gold-winning team.

"Once I knew Bruce was the coach, I was in," Grunfeld said. "It was really that simple. It wasn't much of a recruitment process."

Another inducement was the chance to visit Israel for the first time. Grunfeld had an opportunity while in college, but Israel was engaged in yet another conflict with Lebanon so the trip was put off for the time being.

The Grunfelds have a lot of family in Israel, offering a bit of a comfort factor. "I definitely knew I had people who would support me should I need it, give me the lay of the land, so I do think that was a benefit."

Like his father, Dan characterized Jewish life at home in terms of the cultural if not the ritual aspects: "Being Jewish is definitely important to us." Grunfeld decided at an early age that he wanted to attend Stanford, in part because his grandmother lived nearby. "She never missed a game when I was in college, came to campus every Sunday, and, of course, brought me food . . .

"That story of being a Holocaust survivor, coming to the United States, making a new life for yourself, it's very important to my family," he said, pointing out that his father was also an immigrant.

Grunfeld participated in the communal Bar Mitzvah that has become a highlight of the cultural component of the Games. "There was so much about the Maccabiah Games that was special," he said. "For us, we were lucky because we won the gold medal in dramatic fashion against Israel. It's a great achievement, but the off-the-court stuff is probably/even more special."

There was no one site that Grunfeld could recall as particular standing out in his Maccabiah experience. For him, it was just the simple pleasures of hanging out with his teammates, having dinner on the beach, and marveling that they were in Israel, their ancestral homeland.

"Growing up in the U.S., all you know about Israel is what you hear on the news. Even for someone who has family there, it's hard to escape that perception. And so there's something really amazing about getting there and realizing not only is this a safe place to be, but this is a wonderful, amazing place to be. There's concern before you get there, but once you're there . . . you feel at ease."

Grunfeld felt so at ease, in fact, that he made Aliyah in 2010, play-ing for several teams over the next four years before returning to the United States in 2014. He now works for NBA Entertainment. "I felt in my heart it was the right time to move to something else."

Grunfeld compared the security at the Maccabiah with trips to other areas around the world. "It's in everyone's best interest to be dili-gent and know your surroundings. There *are* security concerns in Israel and the surrounding areas, and there are areas you probably should not go and we were probably made aware of that, but at the same time, we didn't have a ton of freedom. It's not like we had cars and a ton of free time to buzz around the country alone." Grunfeld's assessment of the competition was similar to Coach Pearl's. "It's all relative, right? I can't say it was like the PAC-10 . . . but at the same time, it was certainly good competition. You look at Israel's team, all those guys are pros. [And] that's who we beat for the gold medal. There were some teams that were probably not as strong, but once you got to the medal round, you were playing against pro players."

Like many Maccabiah alumni, Grunfeld does not maintain an offi-cial connection with the national organization, but is willing to help out when called.

"I still have a relationship with the people," he said. "I really appre-ciate all of them and what they did for me. I'm a supporter of the organization always. If they need anything from me I'm always there to help and be involved. For me, the Maccabiah Games was almost a life-changing experience. I had never been to Israel and that's really a formative place in my family's history and then a springboard for me to play four years there and live there with my wife. So we're always a friend of the program."

There's obviously a lot of love and pride shared by father and son, but that doesn't mean Grunfeld, the younger, is above a little good-natured ribbing when he points out that his team won a gold medal while Ernie's won silver. "He then has the trump card because he won an Olympic gold medal," Dan acknowledged.

When I pointed out that the Olympics have been going on longer, and that a gold medal there is more of a rare commodity, Dan Grun-feld agreed.

"Yeah, there you go, I'll use that."

* * *

For every rookie to the Games like Pearl and Grunfeld (see sidebars), there are veterans who keep coming back, such as Mim Chappell-Eber, making her fourth appearance as part of the women's field hockey team.

Like Pearl, Chappell-Eber had the joyful experience of coaching her own child on the squad: Ariel Eber was the goalie for the 2009 team.

"Representing the country with her was a great bonding experience," Chappell-Eber told the JTA. "It's not often you get to coach your children in a setting like that, representing your country."

The coach, then fifty-four, had converted to Judaism at the age of twenty-seven. "You go to the Maccabiah Games . . . you don't see the Ashkenazi Jews you see in America," she said. "Indians, South Americans—every country that has Jews in it, they're all there."

Chappell-Eber also pointed out another distinction that apparently made no difference in Israel. "Me being a black American and being a little different from Jewish white America, it's great to see the differences. So often in the United States, you just think of one type of Jew.

"Near Netanya where we stay, you tell them you're with the Maccabiah, they get so excited, they don't care what color you are." [12]

Maccabiah Profile: Gregg Sulkin, Great Britain, Soccer

British heartthrob and soccer enthusiast Gregg Sulkin was perhaps just as famous for being Miley Cyrus's boyfriend as an actor in his own right, with television credits that include *The Wizards of Waverly Place* and *Pretty Little Liars*. (The title of a *Jweekly* article carried the headline, "Miley Cyrus' boyfriend kicks around Israel.") Sulkin had missed almost a year on the pitch due to injury. He told the media, "The first time I played since my injury was at the trial

---

12 "Field hockey family affair," JTA, July 6, 2009

for Maccabiah, so I was happy I didn't really lose my touch. Obviously I was a bit rusty, but I still hadn't lost it completely."[13]

Sulkin had been in Israel four years earlier, where he celebrated his Bar Mitzvah in a ceremony at the Western Wall. The experience had a lasting effect.

Though you wouldn't think someone as busy as Sulkin could find time to participate in the Games, he seemed to figure it out.

"I heard about them through my father. He always wanted me to participate if I was good enough. There were hundreds who tried out [for the team]." As one could imagine, his celebrity didn't make much of an impression on his teammates. He had to prove he belonged and wasn't just there based on his status. "I'm still good friends with them. We had a great group of talented boys and we all got on very well. Of course, we had a lot of banter. We are from the UK after all."

If not for acting, Sulkin may well have been a professional soccer player. "I've been kicking the ball since I was four years old. Soccer came first, [and] *then* I got into acting," said Sulkin, who described himself as a "massive" avid fan of Arsenal F.C.

Sulkin, who was a starter on the British team, played several positions, including center, midfield, and right back. "I am more of a passer and reader of the game," he said. The Maccabiah was his first taste of international competition and he "loved every second of it."

"It was amazing. Very loud, and a great honor to walk out in front of 80,000 people representing your country," he said, describing the opening ceremonies. "It's tough to describe how special they were. I learned so much about myself, Israel, teamwork, etc. I was thrilled I got to participate."

A lad of his generation was all in to share the experience via social media. "I use Instagram, Twitter, and Facebook. I'm an actor, after all; I sort of have to! It's so easy to connect with friends on the Internet these days."

---

13 jweekly.com/article/full/39367/miley-cyrus-boyfriend-kicks-around-israel/ (July 23, 2009)

Although the fact that Great Britain did not win a medal at the Games may have been a disappointment, Sulkin said he "was simply thrilled to be a part of it all." He would love the chance to compete again at the 2017 Games, but doesn't think his busy schedule will allow a return trip. "If I did have time, 100 percent. But I'm 95 percent sure I won't have that time."

* * *

Among the highlights and oddities at the 18th Games:

Jason Lezak won individual medals in the men's 50- and 100-meter freestyles (both gold) and two more as a member of the 4x100-meter freestyle and medley relay quartets. Teammate Andrew Lagenfeld also impressed, winning silver in the 100-meter butterfly, bronze in the 200-meter butterfly, and bronze in the 50-meter freestyle. Israel's Nimrod Hayet won medals in the 100- and 200-meter butterfly and 200- and 400-meter individual medley as well. In the women's pool, Efrat Rotsztein, another Israeli, won four medals.

There was such a poor turnout for men's gymnastics that the open and junior events were combined. Alexander Shatilov made Israel proud by winning four gold medals (all-around, floor, pommel horse, and parallel bars) and a bronze (high bar). His total was matched by David Sender, an American, who won gold in high bar, rings, and vaults, and silver in all-around and the horse. Only four other American gymnasts have earned five or more gold medals in a single Games: Abie Grossfeld (seven gold medals in 1953), Mitch Gaylord (six golds and a silver in 1981), Sharon Shapiro (five gold medals in 1977), and rhythmic gymnast Tamara Levinson (five gold medals in 1993).

The closing ceremony was held in Latrun, a hilltop overlooking Tel Aviv. More than 11,000 athletes and fans packed the amphitheater to hear compliments, farewell speeches, and invitations to make aliyah and return in 2013.

Once again, Israel overwhelmed the competition when the nearly 1,250 medals were tallied. The totals provided by the media included all categories, not just the open. Israel won more than half of the awards (628), including 239 golds, 216 silvers, and 173 bronzes. The United States was far behind with 255 (84/92/79), followed by Australia with 60 and Russia with 57.

Normally, the Israeli press would wait for the Games to be over before offering their observations. This time, it came in the middle.

A reporter covering the women's swimming noticed that there were only two teams competing for one of the relay events. "No one would win a bronze medal, but at least silver was guaranteed," quipped Jeremy Last.

While some of his colleagues had questioned whether the Games were still relevant—certainly the Maccabiahs were no indication of the best Jewish athletes in the world—Last was philosophical rather than critical when he wrote, "The main focus of the entire two-week event is on Jewish unity first and foremost" while suggesting that most of the athletes' results were more comparable to the "community pride of a local soccer tournament rather than the aura of grandeur at the Olympics."

"This is nothing to be worried about, and it should really be celebrated," he wrote.[14]

---

14 "The truth about the Maccabiah Games," *Jerusalem Post*, July 17, 2009

Chapter 20

The Nineteenth Games
July 18-30, 2013

"The Maccabiah is an extraordinary event which brings together Jews from across the world," Netanyahu said. "Only in the Maccabiah can a 13-year-old Jewish swimmer from Brazil meet an 88-year-old Jewish tennis player from South Africa. The Maccabiah reminds us that we are all one people. The Games symbolize the special spirit of our people that overcame every obstacle to found the State of Israel."

Israeli Prime Minister Benjamin Netanyahu[1]

---

1 "Israel welcomes the world in style. 19th Maccabiah Games open with sensational show, meaningful moments at Jerusalem's Teddy Stadium," *Jerusalem Post*, July 19, 2013

"We have come from different places, but we belong to the same family."

Israeli President Shimon Peres[2]

In honor of the Games' 80th anniversary, *The Jerusalem Post*—which was celebrating the same milestone—made its pick of the top five athletes of all time, who "symbolize what the Maccabiah is all about."[3] The list included:

* Jason Lezak, swimming, "one of those renowned athletes who took part in the Maccabiah in 2009, not due to its significance in the world of sports, but rather because of its illustrious Zionist history."
* Ben Helfgott, weightlifting, "one of only two known athletes to have survived a concentration camp and gone on to compete in the Olympics."
* Tal Brody, basketball, who "fell in love with Israel during his stay for the Maccabiah and has since earned an iconic status in the country."
* Agnes Keleti, a 10-time Olympic gymnastics medalist who came to the 1957 Maccabiah with her "legendary status long secured."
* Mark Spitz, who presaged his Olympic swimming talents when he made his international debut at the age of fifteen at the 1965 Games, winning four medals. He added six more gold to his collection at the 1969 Games.[4]

In one of the more controversial moves, Maccabi Australia decided it would accept non-Jews to participate in some of their events, although not the Maccabiah Games themselves. If nothing else, this gave those athletes who would be at the 19th Games the opportunity to practice

---

2 "Crowd of 30,000 Greets Opening of Maccabiah Games," The Jewish Chronicle Online, July 19, 2013 (thejc.com/sport/sport-news/109633/crowd-30000-greets-opening-maccabiah-games)
3 "80 years, 18 Maccabiah Games, thousands of dreams come true, millions of souls inspired," *Jerusalem Post*, December 12, 2012
4 Ibid

their sports that might otherwise have been abandoned by a lack of Jewish practitioners.

"If you live in a community where you're only 0.5 percent of the population and you resent being discriminated against, you can't discriminate against others," said Rabbi John Levi of the Executive Council of Australian Jewry.[5]

Historically, there has always been some glitch to work out at the Maccabiah, whether it was a track that wasn't quite ready, not enough room at athlete housing, or the banning of one nation or another. This time, it was a strike by workers at Israel's Foreign Ministry department, which threatened to create a red-tape nightmare that would prevent a number of athletes, primarily from the smaller delegations, from obtaining the proper paperwork that would allow them into the country to compete.[6]

Maccabi World Union CEO Eyal Tiberger asked the government workers to make an exception, appealing to a sense of fair play. Many of the athletes had been training and already had their tickets and other arrangements made. The workers' union basically said tough luck. They would provide services again "when the Finance Ministry decides to sit down for proper talks and negotiations."[7]

One of the real feel-good stories of these Games was the return of U.S. softball legend Dave Blackburn, the sole American player to be inducted into the Israel Softball Hall of Fame.

The Bunyanesque figure had led the U.S. men's softball team to Maccabiah glory for six Games as the prominent pitcher in the sport beginning in 1985, then serving as coach until 2009. The following year, while driving with teammates from one of the thousands of games he played over the decades, Blackburn was seriously injured in a horrific car accident. He broke more than two dozen bones, was placed in

5 "Jewish sports teams in Australia to accept non-Jews," JTA, Dec. 4, 2011
6 "Maccabiah athletes may be no-shows due to visa dispute," JTA, July 5, 2013
7 Ibid

a medically-induced coma for two months, and had part of his right leg amputated. Recovery took more than six months.

Blackburn let it be known that he had every intention of returning to the 2013 affair and sure enough, with the support of lots of friends within and outside of Maccabi USA, he was on hand to throw out the first pitch of the softball tournament.

Although he made an inspirational return to the 2013 Games, he died suddenly in May, 2014, of a heart attack at the age of fifty-four.

"He was larger than life: personality, size, and ability," said Jeff Bukantz, United States chair of the Games in 2013.

Bukantz called Blackburn one of his best friends since they day they met during orientation prior to the 1985 Games.

"I was on the [pay] phone with my wife, about to say goodbye for seventeen days . . . All of a sudden I see this gigantic guy come out in a pro wrestler's robe and a championship belt. Dave was a softball player, I was a fencer, but here we had something in common because we were both nutty about pro wrestling. So I immediately said to my wife—even though there was no one on line at the time—'sorry, there's a long line here, I gotta go. Love you, goodbye,' and I went over and immediately introduced myself to Dave and wound up spending the night 'til about two in the morning telling wrestling stories in the dorm with him and his softball buddies. It was the most random meeting."

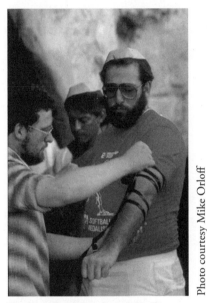

The legendary Maccabiah softball pitcher Dave Blackburn puts on phylacteries at the Western Wall in 1985.

Photo courtesy Mike Orloff

Bukantz has been involved in the Maccabiah since 1981 and aside from his fellow fencers, Blackburn "became my closest friend." Over the years, in addition to their Maccabiah get-togethers, they visited each other's homes in California and New Jersey and remained in frequent contact.

Another thing they had in common: both of their fathers competed at extremely high levels, in fencing and softball. "We always used to talk about the Halls of Fame that our dads were in . . . and how proud we were of them. And after we finished talking about our dads, we said 'Well, what about us? Maybe we could be in some Halls of Fame, too, and follow in our dads' footsteps.' We would talk about that and dream about that."

A few days before the accident, Blackburn called Bukantz to tell him he had been elected to the International Softball Congress Hall of Fame. "I was so happy for him, I said, 'Dave, when is it going to be? Give me the date, I'll be there.'"

Bukantz's voice caught a bit as he recalled the details of the injuries and the healing process. "Here was this guy who was like 6'3", 300 pounds, with calves the size of a world-class weight lifter. The guy was mammoth and all of a sudden here he was, sitting in a wheelchair.

"That was sad, but Dave didn't let you be sad . . . . Whatever was going on inside of him, he kept a stiff upper lip and he was always laughing, whatever sick jokes we were telling."

Bukantz made a decision with Ron Carner, Bob Spivak, and Jed Margolis, the president, chair, and executive director, respectively, of Maccabi USA, before the 2013 Games: "Whatever it takes, we're going to get Dave there. However it is, however much money we have to raise, whatever the logistics, we're gonna get Dave there.

"I think Maccabiah was a huge part of his life," Bukantz said. "We had a three-time rule [limiting athletes to three Maccabiah Games so others can participate]. I think Dave went to six," because of the importance of the pitcher to softball perhaps more than any other position in any other team event. "And Dave was the man, he was always the man, even as he got older . . . , he was still our best guy. He took great pride; he was 'Mr. Maccabiah.'"

Bukantz made Blackburn a banner-bearer for the opening ceremonies. Even though he was in charge of the entire U.S. delegation of more than 1,100 athletes, coaches, assistants, and support staff, "I just went down to the infield and stayed with him almost the whole time because I knew it was an important moment in his life, that he lived to make it to this moment, and I wanted to spend it with him."

The U.S. won the gold medal at every level of softball during those Games: open, juniors, and masters. "The plan was that when it was [all] over, as they're giving the medals out, all the teams would come out, and from each country, everyone who had the number seven would take their [jersey] off and give it to Dave because they were retiring his number . . . ," Bukantz said.

"You wish you could rewrite history," Bukantz said. "But if you had to do it over again, you couldn't write a better farewell than that one night. It was really something else."

* * *

The longer Maccabiah Games were held, the more they resembled a pop festival. The opening ceremonies of the 2013 Games featured performances by pop Israeli music stars Rami Kleinstein and Harel Skaat, Carly Rose Sonenclar (a fourteen-year-old *X Factor* finalist), and hip-hop violinist Miri Ben-Ari. Aly Raisman, the petite heroine of the U.S. women's 2012 gymnastics team, ignited the Maccabiah cauldron at Teddy Kollek Stadium in front of an estimated crowd of 30,000. In addition, 9,000 athletes and delegation members from more than seventy countries—fourteen making their Maccabiah debuts—were on hand before taking part in thirty-four sports, including the implausible ice hockey, which returned after an absence of sixteen years.

Israel's contribution to the competition was 3,000 juniors, seniors, open, and para-athletes. The United States supplied 1,200, a third more than had come to the Intifada Games. Albania, Armenia, Aruba, Bahamas, Bosnia-Herzegovina, Cuba, Curacao, Ecuador, Guinea-Bissau, Honduras, Mauritius, Mongolia, Nicaragua, and Suriname were among those nations attending the Games for the first time.

This represented the first time that Cuba would be participating as a national entity; individual athletes had appeared over the years. Naturally, this was the subject of numerous storylines and articles, describing the challenges of putting together a delegation from the handful of qualified Jewish athletes in that communist country. JLTV aired a profile piece on Rafael and Roxana Gonzales, brother and sister, who comprised Cuba's archery team and two of the twenty-six Jewish residents in the town of Cienfuegos.

Jewish Learning TV carried the opening ceremonies live, allowing its viewers to see the spectacle of the athletes marching into Teddy Stadium. Of course, there were plenty of interviews from the sideline reporters both in the stands and walking alongside the ecstatic athletes during their march in.

In fact, JLTV did an outstanding job of bringing little-known countries and sports to the attention of the rest of the world. There are Jews in Guinea-Bissau? Where the heck *is* Guinea-Bissau? And what the heck are futsal and netball? (The basketball team from Guinea-Bissau lost their first game to Australia, 89-45; they earned $10 for each point they scored towards donations to support the fight against Malaria in western Africa.[8])

With social media becoming a larger part of the lives of people of all ages, many athletes took to posting their experiences via Instagram, Flickr, Twitter, and similar sites. Savvy national Maccabi groups set up Facebook pages where they could offer supporters the latest news and images, as well as adding information to their individual websites. Chloe Rothman, a women's basketball player at Merrimack College in North Andover, Massachusetts, for example, kept a blog about her experience for the school's website. Brie Lizmi, a triathlete from the Washington, D.C., area, posted about her personal triumphs and disappointments (a common theme regarding the organization of many events at the Games) on her own blog, supplemented with Tweets.

Shimon Peres officially opened the Games. President Barack Obama greeted the Maccabiah through a prerecorded video, as did Prime Minister David Cameron. During the parade of nations, giant helium

---

8 "Israel medals in rugby; USA, South Africa grab golds," *Jerusalem Post*, July 22, 2013

balloons bearing the name of each country preceded that nation's delegation.

Obama went first:

> Hi, everybody.
>
> Today's opening ceremony of the 19th Maccabiah Games is a great reminder of the power of sports to bring people together and inspire the best in all of us. It's also a celebration of the deep friendship among the competing nations, especially the unbreakable bond between Israel and the United States. In that spirit, I want to wish my good friend, President Shimon Peres, a very happy 90th birthday. He's an example of vitality and dedication to all of us and his legacy embodies the essence of these games.
>
> So to all the athletes who are about to take the field, the court, or the pool, good luck. And to everyone on Team USA, we're cheering for you and can't wait to see what you all accomplish.

Cameron echoed Obama's remarks, tossing in a reminder of the role his country had played in the most recent Olympics:

> Hi, Everyone.
>
> It's great to speak to you on this very special day.
>
> The Maccabiah Games are a tremendous force for good, bringing Jewish people together from across the world.
>
> Originally the idea of Joseph Yekutieli, a fifteen-year old boy, these Games have grown into a huge sporting celebration with athletes from over fifty nations across the globe taking part. While the competition over these next thirteen days will be fierce, the spirit of friendship will reign supreme. Because as we saw in the Olympics in Britain last year, sports has a unique power to bring people together, to strengthen harmony between nations, and to promote the values of peace.

I send my warmest regards to President Peres, Prime Minister Netanyahu, and all of the Israeli people, and to the 420 men, women, and children, who make up Maccabi GB, I say this: Do your country proud, and bring home the medals for Britain. Every best wish for a successful Game.

In an example of how "you can't please everyone," some members of the media pointedly commented that Obama had slighted Netanyahu. Dr. Aaron Lerner, director of the Israel-based Independent Media Review & Analysis organization, blogged the next day, "In a break from protocol, President Obama declined to mention Prime Minister Netanyahu in his recorded remarks for the opening ceremony last night of the Maccabiah Games in Jerusalem. Instead Mr. Obama wished President Shimon Peres another happy birthday. . . . "

Lerner also pointed out that Obama's remarks were followed by "greetings of the UK PM that, following protocol, do greet PM Netanyahu."[9]

Coincidentally, the opening ceremony took place on Nelson Mandela's birthday. The South African delegation carried with them a large banner reading: "Celebrating our legacy—Mandela Day."

According to a report on the Israel21c website, Maccabiah Chairman Amir Peled said that approximately 70 percent of the 9,000 visitors that summer were in Israel for the first time.

"I want them to have the best summer of their life—two weeks to experience, a lifetime to remember," says Peled.

"They are here for sports and I wish all of them success," he continued. "But they are also here for Jewish identity and education and Zionism, so I hope they leave here with a deep love of Israel. And if the outcome will be that they come again, to study or live, or even if they just enjoy following Israeli sports teams, I will be more than happy."[10]

---

9 "President Obama Slights Netanyahu in Remarks for Maccabiah Opening," imra.org.il/story.php3?id=61546

10 "Let the Maccabiah games Begin!" israel21c.org/culture/let-the-maccabiah-games-begin/

In one of the more unusual "connections," Amar'e Stoudemire, the 6'10", Ft. Wales, Florida-born NBA star, was named the assistant coach for Team Canada. Stoudemire had "discovered" he had Jewish roots on his mother's side and had become enamored of Israel, made several trips there, appeared on the Israeli version of *Sesame Street*, and even having his wedding performed under a chuppah, the Jewish wedding canopy.

"It was a bit of a dream scenario to reach out to Amar'e because of his discovering his Jewish roots and his playing basketball," Alex Brainis, the head of Maccabi Canada's delegation, said. "We figured that if he said yes, this would be a big recruiting tool."[11]

Maccabiah Profile: John Dore, Canada, Basketball

Originally from Queens, New York, John Dore, sixty-two, came to Concordia University in Montreal, Quebec, after an unsatisfying year playing basketball and baseball at a school in southern Georgia. He liked Montreal so much that he stayed there, working in coaching and educational positions at various levels of schools.

Dore is one of the few non-Jews involved in the Maccabi movement. "I was married to a Jew for many years," he said, invoking the "some of my best friends are Jewish" line.

Dore was set to serve as an assistant coach for the Canadian men's basketball team in 1993, but that fell through. He was asked to be the head coach four years later and enjoyed immediate success, winning the gold medal, the first time another country other than the United States or Israel had pulled that off.

"I made a lot of friends over there, I have a lot of friends in the United States," including Herb Brown, coach of Team USA, Dore asserted. "We actually shared scouting reports because we were on opposite sides of the [competition's divisional setup]."

---

11 "Knicks player to help coach Israel games," *Pittsburgh Post-Gazette*, April 12, 2013

Dore has coached the Canadian team ever since.

"I knew the basketball was pretty good [in Israel]," he had experience against the Israeli team at various international tournaments.

Dore brought the Concordia team to the second Friendship Games, which were held in Israel in 2007. To help finance the trip, Dore agreed to hold several basketball clinics in Israel with his team.

Dore has witnessed a lot of changes over the years.

"In '97, the year the bridge collapsed, there were a lot more basketball teams. Maybe sixteen, seventeen teams at that time. And the number has gone down. In 2001, it was the Intifada, so there was about eight or nine teams then. Last time, I don't remember how many teams there were, but the numbers were down. I think it has to do primarily with the cost. You want to have the best players there and if you don't get a sponsor, it's very costly."

The level of competition at the Games compared with the teams in the Quebec Conference—which consisted mostly of local schools in Montreal and other cities in Canada and the United States—was high, said Dore. "A lot of people think everything south of the border is better, which is not necessarily true. But they just look at it that way. The shopping is better, the gas is cheaper, Florida is warmer. I think in the U.S., they just do a much better job of marketing and selling and promoting their sport than we do here in Canada."

For the 2013 Games, Dore had an assistant coach who would bring a lot of attention to the Canadian team.

"I was involved with the [New York] Knicks as a consultant, so I had access to Amar'e [Stoudemire]." Dore queried Glen Grunwald, the team's general manager, to ask the six-time All-Star forward/center if he would be interested in coaching with him.

Dore made this request based on Stoudemire's disclosure in 2010 that he had Jewish roots.

"It just so happened [the Knicks] were in the playoffs at the time and I went in and spoke to Amar'e and he said, 'yeah, I'd be interested.'

"We started talking about it and the Maccabiah Games and what it meant—the Jewish Olympics. I didn't realize how big it was going to be to have him there. His personality, his commitment to Israel . . . He was a major, major celebrity over there."

The NBA veteran gave the Canadian team, as well as the Macca-biah Games as a whole, a wider brand of credibility. "That I was able to steal him away from the States was a little coup for Canada," he said.

Stoudemire "was great with the guys," Dore said. "He got better as coach as we went along. The commitment to coach is different than as a player. You have to study a little but more, you have to scout."

Dore credited his high-profile assistant as being "great with the kids and great with the people of Israel. Because of him, I got to go to Shimon Peres's house,"

Asked if Dore had been concerned about taking a team to the 2001 Games during the Intifada, the question was barely offered when he replied "No."

"I actually tried to speak to some people about going there during the Intifada. I was going; I felt very comfortable going. I feel very safe in Israel. As a mater of fact, at that time we had about a half-dozen kids on the team who had not seen the Wall and for some reason we were not going to get to the Wall. So we were down at Sultan's Pool in Jerusalem and I took the kids myself and walked through five different check-points to bring these kids to the Wall. There was an Israeli solder who was a captain in the army and he came up to me and hugged me and was crying and he thanked me for coming . . . . It was a really moving experience for me. But I wanted the kids to see [it]. I thought it was really important."

Even though Dore never converted to Judaism, he attended a mass Bar Mitzvah ceremony during one of the Games as a symbolic gesture of solidarity.

Even as a non-Jew, Dore understood the importance of the Games. "The Games bring . . . Jews from throughout the world together. I think in the age of the Internet and social media, the world is a much closer place. We've had players in Canada go out with players from South Africa, Australia . . . . An Australian therapist married a guy from Montreal. The world is a small place; it should be open to everybody. The more people we can touch, the more we can learn about each other."

Dore was set to retire from Concordia after the spring 2015 semester. Perhaps he'd consider a coaching job in Israel.

* * *

The smallest piece of equipment got the biggest helping hand when shoe designer Stuart Weitzman donated $1 million to help fund the U.S. table tennis team.

Weitzman, who was a member of the 2009 team, told the media through a statement, "After experiencing the Games myself, I saw how Maccabi USA changes the lives of athletes by enhancing their connection to their Jewish culture and heritage."[12]

The gift, made through the Weitzman Family Foundation, represented the largest single contribution in the history of Maccabi USA.

Weitzman first got involved with Maccabi USA as a member of the Masters Table Tennis team at the 18th Maccabiah Games in 2009. "My participation in the Maccabiah Games was one of the greatest experiences of my life," he stated. "After experiencing the Games myself, I saw how Maccabi USA changes the lives of the athletes by enhancing their connection to their Jewish culture and heritage. I knew that I had to support the work they do so future Jewish athletes can participate in this life-changing event and feel a strong connection to the State of Israel."

He expressed his hope that "this gift spurs other individuals and foundations to support Maccabi USA and the important work they do with similar gifts."

Ron Carner was dumbfounded by Weitzman's generosity and by the fact that he didn't just make a pledge, but actually wrote a check on the spot.[13]

12 "Show bigwig Stuart Weitzman gifts $1 million to Maccabi USA," JTA, Feb. 21, 2014
13 "A Sporting Chance," *Jerusalem Post*, April 19, 2013

Maccabiah Profile: Ron Carner, United States, President

Ron Carner, seventy-six, was elected as president of Maccabi USA in 2009 and reelected in 2014. He has been involved with the organization in various capacities for more than thirty years. In 2009, he became only the fifth North American to receive the Yakir Award, the Maccabi World Union's highest honor, presented every four years in recognition of exceptional activists' dedication to the Maccabi Movement.

With the U.S. the largest foreign delegation by far attending the Games, the work is pretty much non-stop. At our conversation in late 2014, Carner said he expected work on the 2017 Games to get underway shortly after the beginning of the 2015 New Year, even though there are other Maccabi projects scheduled before then, including the Maccabi Pan American and European Games.

Carner said he had been vaguely aware of the Maccabiahs when he was a student and knew a few people who went, but hadn't been involved . . . yet. It just wasn't on his radar at that time.

Post-graduation, he enjoyed a career as a successful lawyer. "In the mid-80s, I said to my wife, things are good; it's time to give back." He examined where his interests lay: Jewish kids and sports, and the State of Israel. So what could be more natural than getting involved with the Maccabiah movement?

His first role in the organization came in the 1987 Pan-Am Games as chair of the men's open basketball team. The responsibilities are quite different for the chair of a committee for an individual sport than president of the whole shebang.

"First and foremost, you have to secure a coach," Carner explained. "The U.S. has had some of the best, including Dolph Schayes. Dolph has a really great Jewish heart. He understands exactly what the program is about; it's much more than just sports. And he loves the idea of giving back, to that extent. Of living his basketball life over again.

"For the last Maccabiah, Brad Greenberg was our coach. Greenberg had been a coach of the year in Israel for his work with Maccabi Haifa in 2012. For Maccabiah in '09, Bruce Pearl was our coach."

Like the players, the coaches come to the Games as volunteers. "They don't get paid," Carner corroborated, "and to a degree, it costs them. Everyone who participates in the Maccabiah raises or pays a certain percentage of the actual costs. It depends on who they are and what they're doing. Even the coaches; even a Bruce Pearl had to raise or pay X amount of dollars."

While getting a high-profile coach like Schayes or Pearl is a feather in the cap for the Maccabiah, the reverse is true as well, said Carner. "It's a feather in their cap, too. They fight like crazy for it. Some of them want to come back but we tell them we want to give someone else the opportunity."

Carner said it cost about $10 million to get the U.S. team to Israel for the 2013 event. "Our subsidies are about $2.5 million." The four-year cycle, he said, costs about $17-18 million and is run by a small full-time staff that operates out of Philadelphia.

Where does all that money come from? "I'd like to say begging. We're out there asking. A very important part of that money comes from the participation of our Masters athletes for the Maccabiah. They have to pay the full cost, plus they have to donate to the organization." That money, however, doesn't necessarily have to come out of their own pockets, but through various fundraising methods such as raffles or dinners.

"It's a Jewish event and sports is the hook," Carner said. "I learned through my years of involvement that sports is an *amazing* hook and so much can be done through sports and it's so exciting that you can reach so many people in so many different ways, through the medium of sports."

"[It's] hugely gratifying, that's what it's about. Yes, but the credibility of the sports program is extremely important in order to be able to verify the whole experience. Meaning, we take the best athletes we can find." Even if that means losing donations from some wealthy patron who wants to play or have their kids or grandkids play?

"Am I going to step in? Absolutely not." Carner likes to joke: "We had 3,000 applicants for the USA team, and we took a team of 1,100. That means we had 1,900 lawsuits."

The 2013 Maccabiah was a huge success, but Carner has been through some lean times, too. The *tsuris* he had from the 2001 Games, he said, "took five years off my life."

"Let's say the team was leaving July 10 [2001]—I can't remember the exact date. On June 2, we had the bombing of the Dolphonarium. We were having a meeting the day after and the executive committee decided that we would not participate but we were going to wait to announce it until after we had a meeting in Israel. I went to Israel with another fellow and the decision was made that the Games would be cancelled, but we would not announce it for another ten days.

"So we come back to the States and in the meantime there's a telephone conference call with the leadership of Israel, several members of the Knesset and ministers and the USA, and while I'm on the phone, I'm realizing my concern. I was concerned that so many countries were dropping out of it . . . that we wouldn't have a legitimate event.

"Well, my thinking was a little bit skewed at that point. That's why I was negative about going." But after further discussion with the leadership of major American Jewish organizations Carner realized, "There's no way we *can't* go. Even if it's going to be a *balagan* (disorderly mess), and we go to events and a volleyball player would have to play [on the softball team].

"We changed our position, and the USA team went. We *had* to go. This was about the 14th of June and we were leaving in three weeks. Well, you can't imagine what it was to put it together."

Carner said he didn't mind people deciding not to go, but when they started trying to convince others to pull out, that was another story.

"We had so many people that did go, and we had all kinds or problems and issues, but it worked and it was a legitimate Maccabiah and it was wonderful. And thank God we did it, because we wouldn't be where we are today."

"It was amazing. To this day some people don't speak to me because we went, because we jeopardized our team and our athletes.

Bullshit. It wasn't for me to make that decision, it would be for the [Israeli] security people to make that decision. [But they] told us what they were going to do and I felt comfortable with it. And it worked out very well."

Coming on the heels of the 1997 Yarkon Bridge collapse, "You can imagine, two Maccabiahs in a row, we had nothing but aggravation."

Carner believes the Israelis are still thrilled to hold the Games, for a number of reasons, if not the same ones as when they debuted in 1932. Certainly they appreciate the boost to the economy all the tourists bring. "In Israel they have the low season, the high season, and the Maccabiah season."

The headaches are incalculable, but the rewards more than make up for it.

"I hear this so many times . . . 'Best experience of my life.' 'Most important experience of my life.' 'One of the greatest times I've ever had.' I hear it all the time. And it's not just because they had a good time; it's because they learned something, they feel good about certain things, and they understand who we are and what we do and to be a Jew as a nation is important to us."

* * *

Seth Greenberg, head coach of Virginia Tech University, took over the men's basketball reins following the gold-winning success of Bruce Pearl in 2009.

"This volunteer position is important to me because any time you can represent your country and your faith in the same event, it's something very special," he said in a statement after his appointment.[14]

So when it comes to basketball coaches, is there a Maccabiah curse, a la the curse that some allege comes with an appearance on the cover of

---

14 "Virginia Tech's Greenberg tapped to coach Maccabiah basketball team," JTA, April 10, 2012

Sports Illustrated? Both Pearl and Greenberg were dismissed from their college positions after being named head coach of the Jewish hoops squad. While Pearl got the boot for NCAA recruitment rules infractions two years after leading Team USA to a gold medal, Greenberg was let go just weeks after his appointment was announced.[15]

Nevertheless, Greenberg was evidently the right pick to lead the Maccabiah squad. For the second straight event, the U.S. men won gold, beating Argentina, 85-76. Israel took the bronze medal, narrowly outdueling France, 64-62.

Basketball legend Tal Brody blasted the team in the media, calling Israel's performance unacceptable. The former Maccabi USA *and* Israel national team player said that while the tournament was at a very high level, Israel needed to send its best team and help the country's sporting reputation.[16]

The American women also won for the second consecutive Games, easily handling the Israeli team 72-56. Team captain Jacqueline Kalin, who would remain in Israel to play pro ball, scored 22 points to go along with seven assists and six rebounds.

The Canadians won the bronze medal.

At the closing ceremonies—another chance to try to convince the visiting athletes to consider making Aliyah—Jerusalem's Mayor Nir Barkat, along with Omri Casspi, the first Israeli to play in the National Basketball Association, presented the Most Outstanding Athlete award to American swimmers Andrea Murez, who won five gold medals and two silver, and Garrett Weber-Gale, who earned two golds.

Normally the Israeli media (as well as others) offer a review of the Games upon their conclusion. But the general public can't wait that long apparently. Three letters to the editor published in the July 22 *Jerusalem Post* had little nice to say about the opening ceremonies. One writer complained about a photo of the U.S. team appearing on the front page, rather than the Israeli hosts. Another was "disgusted and

---

15 "Has the Maccabiah Games developed an SI jinx? (Or is it us?)," JTA, April 26, 2012

16 "US Dominates the Maccabiah team finals," *Times of Israel*, July 30, 2013

left with a sour taste" by the "rehiring convicted criminals responsible for the 1997 Maccabiah bridge collapse! It displays the nepotism and proteksia [favoritism] that are well-known throughout Israeli society." A third enumerated several complaints that the writer hoped would be addressed for the 2017 event, including a better sound system, better deportment, and marching by the athletes to reduce the time for their entrance. The writer also called for better transportation to and from the stadium, shorter speeches by Israeli dignitaries, and, perhaps most important, cleaner restrooms.[17]

Once again, Israel led the way with the most hardware collected in open events by a large margin, with 461 medals (165 gold, 146 silver, 150 bronze), followed by the United States, with 175 (54, 58, 63).

The Final Medal Count (Gold/Silver/Bronze):[18]

Israel 461 (165/146/150)
USA 175 (54/58/63)
Russia 40 (11/16/13)
Canada 28 (9/8/11)
Australia 17 (4/9/4)
Hungary 15 (3/3/9)
Ukraine 14 (8/4/2)
South Africa 13 (4/2/7)
Brazil 11 (3/3/5)
Mexico 10 (0/3/7)
Argentina 7 (0/5/2)
Georgia 6 (0/3/3)
Great Britain 5 (1/0/4)
France 4 (2/2/0)
Holland 4 (1/1/2)
Azerbaijan 3 (1/0/2)
Cuba 3 (1/1/1/)
Czech Republic 3 (0/2/1)
Latvia 2 (0/1/1)

---

17 "Letters," *Jerusalem Post*, July 22, 2013
18 Maccabiah.com/en/medals-count

Belarus 2 (0/0/2)
German 2 (0/0/2)
Guinea-Bissau 2 (0/0/2)
Chile 1 (1/0/0/)
Uruguay 1 (1/0/0)
Lithuania 1 (0/1/0)
Sweden 1 (0/0/1)
Greece 1 (0/0/1)
Hong Kong 1 (0/0/1)
Italy 1 (0/0/1)
Macedonia 1 (0/0/1)
Norway 1 (0/0/1)

Athletes who won medals in both Olympic and Maccabiah competition

Athlete	Country	Olympics	Sport	Event	Medal	Maccabiah	Sport	Event	Medal
Gerry Ashworth	USA	1964	Track & Field	4 x 100 M Relay	G	1965	Track & Field	100 M	G
Albert Axelrod	USA	1960	Fencing	Foil, Individual	B	1961	Fencing	Foil	B
Isaac Berger	USA	1956	Weightlifting	Featherweight	G	1957		Featherweight	G
		1960		Featherweight	S				
		1964		Featherweight	S				
Mark Berger	Canada	1984	Judo	Heavyweight	B	1985	Judo	> 95 kg.	G
James Bregman	USA	1964	Judo	Middleweight	B	1965	Judo	Middleweight	G
Larry Brown	USA	1964	Basketball	Men's Basketball	G	1961	Basketball	Men's Basketball	G
		1980		(Assistant Coach)					
		2000		(Assistant Coach)					
		2004		(Coach)	B				

(Continued)

Athlete	Country	Olympics	Sport	Event	Medal	Maccabiah	Sport	Event	Medal
Lillian Copeland	USA	1928	Athletics	Discus	S	1935	Track and Field	Discuss	G
		1932		Discus	G			Javelin	G
								Shot Put	G
Yves Dreyfus	France	1956	Fencing	Team Epee	B	1965	Fencing	Epee	S
		1964	Fencing	Team Epee	B				
Mitch Gaylord	USA	1984	Gymnastics	Team All-Around	G	1981	Gymnastics	All-Around	G
				Horse Vault	S			Horse	G
				Parallel Bars	B			Horizontal Bar	G
				Rings	B			Vaults	S
								Parallel Bars	G
								Rings	G
								Floor	G
Brad Gilbert	USA	1988	Tennis	Singles	B	1981		Singles	S

Athlete	Country	Olympics	Sport	Event	Medal	Maccabiah	Sport	Event	Medal
								Men's Doubles	G
Scott Goldblatt	USA	2004	Swimming	2 x 200 M Freestyle Relay	G	2005	Swimming	100 M Freestyle	B
								200 M Freestyle	S
Ernie Grunfeld	USA	1976	Basketball		G	1973		Basketball	S
						1989		Basketball (Coach)	S
Allan Jay	Great Britain	1960	Fencing	Epee Individual	S	1953	Fencing	Foil Individual	G
				Epee Team	S			Foil Team	G
								Foil	G
						1957	Fencing	Epee Individual	G
								Epee Team	G

(Continued)

Athlete	Country	Olympics	Sport	Event	Medal	Maccabiah	Sport	Event	Medal
Lenny Krazylburg	USA	2000	Swimming	100 M Backstroke	G	2001	Swimming	Epee	G
				200 M Backstroke	G			100 M backstroke	G
				4 x 100 M Medley Relay	G				
		2004		100 M Backstroke					
				4 x 100 M Medley Relay	G				
Jason Lezak	USA	2000	Swimming	4 x 100 m Freestyle Relay	S	2009	Swimming	50 M Freestyle	G
				4 x 100 m Medley Relay	G			100 M Freestyle	G
		2004		4 x 100 m Freestyle Relay	B				
				4 x 100 m Medley Relay	G				
		2008		100 m Freestyle	B				

Athlete	Country	Olympics	Sport	Event	Medal	Maccabiah	Sport	Event	Medal
				4 x 100 m Freestyle Relay	G				
				4 x 100 m Medley Relay	G				
		2012		4 x 100 m Freestyle Relay	S				
Mariya Mazina	Russia	1996	Fencing	Team Epee	B	2001	Fencing	Epee	G
		2000			G				
Marilyn Ramenofsky	USA	1964	Swimming	400 M Freestyle	S	1961	Swimming	400 M Freestyle	
						1965		400 M Freestyle	
David Segal	Great Britain	1960	Track & Field	4 x 100 M Relay	B	1961	Track & Field	200 M	G
								400 M	B
								Pole Vault	B
Sergei Sharikov	Russia	1996	Fencing	Sabre Individual	S	2001	Fencing	Sabre	G
				Sabre Team	G				

(Continued)

Athlete	Country	Olympics	Sport	Event	Medal	Maccabiah	Sport	Event	Medal
		2000		Sabre Team	S				
		2004		Sabre Team	B				
Shay Oren Smadja	Israel	1992	Judo	Lieghtweight	B	1989		65 to 71 Kg.	G
Frank Spellman	USA	1948	Weightlifting	Middleweight	G	1950		Middleweight	G
Mark Spitz	USA	1968	Swimming	100 M Freestyle	B	1965	Swimming	400 m Freestyle	G
				4 x 100 M Freestyle Relay	G			1500 M Freestyle	G
				4 x 200 M Freestyle Relay	G			400 M Ind. Medley	G
				100 M Butterfly	S	1965	Swimming	100 M Butterfly	G
		1972		100 M Freestyle	G			100 M Freestyle	G
				200 M Freestyle	G			200 M Freestyle	G
				4 x 100 M Freestyle Relay	G				

Athlete	Country	Olympics	Sport	Event	Medal	Maccabiah	Sport	Event	Medal
				4 x 200 M Freestyle Relay	G				
				100 M Butterfly	G				
				200 M Butterfly	G				
				4 x 100 M Medley Relay	G				
Garrett Weber-Gale	USA	2008	Swimming	4 x 100 M Freestyle Relay	G	2013	Swimming	100 M Free	G
				4 x 100 M Medley Relay	G			50 M sprint	G
Wendy Weinberg	USA	1976	Swimming	800 M Freestyle	B	1977		100 M Butterfly	S
								200 M Butterfly	G
								100 M Freestyle	S
								200 M Freestyle	G

(Continued)

Athlete	Country	Olympics	Sport	Event	Medal	Maccabiah	Sport	Event	Medal
								400 M Freestyle	G
								800 M Freestyle	G
Henry Wittenberg	USA	1948	Wrestling	Light-Heavyweight Freestyle	G	1950	Wrestling	Men's Light-Heavyweight Freestyle	G
		1952		Light-Heavyweight Freestyle	S	1953	Wrestling	Men's Light-Heavyweight Freestyle	G

Note: Medal winners as members of team sports are not listed in Maccabiah results and are therefore absent from this list.

Agnes Keleti (Gymnastics, Hungary, 1952, 1956) and Nicolas Massu (Tennis, Chile, 2004) medaled in their Olympic appearances but not in their Maccabiah Games.

Sources: jewishvirtuallibrary.org/jsource/History/jewishmedalists.html; Maccabi World Union; Sports-Reference.com (Olympic medals)

The Yakir Maccabi Award

First bestowed in 1984, the Yakir Maccabi—the Maccabi World Union's highest honor—is given for lifetime achievement to those aged sixty or older in recognition of their dedication and commitment to the Maccabi movement.

1984

Nahum Heth, Israel
Dr. Robert Atlasz, Israel
Mordechair Ben Dror, Israel
Herman Bochner, Belgium
Eugeen Justice Dayan, Israel
David Gluck, Sweden
Nat Holman, United States
Leon Kaplun, Chile
Dr. Alexander Rosenfeld, Israel
Lionel Schality, Great Britain
Haim Wein, Israel

Arthur Haank, Israel
Joel Haskel, Belgium
Benno Hess, Holand
Ian Maltz, South Africa
Rivka Netanel, Israel
Aron Netanel, Israel
Fred Oberlander, Canada
Massimo Della Pergola, Italy
Joe Rosen, Israel
Dr. Emmanuel Simon,
    Israel
Avraham Tory, Israel

1985

Pierre Gildesgame, Great Britain
Isaac Fisher, Brazil
George Flesh, Israel
Manusia Gildesgame, Great
    Britain (Special Award)
Ken Gradon, Great Britain
Theo Haas, France

1986

Moshe Edelstein, Israel
Avraham Fieger, Israel
Carlos Fishbein, Mexico
Louis Gecelter, Israel
Lou Rose, MBE, Australia
Moshe Tov, Argentina
Fred S. Worms, Great Britain

1989

Israel Ben Nun, Israel
Benny Guggenheim, Sweden
Miguel (Mechel) Grynblat,
    Argentina
Herman Deutch, Israel
Yehoshua Hadari, Israel
Shalom Zysman, Israel
Harold Zimman, United Stated
Haim Cahanov, Israel
Erich Sinai, Austria
Alex Fisher, Canada
Dr. Israel Peled, Israel
Dr. Shimon Kotliar, Argentina
Berny Kellen, South Africa
Eric Rayman, Great Britain

1991

Yehoshua Aluf, Israel
Moshe Gradinger, Israel
Werner Gronwitz, Sweden
Mordehai Yampolsky, Israel
Adolfo Mogilevsky, Argentina
Monty Manoim, South Africa
Menachem Novitz, Israel
Salomon Fuchs, Israel
Harry Shapiro, Great Britain

1993

Sam Bulka, Great Britain
Moshe Gitlin, Mexico
George Horn, Holland
Wolfgan Wronkow, Sweden
Itzhak Caspi, Israel
Abe Luxenberg, Canada

Azrikam Milchen, Israel
Julio Pinco, Argentina
Yoshua Kipnis, Mexico
Rivka Rabinowitz,
    Israel

1997

Yitzchak Braz, Israel
Lionel Davidson, Great Britain
Mauricio "Tata" Furmanski,
    Israel
Jose Furmanski, Argentina
Michael Kevehazi, Israel
George Mendelosohn, South
    Africa
Moises Schnaider, Brazil
Max Sheldon, United States
Moshe Soloducho, Uruguay
Richard Urban, Great Britain
Julio Yasiniovsky, Israel

2001

Rina Carmeli, Israel
Arieh Cohen, Israel
Rami Horwitz, Israel
Juan Imel, Argentina
Dov Levin, Israel
Elias London, Mexico
Jacob Nabel, Argentina
Juan Ofman, Argentina
Moshe Resch, Israel
Roy Salomon, Canada
Robert Spivak, United States
Jacques Springer, Holland
Zvi Warshaviak, Israel

2005

Bernie Offstein, Canada
Jose Burstein, Argentina
Bob Glatter, Great Britain
Moises Weinstock, Mexico
Mary Luxenberg, Canada
Uzi Netanel, Israel
Shmuel Ezrati, Israel
Louis Platus, Australia
Leo Kowarsky, Israel
Marcel Koster, Holand
Alan Sherman, United States

2009

Ron Carner, United States
Jeanne Futeran, South Africa
Ishie Gitlin, Mexico
Bernie Gold, Australia
Michel Grun, Belgium

Marcus Kaplun, Chile
Stuart Lustigman, Great Britain
Gideon Osterer, Germany
Eli Roloff, Israel
Avi Shur, Israel
Ran Yegnes, Israel

2013 (No country listed)

Adolfo Finkielsztein
David Fleisher
Allen Gerskup
Tom Goldman
Miguel Litchi
Harry Procel
Mervyn Tankelowitz
Jack Terpins
Motti Tichauer
Victor Vaisman
Toni Wortman

Source: Maccabi World Union

Maccabi USA's Legends of the Maccabiah

The Legends of the Maccabiah are individuals who have contributed greatly to Maccabi USA as athletes, volunteers, and supporters. The Legends program is an annual event where the Legends are inducted geographically and recognized at a gala event each fall.

Additionally, Maccabi USA uses the occasion of the Legends of the Maccabiah Gala to recognize an individual who embodies the 'Maccabi Spirit.' By living the values of the Maccabi Movement, this volunteer uses sports as a means to engage Jewish youth to strengthen their connection with their Jewish culture and identity and their support for the State of Israel.

2011
Leland Faust
Ken Flax
Mitch Gaylord
Brad Gilbert
Dana Gilbert
Paul Klapper
Lenny Krayzelburg
Jason Lezak
Wendy Paskin-Jordan
Max Sheldon
Gary Shemano
Bob Sockolov
Mark Spitz

Maccabi Spirit Award Recipient
Peter Pollatt

2012
Jan Albert
Tal Brody
Larry Brown
Suzan and Allen Fox
Joy and Gary Gordon
Iris and Igal Hami
Ira Kamens
Julian Krinsky
Bob Levy
David Micahnick

Mel Miller
Lou Moyerman
Larry Needle
David Pudlin
Sam Rabinowitz
Brian Roberts
Dolph Schayes
Brian "Shifty" Schiff
Larry Shane
Charles M. Shechtman
Robert E. Spivak
William Steerman
Fred Turoff
Rose Weinstein

2013
Alan Albert
Ellen and Simon "Si" Atlas
Mel Chaskin
Jeff Fleishman
Mark and Brent Goldstein
Ernie Grunfeld
Paul "Jacky" Loube
Michael Oren
Jodi and Ricky Reff
Don Spero
Wendy Weinberg Weil

Source: Maccabiusa.com

Maccabiah Interviews

Carol Benjamin, Nov. 3, 2014

Tal Brody, Dec. 23, 2014

Jeff Bukantz, Jan. 30, Dec. 3, 2014

Ron Carner, Nov. 3, 2014

John Dore, Nov. 25, 2014

Joseph Garrie, Nov. 17, 2014

Mitch Gaylord, Oct. 15, 2014

Bernie Gold, Nov. 2014*

Daniel Greyber, Jan. 29, 2014

Dan Grunfeld, Oct. 15, 2014

Ernie Grunfeld, Aug. 8, 2014

Matt Halpern, May 7, 2014

Allen Jay, Nov. 2014*

Ron Kaplan, Aug. 2014*

Marcus Kaplun, Oct. 2014*

Ashley Kochman, Oct. 31, 2014

Lenny Krayzelburg, Sept. 19, 2014

Ricky Landau, Nov. 2014*

Steve Marche Tormé, Aug. 20, 2014

Donna Orender, Oct. 22, 2014

Bruce Pearl, May 23, 2014

Brad Pomerance, Sept. 11, 2014

Marilyn Ramenofsky, Aug. 8, 2014

Roy Salomon, Sept. 19, Sept. 22, Oct. 23, 2014

Danny Schayes, Nov. 5, 2014

Joe Siegman, Oct. 23, 2014

Bob Spivak, Dec. 18, 2014

Greg Sulkin, Sept. 2014*

*Email interview

Index